THE BUILDING
HERTFC
NIKOLAU

The County of HERTFORDSHIRE

See note at foot of Contents page.

THE BUILDINGS OF ENGLAND

Hertfordshire

BY

NIKOLAUS PEVSNER

★

PENGUIN BOOKS

MELBOURNE · LONDON · BALTIMORE

FIRST PUBLISHED 1953

The author and publishers would be grateful
to any user of this book for having any errors
or omissions pointed out to them
in as much detail
as possible

MADE AND PRINTED IN GREAT BRITAIN
FOR PENGUIN BOOKS LTD
BY WILLIAM CLOWES AND SONS LTD
LONDON AND BECCLES

CONTENTS

*

*

The map on pages 2–3 shows all those places, whether towns, villages, or isolated buildings, which are the subject of separate entries in the text. The index on pages 310–313 gives references to the map square in which each place mentioned will be found

TO JOSEPHINE
Born 4 October 1950

*

FOREWORD

*Most of the facts which appear in the following pages were ex-
tracted and assembled by Miss G. Bondi. I want to place on
record my gratitude to her for the care and circumspection with
which she has worked on the published sources. In addition I had
the privilege of my proofs being checked in great detail by Mr
W. Branch Johnson and a team of members of the Hertfordshire Local History Council. I feel very much in their debt and
should like to mention specially, in connexion with other com-
ments and contributions, Mrs E. M. Hunt and Mr Gordon
Moodey, of the East Herts Archaeological Society. Miss
Robin Place wrote all the entries on prehistory and Roman
antiquities, Mr Rupert Gunness generously helped on the
eighteenth-century monuments, Mr C. H. Aslin, County Architect, provided information on the outstanding modern schools
designed in his department, Miss M. F. Austin, former County
Librarian, and Miss M. Swan, and Mr R. C. Sayell, of the
St Albans Public Library and Watford Borough Library
respectively, and also Mr Ian Nairn divers answers to out-of-
the-way questions. The Reverend W. B. Farrer kindly lent me
the photograph illustrated in plate 36a, and Mrs E. M. Hunt
that of plate 7a (taken by the late Reverend J. W. Fall). To all
of them I am most grateful.*

*I also wish to thank the many rectors and vicars of churches
who gave me specific information, and the many owners of private houses, large and small, who allowed me access. Only one
owner of an important country house refused entirely to let me
see it. Many were most helpful. The least thing I can do for
them is to say here most explicitly that the mention or even de-
scription of a house in these pages must not by any means be
taken as an indication that it is open to the public.*

*As in previous volumes of this series by the courtesy of the
Ministry of Housing and Local Government, who have a statu-
tory duty to compile lists of buildings of architectural or historic*

interest, I have had access to unpublished lists and much other information collected by the Chief Investigator of the Ministry and his staff (here abridged MHLG). I could also once more make use of Mr H. S. Goodhart-Rendel manuscript notes on Victorian churches and Sir Thomas Kendrick's on Victorian glass (referred to in this volume under CR and TK). I have made full use of the photograph collection of the National Buildings Record and should like to express my sincere thanks to Mr Cecil Farthing and Mrs M. Parry for all their help.

In spite of so much help received, I am, however, quite sure I omitted to see and register large numbers of houses, especially among the minor ones, partly because literature on these is scanty, and partly because my own cross-country touring was not extensive enough to secure discovery of everything worth recording. Interiors of houses especially will often be found inadequately treated. The reason here may be that privacy to which I alluded before, or simply the fact that I had not seen for myself. On the whole, however, I have made it a principle in these volumes to examine everything personally before I decide to include and try to describe it. Even so there remain no doubt plenty of errors and omissions.

INTRODUCTION

WITH about 630 square miles Hertfordshire is among the six smallest counties of England. In population it is the fourteenth from the top (1951); that means it is remarkably densely populated. This is due to its proximity to London, a fact which one's eyes are hardly ever allowed to forget. The landscape of Hertfordshire is naturally friendly, green, gently rolling, with no large river, uneventful but lovable. It possesses no grandeur, except perhaps occasionally on the height of the Chilterns, and it tends to be dull towards the NE. It has long been under intense cultivation, and one cannot count on much solitude. London's Green Line buses are likely to appear everywhere, and even the familiar red buses cruise as far as Watford and St Albans. At Barnet and Waltham Cross, London reaches solidly into the county. Still separate, but likewise obviously part of London, is the whole Bushey–Oxhey–Watford neighbourhood. The great number of large hospitals (especially mental hospitals) is also connected with nearness to the metropolis. Negatively the effect of this nearness is the absence of any big city (Watford with 73,000 is the biggest town) and of an old cathedral (St Albans was made a cathedral only in 1877).

In its industries Hertfordshire looks to London too. Paper mills and printing works are as characteristic as market gardening and watercress growing, the latter two chiefly in the E of the county.

More conspicuous than the rivers – the longest of which is the Lea running E from somewhere near Luton past Wheathampstead, Hertford, and Ware and then turning S by Broxbourne and Waltham and so into the Thames – are the ancient roads. The Icknield Way is a pre-Roman track. It comes from Ivinghoe and Luton and crosses the county mainly between Hitchin, Baldock, and Royston. The chief

Roman roads are : (1) Watling Street, which enters Hertford-shire at Elstree. Passing through Radlett, St Stephen's, Veru-lam and Gorhambury Drive it leads across the fields to Bow Bridge and Dunstable, and leaves the county at Markyate. (2) Akeman Street, of which only a small part is traceable, on its route from Aylesbury to Boxmoor, through Tring and Berkhamsted. (3) Ermine Street which enters the county at the hamlet of Ball Cross (in the parish of Ches-hunt) and follows the present road to Hamstead End. Thence it proceeds via Cold Hall, Elbow Lane, Hertford Heath, Little Amwell, and Rush Green Farm to Ware Vicarage, Braughing (where it crosses Stane Street), Bunt-ingford and Royston, where it leaves the county. (4) Stane Street, which enters Hertfordshire at Bishops Stortford, passes through Little Hadham to Braughing, crosses Ermine Street, and there leads through Hare Street, Clothall, and Baldock. There are, in addition, traces of a road from Verulam to Colchester, crossing Hertfordshire at Sand-ridge, Ayot, and Welwyn. Hertfordshire is also crossed by two important canals, the New River built as early as 1609–13 as a conduit from Great Amwell to London, and the Grand Junction (now Grand Union) Canal begun in 1792 and completed in 1805. It connects the Midlands with London and runs through Hertfordshire from Tring by Berkhamsted, Boxmoor, Watford, and Rickmansworth. The railway arrived in 1838. It is in several places con-spicuous by fire brick viaducts.

Brick became the accepted building material in Hertford-shire only during the first half of the Tudor Age, although the Romans had used brick extensively, and early medieval builders had made ample use of Roman bricks (*see* St Albans). But brick-making was not taken up for centuries in Hertfordshire, as indeed in the whole of England. Details of the reappearance of brick in the C15 and C16 will be given later. Before then cottages were universally timber-framed, and for churches and large houses flint was extensively used.* The most usual local stone is clunch; the best local stone is the chalk from Totternhoe across the Bedfordshire

* Shenley church in 1424, etc., is of flint with brick dressings.

border, but oölitic limestone from Northamptonshire also appears. Geologically Hertfordshire is all young rocks, chiefly chalk on top of gault and London clay. The only more elevated land is the parts of the Chilterns which lie in the W of the county, NE of Tring. They are continued NE as a less conspicuous escarpment towards Royston.

The most important prehistoric evidence of Hertfordshire belongs to the area SE of the Chilterns and to as late a period as the Iron Age. Of the Stone and Bronze Ages there is no visible evidence except in museums, and what there is in these needs no special comment here. Cassivelaunus, the Belgic king who defied Caesar in 54 B.C., had his capital near Wheathampstead. His grandson moved it on to Verulamium. A third sizeable Iron Age settlement was at Welwyn, NW of the present road from Stevenage to Hatfield. Verulamium became one of the outstanding cities of Roman Britain, in fact the only *municipium* in the country. Much of the plan has been ascertained by excavations. The Museum possesses a most interesting collection. *In situ*, however, are only the theatre and one mosaic pavement. Roman stations were at Braughing, Reed, Thirfield, Clothall, and Wilbury Hill.

Saxon evidence is minor but not without interest. St Michael's at St Albans has its nave and chancel walls preserved, with window surrounds of Roman brick. Long-and-short work can be seen at Reed and Westmill.

Norman evidence is far more impressive. St Albans, one of the most powerful monasteries of Britain, is of course the prime monument. It was begun about 1078 and built very quickly. Much of the long nave, crossing, crossing tower, transepts, and chancel survives. Originally the E end was of seven stepped apses, two on the E side of each transept, two to the chancel aisles, and one to the chancel. Roman brick was extensively used where strength was required. The details are of the rawest and most severe. The church is specially remarkable for never having possessed a gallery like all the other major Norman churches of England, but only a triforium. Smaller English Norman parish churches have apses only rarely and as a rule only in the SE of

the country. Hertfordshire examples are at Wheathampstead (excavation results), Bengeo, Great Amwell, Great
Wymondley, and Weston. Weston also has a Norman crossing tower and seems to have possessed a transept with
apsidal chapels as well. Hemel Hempstead is an exceptionally complete later C12 town church. It has a square chancel
with rib-vaults – the only example of Norman rib-vaulting
in the county * – transepts, a crossing tower, and a nave
with Norman clerestory and aisles. Saratt is a small Norman church on the very unusual Greek cross plan. Other
Norman crossing towers exist or can be reconstructed at
Anstey and Pirton. Norman W towers are preserved at
Barley, Flamstead, Redbourn, and Stevenage; Norman
arcades, e.g. at Abbots Langley, Redbourn, and Walkern.
Interesting overlaps of Norman and E.E. forms, proving
how long into the C13 Norman detail was still used locally,
can be seen at Kimpton and Kings Walden.

The paramount example of the E.E. style in Hertfordshire is, of course, the W parts of the nave and the retrochoir
of St Albans. The former were begun in 1195 and are thus
amongst the earliest examples of pure Gothic design in
Britain. Most of the work, however, belongs to c. 1215–35.
It is exceptional for its date in having deep W porches and a
triforium instead of a gallery. The retrochoir was begun in
1257. At Royston is an interesting fragment of a C13 parish
church, much obscured by later alterations. Surprisingly
sumptuous chancel arches survive at Eastwick and Standon.
In parish churches E.E. chancels are more frequent than
E.E. naves; for the chancels were for the clergy, and there
was no reason to enlarge them later, whereas naves grow
with congregations in the later Middle Ages. The finest E.E.
chancel is at Anstey. Here the transepts are also of the C13.
The same is true of Hatfield with odd W chapels attached to
its transepts. A rare central plan survives at Flaunden – a
Greek cross like Norman Sarratt. Examples of C13 crossing
towers are Northchurch and Wheathampstead.

* The E aisles of the Berkhamsted transepts are also rib-vaulted.
They are, however, of the C13.

Those attracted by the fantasies of the Dec style of the first half of the C14 will be disappointed with what Hertfordshire has to offer. The Lady Chapel of St Albans, though of *c.* 1300–20, has nothing of the lavishness of Ely or Bristol, and the restoration of part of the nave after 1323 is far from original. The only places showing a more fanciful treatment are the transepts of Wheathampstead. Chancel chapels with Dec details are at Aldbury, Abbots Langley, and Benington. Tracery on the whole is unimaginative. So-called Kentish tracery, that is tracery with a motif of a quatrefoil with spikes between the lobes, can be seen at Ayot St Lawrence and St Paul's Walden. Designers need not have gone to Kent for patterns. They appear as near Herts as, for example, Waltham Abbey.

As in so many parts of England, the later C14 and the C15 and early C16 were the high-watermark of prosperity in wool or cloth towns and villages. Baldock and Ashwell churches are two comparatively early examples of this (early C14 and *c.* 1340–80). The majority of medieval work in Herts churches is of the Perp style and chiefly the C15. Important buildings are at Hitchin, Ware, and Watford. Work in the village churches is not on the whole very inspired. Tracery is of no special merit. There are, however, a number of stately w towers, the most beautiful, still of the C14, at Ashwell. This and that at Baldock are crowned by a recessed octagonal storey and then a thin spire. Extremely thin recessed spikes are a peculiarity of the county. They are known as Hertfordshire spikes.

Piers have a variety of sections. To return for a moment to earlier centuries Norman arcades had circular piers, the C13 usually octagonal ones (e.g. Ardeley, Flamstead, Great Gaddesden, Much Hadham, Offley, Walkern). This latter form was continued into the early C14 (Aldenham, Hitchin, Wheathampstead, etc.). The w parts of St Albans of *c.* 1200 have a variation on this theme with four attached shafts in the main axes. Quatrefoil sections of the piers are to be found at Berkhamsted, Anstey, Gilston, and Sawbridgeworth. St Albans *c.* 1257 added to these four slimmer shafts in the diagonals. Royston Priory did the same, but keeled the diagonal shafts – not an unusual profile, also without the keeling. Without capitals to the diagonal shafts the same profile continues at Baldock and Ashwell, Albury and Benington. Later at Ashwell the main shafts turn 3/8 in section instead of semicircular, and at Clothall, also in the C14, the diagonal shafts are also of 3/8 section. The most usual C15 profile is four attached shafts and four hollows in the diagonals (Cheshunt 1418–48, Barnet c. 1440–50, Bishops Stortford, etc.). With 3/8 shafts instead of semicircular ones, the same section appears at Barkway, Furneaux Pelham, St Paul's Walden, and as late as 1532 at Wyddial. More complex late medieval forms are at Tring and Standon with double hollows in the diagonals, at Hatfield with treble shafts in the four main axes, and at Watton and Ware. Perp piers have often capitals only to some shafts. In Herts this characteristic habit is fully developed already at Buckland (1348?).

With the exception of St Albans and Royston all the churches so far mentioned were parochial. Herts was, in fact, not rich in important monastic foundations. The power of St Albans overshadowed all. To its liberty belonged Abbots Langley, Aldenham, Barnet, Codicote, Elstree, Hexton, Northaw, Northchurch, Rickmansworth, Watford, and divers other parishes, going across the border into Bucks. The other monastic houses in the county of which remains survive above ground were the Augustinian priories of Royston (founded C12) and Little Wymondley (founded C13), the Benedictine nunneries at Sopwell and Markyate (both cells of St Albans), the Carmelite house at Hitchin, the house of the Bonshommes at Ashridge, the Dominican friary at Kings Langley, and the Franciscan friary at Ware.

There is no important medieval sculpture in Herts. The shrines of St Albans Abbey are in a sadly fragmentary state. Tomb-recesses and decorated tomb-chests are at Anstey (c. 1300), Benington (c. 1330?, c. 1358?), Little Munden (late C14), Aldenham (late C14), and Aldbury (1471). More ambitious are the three chantry chapels of St Albans, dating from 1447, c. 1460, and c. 1520. Of stone effigies the best of the C13 are at Eastwick and Brent Pelham. A Purbeck marble effigy is at Walkern, a Purbeck slab with incised effigy at Sawbridgeworth, the former C13, the latter early C14. Alabaster effigies are rare, brasses extremely frequent. The earliest are of *c*. 1340 (Albury) and of 1356 (Berkhamsted); the best are the de la Mare brass at St Albans, *c*. 1396, of Flemish workmanship, and of English workmanship those at North Mimms *c*. 1360, Hemel Hempstead late C14, Furneaux Pelham early C15, Digswell † 1415, Watford † 1415, Sawbridgeworth *c*. 1433, Wheathampstead *c*. 1436, Watton-at-Stone mid C15, Standon † 1474, Broxbourne † 1474, a group of *c*. 1475–80 at Albury, Little Hadham, and Sandon, and Hinxworth † 1487(?).

For medieval wall painting St Albans is of national importance, especially the late C13 paintings of the Crucifixion on five nave piers, but also what survives in the chancel. Apart from St Albans only Flamstead with its C13 and C15 fragments, and smaller fragments at Bengeo (C13) and Widford have to be mentioned. Regarding medieval stained glass the figure of the Virgin at St Paul's Walden (early C14) and the Jesse tree at Barkway (late C15) are the best examples.

In church furnishings also outstanding works are lacking. There are plenty of preserved screens, but none of them first-rate. Of special historic interest is the one at Gilston, because it is clearly of before 1300 – a very early date. The stone pulpitum at St Albans is of the late C14, the stone reredos with its Victorian figures later C15. The best C15 timber screens are those of Hitchin. The coving of the rood loft is preserved at Redbourn and Kimpton. A great rarity is the Feretrar's Watching Loft at St Albans (*c*. 1500). Stall-work might be mentioned at Stevenage, misericords at Bishops Stortford, and a C15 font with carved figures at Ware. Decorated iron door-hinges survive at Little Hormead of a Norman date, at St Albans of the late C13. Also of the late C13 is the exquisite iron railing round the Gloucester Chantry at St Albans.*

* As in previous volumes of this series, church bells are not recorded.

That finishes the survey of medieval ecclesiastical architecture in the county. As for secular buildings, Berkhamsted had the most important castle. It dates from the C12 and is very poorly preserved. But its large circumference is still impressive. At Bishops Stortford the mount of the Bishop of London's castle survives, at Hertford also the mount and some bits of masonry. Bennington has a small keep, now part of a Neo-Norman domestic fantasy, Anstey big earth fortifications and again a mount. Homestead moats, that is moats originally surrounding manor houses, are a speciality of Herts. The Royal Commission counts 141 of them. They seem to date from the C13 to the C16. Hardly any of them are mentioned in this volume.

With regard to manor houses the earliest at least partly preserved examples are the Old Palace at Hatfield, Hinxworth Place, and the Rectory at Therfield. Hatfield, the former country seat of the Bishops of Ely, is far more ambitious than the others can ever have been. It has a fine hall with braced roof and is built of brick. Its date is c. 1480–90. It marks the moment in the county when brick became fashionable. Only slightly later is the brick gatehouse of Hertford Castle and the brick frieze at Rickmansworth Vicarage. Hinxworth and Therfield have characteristic late C15 windows. In addition there exists another late C15 hall at Cheshunt Great House. This was originally much larger than it is now. It belonged to the courtyard type also represented by Hadham Hall in its original form and by The Lordship, Standon. The Lordship is of brick, dated 1546. Its principal surviving feature is the gatehouse.

Another big Early Tudor gatehouse of brick stands at Rye House; and Hunsdon, which is now a much altered rectangular brick block, has yet another brick gatehouse close by. The surviving house at Hunsdon was once one projecting wing of a symmetrical E- or half-H-shaped house. At Knebworth fragments of the brick mansion of c. 1500 have in the C19 been built into a new gatehouse. A characteristic early C16 motif in Herts and altogether the brick districts NE of London is the stepped gable (of Dutch and Flemish derivation). It is to be found at Great Hormead, Furneaux Pelham, etc.*

The proof that brick had become equal in social status to stone is provided by its acceptance for church architecture. In Herts this is marked by the N aisle and N chancel chapel at Wyddial (1532) and the s porch at Meesden (c. 1530). The chancel chapels at Hunsdon and Stanstead Abbots (1577), and the tower top at Sarratt followed. They take us into the Elizabethan Age.

The wealth of Elizabethan and Jacobean houses in Herts is exceptional. It is no doubt to be explained by the nearness to London. They range in size from the Early Elizabethan hunting lodge of Queen Hoo to such palaces as the all but demolished Gorhambury (1568, etc.), the demolished Theobalds, and the gloriously surviving Hatfield of 1607–11. The Elizabethan style is complete in the Gorhambury porch with its classical columns and niches, and in the remaining range of Hadham Hall of c. 1575 with its classical pediments above many-mullioned and transomed windows. Of about the same age is Berkhamsted Place, built on the popular E-plan. The same plan occurs, for example, on a large scale at North Mimms, early C17, and on a small scale in the charming Water End Farm of c. 1610. Other examples of the style are Great Nast Hyde, Upp Hall, Delamere House Great Wymondley, Bride Hall Sandridge, and Letchworth Hall. The straightsided Elizabethan gables are still used in the early C17, but shaped gables consisting of concave and ogee curves are the more fashionable form (Astonbury, Barkway, St Monica's Priory Hoddesdon 1622). These are replaced from about 1630 onwards by a type of gable which is finished at the top by a pediment – a first concession to classical standards. Examples of this are at Rothamsted, at Hoddesdon in a house dated 1637 which also displays the novel scheme of orders of superimposed pilasters on the façade, and still in 1665 at Mackery End, otherwise a front belonging in its character to the time after the Restoration.

The dating of cottages is not easy. There are plenty of timber-framed structures in the villages which may in parts

* And as late as 1576 at Little Gaddesden Manor House.

go back to the C15 and in considerable parts to the C16. But changes were slow, and a wholly new type of cottage was developed only after a change of legislation in 1775. Only then do the long low two-storeyed brick cottages with brick modillion friezes appear. Anyway, the recording of cottages in the pages of this volume is entirely inadequate, partly because their strictly architectural interest is so small, partly because there is little printed evidence beyond the Royal Commission volume, and partly because I have not inspected them systematically. The rule that narrowly spaced uprights in a timber-framed house are an indication of early date holds only in a very general way. Chimney-stacks also help in dating, their length, and their position diagonally or otherwise.

A few specially fine barns may here be added, especially the timber-framed weatherboarded C15 barn at Croxley Hall Farm, Croxley Green, and the splendid brick barn, 140 ft. long, at Upp Hall, Braughing.

Of secular buildings other than houses, schools and almshouses begin to appear in the C16. The Berkhamsted Grammar School of 1544 is the best remaining example. It is built of brick and keeps still entirely within the Perp tradition. Other contemporary schools are at Chipping Barnet and Standon, and fragments at Buntingford and Stevenage. Hale's School at Hertford is early C17, the Dewhurst School at Cheshunt 1640. The earliest almshouses in Herts date from 1580 (Watford), but the largest ones are later than the Restoration.

The foundation of schools and almshouses took the place, after the Reformation, of the foundation of chantry chapels in churches. Church architecture between the middle of the C16 and the middle of the C17 was stagnant. The only complete church built during the century is St Peter at Buntingford (1614–26), a Greek cross in plan. The chapel at Oxhey (1612) is still entirely Perp in character and details. The N transept at Little Hadham has intersected tracery dating apparently from the late C16, the chancel chapel at Aspenden octagonal piers of 1622. However, these carry semicircular arches decorated with strapwork, and the Morrison Chapel

at Watford of 1595 and the Salisbury Chapel at Hatfield of
c. 1610 replace Perp piers by Tuscan columns.*

The same development can be followed in much greater
detail in the monuments of c. 1550 to c. 1660. Again in
connexion with the Reformation they tended to grow more
and more self-confident and worldly. It is hard to choose out
of three dozen and more major examples what is to be regarded as outstanding or specially characteristic. The first
sign of dissatisfaction with the Perp motifs of decoration
appears in a tomb-chest of alabaster at Wheathampstead,
which is dated 1558. Strapwork, the new abstract art of
ornament which the Elizabethan style took over from the
Netherlands, appears in full maturity at Aldbury in 1570,
but the majority of the more ambitious monuments belong
to the C17. Some are good enough to be in Westminster
Abbey, first and foremost that of the Earl of Salisbury at
Hatfield, by *Colt*, a large free-standing composition with
kneeling allegorical figures at the angles and the effigy of the
Earl above and as a cadaver below. At least as good *Nicholas
Stone's* moving figure of Sir Richard Cyrle † 1617, in a
shroud. This is also at Hatfield. Works like these would
hold their own in any county. Many others are cruder in
style and showier in decoration. The chief types are one
with kneeling figures facing each other across a prayer-desk,
usual mostly for epitaphs on a smaller scale but occurring
also in standing wall-monuments, and another with a recumbent effigy (or two, one being placed behind and a little
above the other) or a semi-reclining effigy, under an arch,
shallow or deeper and coffered, between columns carrying
an entablature with an achievement. Particularly good
are the examples at Bayford (1612) and Hunsdon (1617).
Others at Braughing (1625), Broxbourne (1609), Hatfield
(1612), Hertingfordbury (1622, c. 1650), Hunsdon (1612),

* Elizabethan and Jacobean CHURCH FURNISHINGS are of no
great interest. It is sufficient here to mention the Early Renaissance
decoration (the earliest in the county) of the screen of c. 1540 at Digswell, the early C17 screen at Wyddial, and the screen and family pews
at Hunsdon of about the same date. The style remained unaltered for a
long time. The pulpit of 1658 at Bishops Stortford is still wholly in the
Elizabethan tradition.

Sawbridgeworth (1625), Standon (1587, 1606), Watford (1599, 1628), and Wheathampstead (c. 1630–5). An odd case of Gothic survival is the canopy of the Ravenscroft Monument at High Barnet of 1630. Rarer types are those with busts (an early example at Braughing, 1597, wider popularity during the reign of Charles I: Hadley, by *Nicholas Stone*, 1616, then Berkhamsted 1627 or 1634, Aspenden 1634 or 1623, Meesden 1626, Buckland 1634, Sawbridgeworth 1637, Willian 1656), those with seated and those with standing figures. The most famous seated effigy is Sir Francis Bacon at St Michael's St Albans, 1626 (an earlier example 1605 at Radwell); the only standing figure is Bridget Gore † 1659. She is in her shroud, a type made popular by the Donne Monument in St Paul's Cathedral.

The Restoration brought a noticeable change in the style of monuments. It is clearly indicated in the beautiful epitaph of Judith Strode at Knebworth (1662) with its purely Italian, nobly handled bust and extremely restrained detail. One type specially favoured shortly after the Restoration has no effigy, though often two mournful putti, and Italian detail in a grand Baroque manner (several examples at Little Gaddesden, also Cheshunt). Busts remain in fashion. (Ardeley 1673, Barnet 1680, 1689, Wyddial 1687, etc.) Semi-reclining figures occur even more frequently than before and their style now becomes more spectacular. Roman costume appears, and the proudly carried wigs of an extremely self-assured age. One of the earlier displays of this self-importance of the prosperous nobleman at the time of William of Orange is the Viscount Hewyt Memorial at Sawbridgeworth (1689). He is portrayed standing in front of us in an attitude as if he were Louis XIV himself. A standing statue also Mr Lytton † 1710 at Knebworth (by *Thomas Green*?). The Lytton Chapel at Knebworth contains the most sumptuous series of monuments in the county. The large monuments to Sir William Lytton † 1705 and Sir George Strode † 1707 by *Edward Stanton* have stately semi-reclining figures wearing wigs and big reredos backgrounds. Two semi-reclining effigies (arranged à la Guglielmo della Porta's tomb of Pope Paul III) at Tring (by *Nost*, 1707). As the C18 progressed, the composition of monuments became more varied. The sources are Italy and France; the style moves from a somewhat ponderous Baroque to a remarkably elegant Rococo. Herts is rich in many types and examples by many hands. Reclining figures with assistant allegories at Offley 1699, at Abbots Langley (by *Cheere*) 1732; two standing figures with a tree in the background at Offley (by *Nollekens*) 1777; allegories singly or in pairs, seated or in other attitudes, without effigies at North Mimms 1716, Offley (by *Taylor*) 1752, Abbots Langley (by *Scheemakers*) 1756, Throcking (by *Nollekens*) 1770, Flamstead (by *Flaxman*) 1782. Of other sculptors *Rysbrack* is represented by four or five works, none amongst his most important, *Roubiliac* by one extremely charming but minor piece (Hertingfordbury 1727), *Bacon* by two (Sawbridgeworth; Watton 1793). The *Stantons* appear at Flamstead (1690) and Barkway, *Scheemakers* made the Freeman Monument at Braughing to *Athenian Stuart's* design (1772). Lesser sculptors of monuments are *T. Bull* (Redbourn), *B. Palmer* (Graveley), *John Richards* (Buckland), and *W. Woodman* (Cheshunt). The last Georgian decades have produced less interesting monuments (two more *Flaxmans*, at Great Gaddesden 1782 and Sacombe 1815, one *Thorwaldsen* at Wheathampstead, an excellent *Westmacott* at Little Gaddesden 1823, more *Westamcott* at Kings Langley, *Chenu* 1796 and 1820 at Barkway, *Kendrick* at Barkway and Great Hormead). Not all the best monuments are signed. There are, for exmple, in various places, a number of delicate epitaphs of *c.* 1760–80 in white, pink, and biscuit-coloured marbles with portrait medallions, cherubs' heads, etc., whose authors are unknown.

In houses the classical style which Inigo Jones opposed to the current Jacobean made an early appearance in Herts; but the first examples are of a characteristically impure, though by no means transitional, kind. They do not employ Jacobean motifs any longer, but use the Italian idiom awkwardly and with a broad accent. The result is academically objectionable, but original and robust. Balls Park of *c.* 1640 is one of the earliest examples of this peculiar Carolean style which has recently been connected with the name of the London architect *Peter Mills*. Tyttenhanger of *c.* 1655–60 belongs to the same group, though its brick quoins, window pediments, hipped roof, and squat cupola are in keeping with the correct style of Pratt at Coleshill, etc. The staircase at Tyttenhanger is one of the earliest in the country to have a railing of openwork foliage panels. Of the late C17 and the early C18 there are quite a number of pleasant, simple, comfortably proportioned brick houses (Brent Pelham Hall, Golden Parsonage 1705, Redheath 1712, Chipperfield Manor House 1716, Temple Dinsley in its original form 1717, and so on to Much Hadham Hall, Cumberland House Redbourn, and many others in villages), but nothing on a grand scale. Grandeur appears only with *Leoni's* Moor Park, a stone mansion with splendid giant Corinthian portico and a hall with paintings by *Amigoni*. The chief country houses after 1750 are Brocket Hall by *Paine* (*c.* 1755–75), curiously solid and unadorned outside, Gaddesden Place by *Wyatt* (1768–73), Gorhambury by *Taylor* (1777), and Woodhall Park by *Leverton* (1777), the latter three Palladian of characteristically different idioms. In 1782 at Pishiobury *Wyatt* appears mildly medievalizing; in a thoroughly Neo-Gothic style Panshanger was built about twenty years later by the younger *Repton*. *Soane* did some of his most original Neo-Greek work at Marden Hill, and one should regard Hyde Hall near Sawbridgeworth of 1806 and the enlargements at Bayfordbury of 1809 in relation to his style. A specially handsome small Neo-Greek villa is Tewin Water of *c.* 1815.

There are plenty of pleasant Georgian town houses in such towns as St Albans, Hitchin, Hemel Hempstead, Ware, Hertford, etc.

Secular buildings other than houses are *James Adam's* Shire Hall at Hertford (1768–9), the Corn Exchange at Bishops Stortford of 1828, and the Town Hall at St Albans by *George Smith*, who did much work in the county (1829). The most extensive almshouses are those of Bishop Ward at Buntingford 1684, and the Duchess of Marlborough's at St Albans 1736. The Old Hall Academy was built as a Roman Catholic College in 1795–9 and enlarged in 1805, a building much more extensive and unified in composition than school buildings other than Catholic were in the C18. However, in 1809 Haileybury College appeared with its long Neo-Greek façade and quadrangle by *Wilkins*.

The only church building of a comparably representational character is *Nicholas Revett's* at Ayot St Lawrence 1778–9, on an unusual plan and with a severe Greek Doric portico. Church work before 1800 otherwise is negligible (St Paul's Walden Chancel 1727, Offley Chancel *c*.1750, Totteridge 1790). Several village churches have their box pews and three-decker pulpits (Stanstead Abbots) preserved. The most remarkable font is that at Essendon, of Wedgwood black-basalt earthenware. Excellent early C18 ironwork is at Hatfield churchyard (from St Paul's Cathedral) and in Hatfield church (from Amiens) and Knebworth church.

Early C19 churches are of no special architectural merit, some classical, some of that starved Gothic which characterizes the period of the so-called Commissioners' Churches. A number are Neo-Norman, and London Colney of 1825 by *G. Smith* must be one of the earliest examples of a Norman Revival in Britain.

Several of the leading Victorian church architects are represented in Herts : *Pugin* with the ambitious chapel at Old Hall Green 1845, *Butterfield* with Holy Saviour Hitchin 1865 and the successful re-modelling and enlarging of the High Barnet Parish Church 1876, *Bentley* with the outstandingly fine Holy Rood Watford 1883, etc., and so on. *Pritchett's* High Wych of 1861 deserves to be specially mentioned as an eminently typical example of High Victorian design at its most revolting, *Seddon's* Ayot St Peter of 1875 as a work by an early adherent of the Morris reform. Other churches by *Blomfield* (Stevenage), *Jekyll* (Lilley), *Norman Shaw* (Boxmoor), *Carpenter & Ingelow* (Long Marston), and so on to *Lutyens's* remarkably original and forceful but unfinished St Martin's Knebworth 1914.*

* The best Victorian Stained Glass is that of *William Morris* at Furneaux Pelham 1866, 1873, Kings Walden 1867, Rickmansworth 1891, and Hatfield 1894, of *Kempe* in his early years at High Cross 1876 and Bishops Stortford 1877, and of *Selwyn Image* at High Cross 1893.

Lutyens married into the Lytton family at Knebworth, and so got several jobs at Knebworth. Homewood of 1900 is one of his most original early houses, Temple Dinsley of *c.* 1908 one of his biggest enlargement jobs. The Early Georgian house sinks into insignificance under the weight of *Lutyens's* Neo-Georgian wings. The chief Late Victorian houses are Goldings by *Devey* (1870), Denham, Totteridge by *Norman Shaw* (1877), New Place, Welwyn by *Philip Webb* (1880), and the American *H. H. Richardson's* Lululand at Bushey for Herkomer the painter (*c.* 1885). Of this only the massive entrance is preserved. *Devey* also built Blakesware, *Waterhouse* Easneye (1868). Of the next generation, *Lutyens's* generation, *Voysey* is represented by some of his best work, The Orchard at Chorleywood (1900) and other houses at Chorleywood, Bushey, and Eastbury, *Walton* by The Leys Elstree (1901), and *Macartney* by Firthwood House Eastbury (*c.* 1900). *Leonard Stokes's* All Saints Convent at London Colney (1899) is institutional architecture of the same generation at its best, a very free Neo-Tudor.

For architectural development in the C20 few counties are as interesting as Herts. Here the first independent garden city was built: Letchworth; and the second: Welwyn.* Here of the seven planned satellite towns of London three are situated: Stevenage, Hemel Hempstead, and Hatfield New Town.‡ Letchworth was designed by *Parker & Unwin*, the pioneers of town planning of their generation, Welwyn by *Louis de Soissons*. The Stevenage plans are by Ash Gordon, those for Hemel Hempstead by *G. A. Jellicoe*, those for Hatfield by *Lionel Brett*. The principle behind their creation is a logical development of that underlying Ebenezer Howard's book on *Garden Cities of the Future* and Parker & Unwin's designs for Letchworth. The satellite town as well as the garden city is meant to be an independent town with its own factories and all urban amenities. The creation of more such cities than Letchworth and Welwyn

---

* More on the principle of the garden city will be found under Letchworth, p. 153.

‡ And Harlow in Essex is only just across the border.

became urgent when *Sir Patrick Abercrombie's* and *Mr J. H Forshaw's* plans for the County of London and for Greater London had shown up conclusively the necessity of 'decanting' some of London's growing population. The necessity seems alas to be for one whole town of 50,000 inhabitants to be completed every year, or else the desired relief for London will not take place. As it is six new towns were begun near London: Harlow and Basildon in Essex, Crawley in Sussex and the three mentioned above in Hertfordshire. They were started on paper with much enthusiasm. The idea had been to progress beyond Letchworth and Welwyn by giving them a more urban character. But as nowhere building has started in the natural way from the centre, what can so far be seen is nearly as suburban and loosely laid out as the garden cities. The only difference is the consistent use of terraces of houses and the occasional interjection of blocks of flats (Stevenage). The only completed shopping centre at the time of writing was at Hemel Hempstead. However, things may look very different in a few years time, if, as much be hoped, the rate of growth can be geared up. So far building of houses seems to be slower than in many less convincingly planned housing estates in Herts built, for example, by the London County Council. If in the end the New Towns come to be anything like their present plans, then they will be the first towns in England since Bath of which their inhabitants and the country can be unreservedly proud.

In addition the *Herts County Architect's Department* is remarkably active in taking over, converting, adjusting, and thereby saving, good Georgian and Victorian houses and in erecting new buildings which are intelligently designed and built. The outstanding case is that of the county's schools programme. The case has rightly received wide publicity at home and abroad, but must here in conclusion be summarized, especially because it will not be possible to mention all the exemplary new schools built since 1946. They now (Summer, 1952) total over fifty. The programme was based from the beginning on extensive, very ingeniously conducted research, as to how materials can be ordered beforehand

and stocked by the manufacturers, how delays in sanc-
tioning can be avoided, and how local contractors can
be made use of. The answer to these questions is a system
of galvanized steel frame units bolted together on the site,
with pre-cast vibrated concrete units for walls and roofs.
This very complete system of prefabrication allows extremely rapid assembly, and as only the basic units (on a
module originally of 8 ft 3 in. now of 3 ft 4 in.) are stan-
dardized, also extreme freedom in grouping. At first the
system was used only for single-storey primary schools,
but it has now been extended to two- or three-storey buildings, so as to allow the construction of secondary schools.
Recent developments have also taken place in the use of
concrete and timber frames to overcome the steel shortage
and also in the use of plastic and other cladding materials.
These experiments have been designed on the new 3 ft 4 in.
planning module. However, in spite of all this research and
technical ingenuity, these schools would be merely an
achievement of engineering and organization if the composition and finishes were not the work of a team of exceptionally sensitive and modern-minded designers. From
the balancing of block against block down to the colours of
the walls, the curtain patterns, and the door handles, everything is carefully considered and elegantly done. It is a
delightful experience to walk around and through some of
these schools. In the following pages only a dozen selected
examples are mentioned.*

So this account of the history of architecture can end on a
note of cheer and optimism, which is more than one can say
of modern developments in many parts of Britain.

A few lines must be added on the printed sources on
which the information contained in the following pages is
based. The chief sources are the *Victoria County History* (4
vols, 1908–14) and the Hertfordshire Volume of the *Royal
Commission on Historical Monuments*. This, however, being
the earliest volume published by the Commission (1910) is

* *See* Boreham Wood, Cheshunt, East Barnet, Essendon, Hemel
Hempstead, Hertford, Hitchin, Oxhey, St Albans, Stevenage, Ware,
Welwyn Garden City.

not as detailed as its successors. In addition such guidebooks as the *Little Guide* (by H. W. Tomkins) and *Kelly's Directory* were used. Of more specialized literature the histories of Herts by Chauncy, Clutterbuck, and Cussans are of value, of periodicals *Country Life* and the *Transactions of the East Herts Arch. Soc.* and of the *St Albans and Herts Arch. & Arch. Soc.* On the whole, however, not much strictly architectural research has been done in Herts monuments, and the present volume will no doubt reflect that shortage.

HERTFORDSHIRE

*

ABBOTS LANGLEY

ST LAWRENCE. A church of exceptional architectural interest, thanks to its Norman nave arcades and Dec s
chancel chapel. The church is not large. It has a low w
tower with diagonal buttresses on the lower stage only.
That stage is of the C13, as indicated by its small lancet
windows. Its top is a plain brick parapet. The nave is
short, of two bays, the chancel lower than the nave. Its
windows have Early Perp tracery. The aisle windows are
later Perp. So is the clerestory, although remains are
noticeable of an earlier clerestory (c. 1300) with pointed
trefoil-headed windows. The s chancel chapel has a sumptuous exterior with a chequer pattern of flint and stone
mixed with brick, while the rest of the church is flint with
stone dressings. The tracery of the windows in the chapel
is typical Early Dec. Remains of the w window show that
the s aisle was renewed later. A s, and also a N, aisle had,
however, existed long before. On entering the church one
sees at once that the nave arcades belong to the C12. The
N arcade has one circular pier with scalloped capital and
w and E responds of the same design. The roundheaded
arches are decorated with zigzag placed at right angles to
the wall surface and an outer billet. The s arcade has the
same arches and responds, but the pier was renewed in
the early C13 with a shallow stiff-leaf capital, at about the
same time at which the tower was built and received its
arch to the nave with an elaborate moulding and large and
more expressive stiff-leaf capitals. The w window of the s
aisle proves part of that wall also to be a Norman survival.
The nave arcades were continued in the late Middle Ages
(four-centred arch on the s side). The Dec s chancel
chapel opens to the chancel by a two-bay arcade with

sharply pointed two-centred arches of double-chamfered moulding. The nave roof is handsome C15 work of king-post type with the closely set rafters showing and the spaces between them plastered.

FURNISHINGS. FONT. Octagonal, Perp, with shields inside quatrefoils (in two panels coarsely carved angels instead). – PAINTING. SS Lawrence and Thomas, high up on E wall of S chancel chapel. Much of what is seen now is Professor Tristram's 'restoration'. The style is clearly that of the chapel itself, that is first third of the C14. – COFFER. German, C16, with reliefs alluding to original sin and redemption, no doubt from the Protestant North, as the dialect of the inscriptions also proves. – STAINED GLASS. S chapel E window, 1909, with a lush display of white foliage between the small scenes. By *Powell's* of Whitefriars. – MONUMENTS. Unimportant brass of 1607 in the N aisle. – In the S chapel Anne Combe † 1640, the usual epitaph with kneeling figure, and Dame Anne Raymond † 1714, an epitaph of unusual design, with the principal figure in timeless costume seated frontally, dignified and urbane. The representation of the three grandchildren in their cradles on the plinth is, however, still in the naïve C16–C17 tradition. – The two principal monuments are placed against the aisle W walls : the first Lord Raymond † 1732, by *Cheere*, semi-reclining figure with wig, with a seated allegory on the l. holding a portrait medallion, and putti on the r., the whole against a broad pyramid ; lively diagonal composition. – The second Lord Raymond † 1756 with black sarcophagus against black obelisk in the centre and seated allegories of hope and plenty to the l. and r. By *Scheemakers*.

THE VICARAGE, big and square, Georgian, behind the church, the gabled and cemented MANOR HOUSE, neglected at the time of writing, to the SW. To the NE the Georgian LANGLEY HOUSE (Breakspear R.C. College, so called because Nicholas Breakspear, later Hadrian IV, the only Pope of English nationality, was born at Abbots Langley), *c*. 1770, the usual five-bay, two-and-a-half-storey structure, stuccoed *c*. 1830 and enlarged.

Other buildings around: the large, ugly, yellow and red brick LEAVESDEN MENTAL HOSPITAL (1868–70), by *Giles & Biven*. Between it and the village one of the pairs of MODEL COTTAGES has been erected in 1856 which *Henry Roberts* designed at Prince Albert's request for the Society for Improving the Conditions of the Labouring Classes. The first of them could be seen at the Great Exhibition of 1851. The cottages are characterized by open recessed staircases and some Neo-Jacobean trim. They were meant to be model units for larger and higher blocks of flats.

LANGLEYBURY *see* p. 152.

ALBURY

ST MARY. As in so many churches in this neighbourhood the chancel is the earliest surviving part: C13 with original N and S lancet windows. The nave and aisles are mid C14, as shown by the aisle windows with very unusual, rather ugly, heavily flowing tracery. The arcades have piers with big round shafts and thin shafts in the diagonals. The arches are two-centred and double-chamfered in the S, more complex in the N. The chancel arch is of the same style, the very tall tower arch evidently a hundred years later. The tower has diagonal buttresses, a low stair-turret, and a spike. – PULPIT. C18 with inlaid shield. – SCREEN. Tall, C15. – PLATE. Chalice, 1626. – MONUMENTS. Tomb-chest with five quatrefoils with shields. On it the defaced effigies of a Knight and a Lady of *c.* 1400. – Brass to a Knight in armour and his Lady, elegant somewhat mannered figures of under $1\frac{1}{2}$ ft length, *c.* 1475 (nave floor). – Brass to Thomas Leventhorp † 1588 and wife and children; husband and wife turned towards each other (s aisle). – Brass to John Scrogs † 1592 with wife and child; one plate with tapering sides.

ALDBURY

An exceptionally charming village green. To the E the woods up the hillside towards Ashridge. The church recedes

H.—2

from the sw end of the green, and several excellent cottages lie NE and w of the church (especially Nos 11–13) and N of the green along Stocks Road. In the distance on the brow appears the MONUMENT (a Greek Doric column with an urn) to the third Duke of Bridgewater, erected in 1832 to commemorate his pioneer work for English canals.

ST JOHN THE BAPTIST. Tall, slender w tower with slim diagonal buttresses. In contrast to its vertical elevation the long, relatively low nave and yet lower chancel, an impressive opposition of vertical and horizontal. The chancel is embattled. Its masonry is the oldest part of the church, as proved by a small C13 lancet window in the N wall and a low-side lancet in the S wall. The nave arcades are early C14 with octagonal piers carrying moulded capitals typical of that date and double-hollow-chamfered arches. One pier on the S side is broader than the others, perhaps for a screen. The staircase in the S aisle does not, however, correspond to it. It led to the parvis above the porch. The E bays have renewed piers. The N chancel chapel must also be early C14. The tower arch is a little later. – In the N aisle wall is a figure CORBEL, very coarse, yet probably later than the C13, which is the date suggested by the Royal Commission. – LECTERN. C16, of timber. – PLATE. Cup of 1514; secular.

The most remarkable part of the church is the PENDLEY CHAPEL. It is divided from the aisle and the chancel by an excellent stone SCREEN with original Perp tracery and a castellated top. In it is the MONUMENT to Sir Robert Whittingham † 1471 and his wife, two recumbent stone figures on a tomb-chest with weepers alternating with shields. The monument and the screen came from Ashbridge in 1575–6. Against the E wall the later epitaph to Sir Richard Anderson †. 1699 and his wife, with two elegant busts. – MONUMENTS in other parts of the church; Sir Ralph Verney † 1546 with wife and children, large brasses on stone tomb-chest decorated with shields. Also from Ashbridge. – Tiny brass to John Davies (E respond, N arcade), late C15. – Epitaph to Thomas

Hyde † 1570 and his son † 1580 (N chancel chapel) with exquisite strapwork decoration but no figures.

ALDENHAM

St John the Baptist. The church stretches out im- 12 pressively s of the Green, long and well-proportioned, with a w tower, nave, and aisles of four bays, and chancel and chancel chapels. Exterior and interior look at first a unity, but they represent quite a long and complex building history. The exterior is all flint with stone dressings, the window shapes will be mentioned later. The w tower has diagonal buttresses, a NE stair-turret higher than the tower battlements, and a thin, long (renewed) timber spire. The oldest remaining fragment is a Norman window at the w end of the s aisle, perhaps not in its original position. The lower parts of the w tower (see windows) are C13. C13 also is the chancel, with deeply splayed lancet windows, completely renewed sedilia, and a trefoil-headed piscina recess.* The s chancel chapel has windows with typical tracery of c. 1300, with trefoils and pointed trefoils. It is separated from the chancel by short octagonal piers with broadly moulded capitals and double-chamfered arches. The nave and s aisle were rebuilt about 1340 (see the octagonal piers with capitals decorated by fleurons and the double-chamfered arches and also the tracery of the two-light windows). To the Perp style belong the N arcade and wide N aisle (the capitals of the piers are finer and have faces as well as fleurons as decoration), the N windows, the N chancel chapel, the tower arch towards the nave, the upper parts of the tower, and the clerestory with small two-light windows. The brick N porch is C19. The roofs are good C15 work, especially in the nave and N aisle. Both are of very flat pitch.

FURNISHINGS. FONT. Square, C13, undecorated, on five supports. – SCREEN. Between s aisle and s chancel chapel, C15, much renewed. – COFFER. 10 ft long, oak

* The E window was inserted by *Sir Charles Barry* during the restoration of 1840.

trunk scooped out; the sides are 3 ft thick. With iron bands and many hinges. Dated C14 by Roe. – STAINED GLASS. By *Kempe*, 1891–1900; the earliest the Crucifixion in the N chancel chapel. – PLATE. Cup, 1565; Cup, 1635; several C19 pieces. – MONUMENTS. An unusual wealth of BRASSES, not of high aesthetic quality, but interesting as illustrating the changes of costume: in the chancel man, woman, and eight children, C16; man, woman, and eleven children, C16; Lucas Goodyere, 1547, draped in a shroud; in the S chancel chapel a series from the early C16 to the early C17 (man and wife, *c.* 1520; man head missing, *c.* 1520; man and two wives, *c.* 1525; lady, *c.* 1535; Joan Warner † 1538; E. Brisko † 1608 and wife). – Of stone monuments the most important is that to two ladies of the Crowmer family in the S chancel chapel. Two identical tomb-chests with quatrefoil decoration. Recumbent effigies on them in late C14 costume. Canopies above with cusped four-centred arches and embattled top cornices. The two monuments form one composition. – John Coghill † 1714, ascribed by Mrs Esdaile to *R. Crutcher*, two effigies on tomb-chest; he reclines and seems to talk to her; she is behind him in a half-sitting position. Contemporary costumes. – Robert Hucks and his wife † 1771, good unsigned epitaph in various marbles, with double profile medallion. – Vice-Admiral Sir John Chambers White † 1845, Gothic epitaph, very Dec in style, made by *Poole* of Westminster. – In the churchyard big urn on pedestal to Lt-Gen. R. Burne † 1825. On the pedestal the places in Europe, Asia, [and America are enumerated where he fought; amongst them Buenos Ayres and The Suburbs of Buenos Ayres.

EDGE GROVE, N of the church. Late C18, with four-column Ionic porch, much altered in Edwardian days.

WALL HALL, N of Edge Grove. Castellated, turreted, and cemented house of *c.* 1800 (then given the fancy name Aldenham Abbey) and *c.* 1830. Big Gothic conservatory, some artificial ruins, an Ionic covered garden seat and an ice house in the grounds.

At PATCHETTS GREEN, s of Aldenham, a pair of exceedingly picturesque farmhouses with weatherboarded outbuildings.

At DELROW, SE of Patchetts Green, gabled cemented house with a few preserved Jacobean-looking fireplaces. One rainwater-head bears the date 1666.

At BATLERS GREEN, 1 m. E of Aldenham, an excellent C16–C18 house. The street front is of eight bays, early C18. Behind, an L-shaped Tudor house with a plastered and pargetted gabled E front and contemporary timber and brickwork. In one room ceiling with moulded beams.

ALDENHAM HOUSE, 2 m. SE. A fine brick house of c. 1700, much enlarged c. 1870 and later, for instance by an incongruous tower. *Sir Arthur Blomfield* is supposed to have been the architect of 1870. The earlier house has a W front of seven bays with two storeys, hipped roof, dormer windows, a carved pediment, and a pedimented porch on detached unfluted Ionic columns, and a s front with central polygonal bay window and crowning vases. The Venetian window to the l. of the W front is Early Georgian. What valuable features the interior possesses are all boarded up at the time of writing.

ANSTEY

ST GEORGE. An architecturally interesting and externally very impressive church. Internally the aesthetic effect is spoilt by the very features which make the building archaeologically remarkable. The crossing tower seems Norman in its lower stages: four narrow roundheaded arches inside with shafts with extremely primitive volute or spiral capitals on the W side of W and E arches. The arches have roll-mouldings thickening at narrow, regular intervals into a kind of Norman shaft-rings, a motif used in the mid C12 decoration of the Slype at St Albans Abbey. The shafts also have such rings, but here they seem the proper shaft-rings of the Early Gothic style which were introduced in France about 1150 in a completely different context and do not appear in England before Canterbury in 1175. So this 'Norman' work is probably as late as *c.* 1200, a time-lag worth remembering. The chancel and both transepts were rebuilt late in the C13. The S transept front seen from the S is a fine sight, with C13 lancet windows and a round stair-turret. Behind it appears the crossing tower with diagonal buttresses right up to the top, C14 bell-openings and a Herts spike. The chancel has on its S and N sides typical late C13 windows with two lights with pointed trefoil heads and quatrefoils above (no bar tracery yet). Inside the chancel is a fine display of C13 detail. The E end has two blank lancets to the sides of the C19 E window, the N doorway a label on very unusual stops, and the S side an equally unusual piscina and sedilia arrangement combined with the windows and a doorway. It is all so odd that one wonders whether it has not been, in some way, tampered with. In the S transept S wall an exquisite though, alas, mutilated tomb-recess with a canopy and pinnacles. The canopy of the same type as those of *c.* 1300 in Westminster Abbey (blank trefoil in the top). It rests on naturalistic leaf stops. The pinnacles have blank tracery and also naturalistic leaves. Under the cusped arch of the canopy a woman's head with a wimple. The effigy in the recess (cf. below) does not seem to belong. The date of the canopy is probably the earliest years of the C14. Only a little, if at all, later the nave arcades (four bays) with big quatrefoil piers with moulded capitals and two-centred almost straight arches. The C15 clerestory windows are quatrefoil-shaped. The aisle windows are Late Perp, as is the S porch with two-light windows and blank panelling. The inner and outer doorways of the porch have blank quatrefoils in the spandrels. – FONT. Very crude Norman with four mermen holding their split tails with both their hands; the design makes a symmetrical pattern along the four sides of the bowl. – CHANCEL STALLS. Plain C15 or C16 with MISERICORDS (large leaves, a shell, a head with tongue out, two profile heads). – STAINED GLASS. S aisle window by *Heaton, Butler, & Baines*, 1907. – PLATE. Set of C18.

LYCHGATE. C15 or earlier. Tripartite; but one third altered into a lock-up.

ARBURY BANK see ASHWELL

ARDELEY

ST LAWRENCE. Unbuttressed W tower with spike. The W window C14. Embattled aisles, clerestory, and chancel. The aisle and clerestory windows mostly Perp. The N porch tall with two-light windows, also C15. Only in the chancel do two lancet windows show an earlier stage of the church. The windows are matched by the fine piscina and the N recess, both with short shafts and dog-tooth ornament. The nave N arcade consists of three bays with octagonal piers, and these must also be C13 (simple moulded capitals, double-chamfered arches). The s arcade is a little later: C14, as is presumably the chancel arch. The nave and aisle ROOFS of the C15 have bosses, angel brackets, and some tracery in the brackets. – The ROOD LOFT with painted rood and rood canopy (but no screen) was given in 1928. It was designed by *F. C. Eden.* – FONT. Octagonal with big faces in the four diagonals. The date is difficult to determine; probably C14. – PLATE. Chalice, Paten and Almsdish of the late C17. – MONUMENTS. Brasses to Philip Metcalffe, Vicar of Ardeley, † 1515, to Thomas Shotbolt with wife and children † 1599, and to W. Wyndham Malet, Vicar of Ardeley, † 1885 (profile, turned towards the altar). – Mary Markham † 1673, epitaph with lively demi-figure in niche with telling gestures. On a ledge in front her baby. Fine quality. – Cartouche to Henry Chauncy † 1703; also very good.

ARDELEY BURY. A Late Tudor house of brick of which little remains except some walls. The rest mostly the work of a fanciful architect of 1820 who converted the manor house into an enchanted castle. He added a circular flint tower, two polygonal brick turrets, divers pinnacles, and so on, made the windows Gothic, erected a baronial hall with a big fireplace, a minstrel's gallery and a plastered timber roof, and inserted Gothic vaulting in other rooms. Long avenue, lake, and Tudor boathouse.

THE GREEN was made in 1917 by the Lord of the Manor. A brick well in the middle, white thatched cottages, Village Hall, and terraces of cottages around, designed by *F. C. Eden* (a Blaise Castle Revived, though without the capriciousness of the original).

At Cromer, 1 m. NW, CROMER FARM, a specially attractive farmhouse with overhangs, exposed uprights, and gables.

ARKLEY

ST PETER. Rough brick church of 1840 with aisleless nave and transepts. Lancet windows. The chancel was added in 1898 (by *Traylen*; GR). – STAINED GLASS. E window 1903 by *Kempe*. – MONUMENT. Very simple epitaph to Enosh Durant † 1848, at whose expense the church was built; the epitaph is signed by the *Westminster Marble Company*, not by an individual sculptor, a sign of the coming Victorian times.

WINDMILL. NW of the church. Built probably early in the C19. Repaired in 1930.*

ASHLYNS *see* BERKHAMSTED

ASHRIDGE *see* LITTLE GADDESDEN

ASHWELL

13 ST MARY. The glory of the church is its W tower, in four stages with tall angle buttresses. It is 176 ft high, crowned by an octagonal lantern with a leaded spike, the same pattern as at Baldock.‡ The tower is clunch-built and more ambitious than any other of a Herts parish church, and it has never been explained why just Ashwell should have gone to such an enormous expense. It was begun in the

* Information kindly provided by Mr Rex Wailes.
‡ The leading was last renewed in 1948.

first half of the C14.* The church itself is of the same
date, the chancel was apparently completed in 1368, and
the whole building in 1381. The body of the church is of
clunch and flint, relatively low and not embattled except
for the chancel. Most of the windows are usual C15 Perp,
but the clerestory windows and the tower W window prove
that the Dec style was still alive when the building went
up. The S porch is two-storeyed, higher than the aisle,
with a fine outer doorway and two-light windows (the
vault is C19). The N porch of one storey has three-light
windows. Both porches are of the second half of the C15.
The interior bears out the building history surmised for
the exterior. The arcades of the nave look indeed a little
earlier than 1350. They change their details from E to W
(piers with big attached shafts and thin ones without
capitals in the diagonals, then piers with the big shafts
slightly thinner, then with the big shafts of semi-octagonal
section). The aisle roofs are good, solid C14 work. The
chancel arch corresponds to the earlier parts of the nave,
the tower arch to the later. To link up nave and tower a
blank piece of wall was left standing and decorated with a
blind two-light Perp arch as high as the whole nave. The
clerestory windows stand above the spandrels, not the
apexes of the arcade. The chancel is aisleless with large
windows, and as these have no stained glass it appears
very light. The whole church is indeed spacious and
broad, rather than tall. The walls are whitewashed, the
stone parts light. The effect is decidedly puritanical, especially as the church has surprisingly little of furnishings. –

* This is proved by the extremely interesting graffiti inside the N
wall of the tower. They say in Latin: 'MCterX Penta miseranda ferox
violenta . . .(? pestis) superest plebs pessima testis' and 'In fine ije
(secundae) ventus validus. . . . . Maurus in orbe tonat MCCCXI,
1350, wretched, wild, distracted. The dregs of the mob alone survive
to tell the tale. At the end of the second (outbreak) was a mighty
wind. St Maurus thunders in all the world.' The date of this exceptional gale was 1361. Higher up on the tower wall (N) there is a further inscription, in much smaller script: primula pestis in MterCCC
fuit l.minus uno. Also on the N wall a remarkably detailed and accurate
scratching of the S side of Old St Paul's cathedral.

PULPIT. 1627. The usual blank arches in the panels are made up of diamond-cut pieces. – LADY CHAPEL SCREEN. Very elementary C15 tracery. – STAINED GLASS. Small C15 fragments in clerestory windows. – PLATE. Paten, 1632; Chalice, 1688. – No monuments of importance. – LYCHGATE. Attributed to the C15.

4 The village has perhaps more architecturally worthwhile houses than any other in the county, and they are besides, thanks to an uncommonly discriminating and public-spirited landowner, in a very good state of preservation. But the village is so big that the houses cannot be taken in visually as a whole. They are nearly all of the timber-framed or the gabled brick type. The C18 has not added much (chiefly two houses near the E end of the High Street, one of five bays with a hooded doorway, the other of seven bays). In the centre of the High Street, especially excellent, the long ST JOHN'S GUILD HALL with its narrowly spaced timber uprights and the neighbouring cottages with bold rustic fancy pargetting of 1681. Remains of C15 houses have been analysed recently in *Country Life*. Towards the W end of the High Street the CHANTRY HOUSE with a two-light C18 window, and opposite WESTBURY FARM, plastered with symmetrical gables. S of the church the TOWN HOUSE (Museum), two-bay gabled C16 house with overhang and narrowly spaced timbers. (In the Museum a C15 silver Reliquary originally of the Guild of St John.) – W of the church the humble two-bay brick house which was founded by the London Merchant Taylors as a school in 1681. To the S of the grounds of Ashwell Bury DUCKLAKE FARM, a house with bold, good ornamental Tudor wall paintings in one room.

ASHWELL BURY. A sizeable Early Victorian house re-modelled, chiefly inside, by *Lutyens* in 1922–3. The sky-lit staircase is particularly notable. The lowest steps fill the well right across, before the staircase narrows to the width of the second and third flights. In a very Lutyensian way, the architect left one window in an inconspicuous position unaltered so as to show what he started from.

ASHWELL END, BLUEGATES FARM (N of Ashwell Bury).
Two more C16 farm-houses, a little further out.

ARBURY BANK, ¾ m. SW, between Claybush and Newn-
ham Hills. Iron Age hill-fort in the shape of an elongated
horseshoe, SW–NE across a hilltop. The size is 300 by 220
yd. The bank is highest at the SW, where the ground is
steepest.

ASPENDEN

ST MARY. Cemented and much restored (1873, by *Sir A.
Blomfield*). Unbuttressed W tower with spike. The interior mostly Perp and much C19. In the chancel lancets,
proving its C13 date. The S porch is quite lavish with a
decorated doorway and two-light window. It was built *c.*
1525 and paid for by the widow of Sir Robert Clifford.
Inside, the S aisle arcade (octagonal piers, moulded
capitals, two-centred arches) must belong to the mid C14.
The S chancel chapel is the most interesting part of the
church. It was remodelled in 1622. It opens to the chancel
in two bays with the usual octagonal piers, but the arches
are now made semicircular, and strapwork decoration
is applied. – C15 Roofs in nave, S chapel, and S aisle. –
Perp RECESSES in the N chancel wall (ogee canopy and
crenellation) and the S chapel. The latter houses the tomb
of Sir Robert Clifford † 1508. Tomb-chest with shields on
three lozenges. Depressed panelled arch. Against the back
wall brasses of the Clifford family. Quatrefoil frieze above
the arch and top cresting. – *Morris & Co.* windows of
1913 in the S porch. – MONUMENTS (cf. above): Man and
woman, 1500, 18 in. figures (nave, N wall). – Ralph and
William Freman † 1634 and 1623, big epitaph with
broken segmental pediment and beneath it, not in niches,
two frontal busts. The two brothers hold each other's
hands. – John Boldero † 1789, with urn above inscription; white, grey, and pink marble.

ASTON

ST MARY. The chancel shows signs of its erection in the
C13 (one lancet window, Double Piscina). The rest, as far

as visible, is C15 (W tower with diagonal buttresses with five set-offs) or C19 (S porch, nave S windows, whole N aisle). – PULPIT. C17, very simply panelled. – SCREEN. Simple, but handsome, *c.* 1500. – PLATE. Chalice and two Patens, 1571; Chalice, 1612. – BRASS. John Kent † 1592 and wife (nave, E end).

ASTON HOUSE. Brick house of *c.* 1700, remodelled in the C19. The old work well visible on the E side. The stables are more interesting in design than the house: also *c.* 1700, brick chequer with rubbed dressings. Blank arcades on the ground floor, alternating circular and oval windows on the upper floor. Lantern turret.

ASTONBURY HOUSE. Three-storeyed Jacobean brick mansion with remains of a first building period of *c.* 1540. Symmetrical S front (with big trees close to the E end). Two broad gabled projections contain two original staircases; two chimney stacks in the angles between the projections and the centre of the house which is occupied by the hall. On the N side a porch (rebuilt) leads into the Hall. The gables here are shaped with ogee above convex curves. The principal windows are mullioned and transomed. Handsome open well timber staircase (E) with tall obelisks on the newel posts and banisters whose upper half is the mirror image of the lower part.

FROGMORE HALL. Red brick Neo-Gothic mansion with big square tower (chequered parapet, two large Perp windows). Whom by?

AUBREYS, THE, *see* REDBOURN

AVENUE FARM *see* IPPOLLITTS

AYOT ST LAWRENCE

OLD ST LAWRENCE. The old church in the village is in ruins. Tradition has it that Sir Lionel Lyte began to pull it down when he had decided to build (as one would then have called it if to-day's jargon had already existed) an ultra-modern church in the grounds of his house. The

Bishop heard of this when demolition had gone some way, and prevented further destruction. The damage was not repaired, and so the picturesque ruin which we see to-day resulted, a sight which would no doubt have pleased Sir Lionel and his friends. What survives of the building shows that the church had a NW tower, nave, chancel, N aisle, and N chancel chapel. The windows in the N wall of the N chapel tell of Dec tracery (one has a combined star and quatrefoil motif in the head, known as Kentish tracery). The W arch of the same chapel with early C13 stiff-leaf capitals was originally that of the nave arcade. – A decayed C15 tomb-chest under the tower with recumbent effigies of a Knight and Lady.

The house, AYOT HOUSE, looks an early C18 building, with its segmentheaded windows and the characteristic vertical strips and window trim of rubbed bricks. The main front is of three storeys and five bays with the middle bay slightly projected. Additions were made c. 1850 and in 1933. STABLES with cupola and a portico or verandah of tall thin polygonal timber posts. The old manor house close by is of Tudor construction, with a front renewed in the late C17.

NEW ST LAWRENCE was designed by *Nicholas Revett* and 14b built in 1778–9 partly to replace the old church, partly to serve as an eye-catcher from the house. Hence its 'gloriette'-like far-spreading front. The church itself, no larger than, and rather similar to, an early C19 cemetery chapel, has a Grecian front, a thing unheard of at that time. The Grecian Revival had only just begun with *Revett's* and his colleague *James Stuart's* voyage to Athens and their publication of the *Antiquities of Athens* (vol. 1, 1762). To let one of them do a church or chapel with a real Greek temple roof proved a client to be eminently progressive (or ambitious, or perhaps just wanting to be fashionable). The portico with its columns only fluted at the top and foot is copied from the Temple of Apollo at Delos. But the whole composition with side colonnades and little outer aedicules is not at all Grecian. It is a purely Palladian composition, that is the type of composition which was customary for English country houses right through the c18. To have churches really copying Greek temples another fifty years had to go. The ground plan of *Revett's* church is remarkably original. A rectangular centre with coffered ceiling and a short W arm with a screen of two columns and a coffered tunnel-vault. Transepts of the same length and height, also tunnel-vaulted. The E end is a coffered apse, again of the same height and width, with two curved recesses. The small organ is original. – In the outer aedicules stand the urns to Sir Lionel Lyte and his wife.

BRIDE HALL, 1 m. S. Jacobean manor house of brick, built on the E-plan with central two-storeyed porch. The l. projecting wing has a straight gable. On the r. wing this has been replaced by a hipped roof. The windows are renewed. Staircases, door frames, and in the Hall a fireplace and moulded ceiling-beams remain. Weatherboarded barns to the r. and l. The area between them and in front of the house handsomely turfed by the present owner.

AYOT ST PETER

ST PETER. 1875, by *Seddon*. Red brick with blue brick decoration and stone dressings. Asymmetrically placed thin tower with broaches connecting the square with an octagonal upper stage on which rests a spire. Clock with fancifully designed face in a shade of blue. Nave and apsed chancel plus a polygonally projecting S organ chamber. Corresponding to this on the N side a large rose window on the ground floor flanked by lancets. It is all very capricious and deliberately original. The interior is an exceptionally complete example of church furnishing about 1880 by an architect in sympathy with the then recent Arts and Crafts tendencies : chancel arch, an early work of the *Martin Brothers*, who had their pottery at Southall from 1873 to 1915, thin iron chancel screen, elaborate tiling of the chancel, font with mosaic-work on the circular bowl. – STAINED GLASS in the W window (1880) designed by *Seddon* and incompetently executed,

in the apse windows (1879) by an unknown glass artist. –
PLATE. Chalice and Paten of *c.* 1640–50.
In the small cemetery, ½ m. W, a mortuary chapel, once the
E end of a previous church of 1863 by *Pearson*. Pearson's
church replaced one of 1732 which was octagonal and had
a campanile.

AYOT PLACE. Excellent though modernized farmhouse of
1615, partly timber-framing and plaster (N wing), partly
timber-framing and brick (E wing). The hall is in the E
wing and has a 'minstrels' gallery'.

AYOTBURY. A fine well-kept house, the centre block of
which is of 1672. Additions of 1913.

BALDOCK

ST MARY. A roomy church, architecturally in several points
the sister of Ashwell, a few miles away. Big broad W tower
of the early C14 with Dec windows, and on the embattled
parapet a small octagonal lantern crowned by a Herts
spike. The body of the church also embattled, mostly of
flint. But the lower part of the chancel is of stone. Here
traces can be found of C13 windows and a Double Piscina
with a C13 shaft. The S porch is two-storeyed with a turret
in the NW angle and an outer doorway of the early C14.
The other windows are Perp. The interior is in its appear- 18b
ance almost completely early C14: tower arch, arcades of
six bays, chancel arcades of two bays, Sedilia and Piscina
in the S chapel with nodding ogee arches. The piers are
quatrefoil with additional thin shafts (without capitals) in
the diagonals (just as at Ashwell), typical moulded capitals
(on the S side slightly more finely detailed than on the N),
and double-chamfered arches. Good contemporary head
corbels for the outer labels. C15 clerestory roofs (on head
corbels). The aisles are wide and on the low side. The
church is generally broad and roomy: a wealthy town
church. – FONT. Octagonal, on nine shafts; C13. –
SCREENS. A complete C15 set across aisles and chancel
arch, the rood screen, of course, more ornate than the
others, but all three relatively elementary in their tracery.

– STAINED GLASS. W window 1849, looks as if it might be by *Wailes*; E window similar; N aisle Simpson Window 1881, a typical early *Kempe*. – PLATE. Chalice and Paten, 1629. – MONUMENTS. C13 Purbeck marble coffin-lid with cross (N chapel). – Brasses to a nun, *c*. 1400, small (nave, W end); to a man and woman, *c*. 1400, smallish (N chapel); to a man and woman, later C15, larger figures (N chapel); to a man and woman, shrouded, *c*. 1520, *c*. 3 ft long (N chapel). – Monument to Georgiana Caldecott † 1846, by *Baily*. She lies on a couch mourned by a kneeling young woman, while an angel in the background of the relief carries her soul up to heaven. – Many minor epitaphs (e.g. by *Gaffin*).

PERAMBULATION

To judge from the houses of Baldock its wealth was of the C18 rather than the C16–C17. One remembers Georgian but no Tudor or Jacobean houses, red brick but no half-timber. What one chiefly remembers, however, is the interesting way in which the four main streets meet at the centre. They arrive from the four main directions ready to form the usual cross, a visually unsatisfactory thing for a town centre, because the unimpeded views across do not allow the eye to come to a halt in the middle of the town. At Baldock instead islands are inserted at the N end of the High Street and the W end of White Horse Street so that, from wherever one approaches the cross, the eye is always stopped by a wall of houses or at least a house projecting into the facing street. The most ingenious arrangement is at No. 1 HIGH STREET (Late Georgian) with a canted corner towards White Horse Street. The High Street is much wider than the other streets, especially after the island is passed. Part of the island (opposite No. 1) is the FIRE STATION BUILDINGS of 1897 (by *Talbot, Brown, & Fisher* of Wellingborough), uneventful red brick with a tower at the corner. In the High Street the best houses are near the N end. On the E side No. 9, the most ambitious house of Baldock, now unfortunately half hidden by trees. Early Georgian with segmental pediment to the door and an order of giant Corinthian pilasters of rubbed brick, with finely carved stone capitals and entablature. No. 11 is early C18, No. 21 late C18. No. 21 lies back, has seven bays of which the middle three project slightly and carry a pediment into which cuts the arched central window. Plain porch and pretty cast-iron gateposts. – Opposite is an equally stately group : Nos 12–14a (Early Georgian) with plainer details. Otherwise on the W side only Nos 32–42, WYNNE'S ALMSHOUSES of 1621, one-storeyed, brick, with a raised gateway in the low brick wall separating the front area from the street and Victorian bargeboarding to porches and dormers. On the E side Nos 21–23 is SIMPSON'S BREWERY, Late Georgian. It consists of a five-bay, three-storeyed, chequer brick dwelling house and the brewery proper with a seven-bay façade plus lower detached side buildings. The centre is refaced in yellow brick. Behind it the manufacturing parts with one range with giant blank arches, all of chequered brick.

Much less of note in the other streets. HITCHIN STREET is quite short and has on the S side some plastered gabled cottages, especially No. 27 with overhang on canted bays. No. 31, very narrow, is dated 1632. No. 33 lies back. It is early C18 brick and has seven bays. Opposite is No. 16, mid C18 with quoins and a pedimented doorcase with fluted pilasters. At the W end No. 37, three-storeyed, red brick with white brick quoins, a doorcase with fluted pilasters and a plaque with the date 1755. – In CHURCH STREET Nos 4–16, a Late Georgian terrace of two-storeyed brick cottages, No. 3 a large C16 plastered half-timber house with its r. half handsomely refronted in the early C18 (typical doorcase with frieze rising in the middle). At the far end No. 50 (BULL'S HEAD) with close vertical timbers. – Finally in WHITE HORSE STREET, which has the width of a High Street, No. 13 with a later Georgian three-bay, three-storey brick front and a doorcase with fluted Ionic pilasters, No. 22 on the other side, also later Georgian, but two-storeyed with giant angle pilasters and parapet. Back on the other side

No. 31 of five bays and two storeys with doorcase with
fluted pilasters and pediment, and No. 35 with two C17
brick gables and the rest of the front remodelled in the
late C18.

BALLS PARK

Balls Park is one of the most puzzling houses of Hertfordshire. At first sight it appears to be Early Georgian, and it
is only when details are examined that plenty of motifs
are noticed which are far too individual, even perverse,
even uncouth, to be possible in the Augustan Age. The
dates as recorded in fact point to a date about 1640, and
that again seems extremely unlikely considering the total
absence of those semi-Jacobean, semi-Dutch elements
(pedimented curved gables) which occur in such houses
as Swakeleys (Middlesex; 1629–38). Yet the dating is
fairly reliable. The house is illustrated in Chauncy, that is
in 1700, in exactly its present form, except for the pediments and one or two other features. Chauncy also says
that the house was built by Sir John Harrison who was a
rich supporter of King Charles, deprived of his estates in
1647 and only reinstated after the Restoration. He died in
1669, and it seems unlikely that he could have spent
money on a new house at any time later than c. 1640.*
Does the house then go with such a date? What contra-
dicts it is its unbroken block shape, 7 by 7 windows. One
expects a more lively, restless general relief of the façades.
But Tyttenhanger c. 1654 is no less plain and even. Moreover a close study of the main entrance on the N side with
the window above reveals some inconsistencies and mannerisms characteristic of the first coming of the classical
idiom. Tuscan pilasters with waist bands are placed l. and
r. of the doorway so that they half hide slightly higher
Ionic pilasters. The Tuscan pilasters are of stone, the
Ionic pilasters of brick. The doorway is arched and on its
apex stands a flat panel with a stunted pilaster in it. On
the capitals of the Tuscan pilasters are two big corbels,
incongruously placed. They support a balcony (with an

46b

* John Evelyn noted the house as newly built in 1643.

C18 railing). The arched door to the balcony has a frame with typical angular ears (cf. Tyttenhanger) and volutes scrolling out at the foot. The composition was originally continued in a semicircular pediment flanked by unicorns. The two storeys of the house are divided by a broad band of shaped bricks. The angles have brick quoins and two orders of brick pilasters. Of the three plus three windows to the l. and r. of the doorway the middle ones have equally odd stresses (short pilasters on the ground floor, arched heads on pilasters on the upper floor). All these details point to exactly such a date as tradition tells. They place the house near the beginning of a series of about six others which Professor Geoffery Webb grouped together some twenty years ago and called his 'six houses in search of an architect.' That architect has partly been found by Howard Colvin to be *Peter Mills* who practised in the City of London. Balls Park is not ascertained by him or Professor Webb, yet undoubtedly is in the same style. On the other hand, the pediments, the S porch, and some other alterations tally with Salmon's statement in 1728 that the house was 'greatly augmented and improved' by Sir John Harrison's sons who were in possession from 1705 to 1725.

Inside is a big central hall originally in all probability an open courtyard. The whole E side on the upper floor is filled by a long gallery. Several rooms have noble plaster [47] ceilings with that very division into large panels, octagonal, circular, semicircular, and so on, which the mid C17 liked.

A new N wing with a large Dining Room and main staircase was added in 1924–5 by *Sir Robert Lorimer*, and, for the purposes of the Training College which now is installed at Balls Park, a GYMNASIUM standing on its own. It is very handsome work of the H. C. C. Architect's Department (*C. H. Aslin* and *J. T. Pinion*).

BARKWAY

ST MARY MAGDALENE. A big, broad, spreading-out church with a W tower (diagonal buttresses; tower arch

Perp), rebuilt in 1861 with pinnacles (not a Herts pattern). The S porch is also C19. The chancel is the oldest part, C13, as proved by the lancet windows (E window tracery C19, chancel arch Perp). The N and S aisle arcades are characteristically Late Perp with piers consisting of semi-octagonal shafts and hollows in the diagonals. Characteristically Late Perp windows with very depressed, almost straight-sided, two-centred arches at the tops and elementary 'panel' tracery. – FONT. Octagonal, Perp, with fleurons on the coving. – STAINED GLASS. Remains of a Jesse window (E end S aisle): In the centre light four kings above each other, surrounded by leaf scrolls; other figures in the side lights; late C15. – PLATE. Chalice, Paten, and Flagon, 1714; small Chalice, 1807. – MONUMENTS. Brass to Robert Poynard † 1561 with wives and children (S aisle wall). – Standing wall monument to Sir John Jennings, Rear-Admiral, a Governor of Greenwich Hospital, Ranger of Greenwich Park, M.P., etc., † 1743 (against the tower w wall). For the great London man the most successful London sculptor was engaged: *J. M. Rysbrack*. The monument is signed. Tall broad base with inscription and very classical, typical *Rysbrack* detail. On it bust on plinth with two fine putti l. and r. – Several earlier epitaphs, e.g. Judith Chester † 1702, signed *Stanton*; Mary Chester † 1703, Stantonish; Thomas Smoult † 1707, signed according to Mrs Esdaile by *R. Hartshorne* (Stanton workshop). – James Andrew † 1796 and Thomas Talbot Gorsuch † 1820, both epitaphs by *P. Chenu* and done as *pendants*. They are also placed side by side. The earlier with a seated figure of Hope, the latter with Father Time. The change of style in the details is instructive. – John Baron Selsey † 1816, epitaph with a draped urn and bits of willow branches behind; by *Kendrick*.

MANOR HOUSE, S of the church. Brick, L-shaped, first half C17, with mullioned and mullioned-and-transomed windows and shaped gables.

NEWSELLS PARK, 1 m. N. The big house was accidentally burned during the Second World War. Newsells Bury lies immediately to its W, in the grounds, a small brick house of the late C17.

COKENACH, 1 m. NE. Formerly known as Cockenhatch. A composite history. The core is of 1716. Hence the segmentheaded windows. Additions of 1833, and more ambitious additions in 1925.

BARLEY

ST MARGARET. 1872, by *Butterfield*, except for the W tower and the S aisle. The W tower is of the C12 with a typical Norman tower arch, a ground-floor window with deep splay and also roundheaded upper windows. The top stage Early Perp. The S doorway with the aisle is of the C14. The S arcade may be a little earlier than this doorway: octagonal piers, plainly moulded capitals. One typical C14 window. The Butterfield interior is not impressive. The master's hand is only noticeable in the tower top, not a Herts spike but a Butterfield spike. – SCREEN. C15. Parts of the tracery re-used against the N wall of the chancel. – PULPIT. Good 'Jacobean' work, with bookrest, fine back, and fine tester with pendants. The actual date is 1626. – STAINED GLASS. Crucifixion N aisle E window and Head of God N aisle W window, C14 to C15. Some demi-figures of 1536. – PLATE. Steeple Cup, 1612; small Paten, 1618. The inscription in an exquisite script. – BRASS. Andrew Willet † 1621, praying, not quite frontal.

TOWN HOUSE. Early Tudor with outer stair to the upper floor which is one room with original timber roof. It was, amongst other purposes, 'used and employed for the keeping of maides' marriages'.

BIG HOUSE. Shaftenhoe End. E and N fronts early C18. Doorways with hoods on carved brackets. But on the S side porch with overhang on figure brackets and the inscribed date 1624, and longer wing with big outer chimney and diagonal chimney stacks.

Pretty overhanging cottages by the entrance to the village from the N.

BARNET *see* CHIPPING BARNET, EAST BARNET,
NEW BARNET

BATCHWORTH HEATH
1¾ m. SE of Rickmansworth

BATCHWORTH HEATH HOUSE is a nice three-bay Georgian red brick house.

The S ENTRANCE GATES TO MOOR PARK, *see* Moor Park.

BATLERS GREEN *see* ALDENHAM

BAYFORD

ST MARY. 1870, by *Woodyer*. Stone, in the E.E. style, with brick quoins and a flèche. The S vestry roof is the nave and chancel roof carried lower down without a break (a happy effect). – FONT. Perp, octagonal with simple tracery and quatrefoil motifs. – MONUMENTS. George Knighton † 1612, excellent recumbent marble effigy in armour. Let into the back wall the brasses of two men in armour, *c.* 1550 and *c.* 1590.

BAYFORDBURY. The long white façade of twenty-five bays, stepped up gently towards the centre, makes an exceedingly fine effect of Regency elegance, set behind an ornamental lake. In fact the house belongs to two periods, 1759–62 and 1809–12. Of the first are the seven-bay centre and the pedimented outer wings with their cupolas, of the second the connecting links containing one large room each towards the garden, and the porticoes. The garden portico is of unfluted Ionic columns, that towards the entrance of heavy Greek Doric columns, and attached Greek Doric columns are also used on the same side for the new intermediate parts. An iron balcony on thin iron shafts runs all along the garden façade which is also extended still further by an orangery wing on the r. and a screen-wall of the same design on the l. Inside, the Entrance Hall has still its stucco ceiling and fireplace in the

Rococo taste of 1760, and the stucco work of the room to the l. of the Entrance Hall is of the same date. The rest, as far as it has datable decoration at all is in the style of 1810, notably the staircase with its curved sweep up to the upper floor gallery, its iron balustrade and circular dome, and the two ingeniously contrived corridors with an excessively elongated groined vault and small saucer domes decidedly Soanian in character. The fireplace in the present Library was originally in the Egyptian taste which was the latest fashion in 1810 (thanks to Napoleon's Egyptian campaign and Denon's publication of 1803). The two side figures of mottled marble are preserved.

The grounds are of famous beauty. A group of cedars on the E side of the lawn was planted in 1765. Close to the kitchen garden are the stables, plain and utilitarian but dignified (1812).

BEECHES see BRENT PELHAM

BEECHWOOD
1½ m. SW of Flamstead

The house stands close to the site of a suppressed nunnery. ₅₀ₐ But no remains exist now older than the Elizabethan period, and what there is, is quite minor. The beauty of the house is its NE façade of 1702. It is of red and purple brick chequer with stone quoins and lively stone surrounds of the windows. The central doorway of the nine-bay, two-storeyed front has a broken segmental pediment on fluted Corinthian pilasters. – Central three-bay pediment, hipped roof, and dormer windows. The central courtyard of the house was converted into a Hall with skylight in 1859. To the SE front a wing was added in 1819 with the Library. *Soane* had something to do with the house (according to information kindly provided by Miss Dorothy Stroud), and the blue marble fireplace of the Library may indeed well be his. – Splendid fireplace, door frames, and ceiling of *c.* 1740 in the drawing room to the N of the Entrance Hall.

BENGEO

ST LEONARD. The rare example of a virtually intact Norman village church; nave and chancel with apse. This
again is a rarity, at least in Herts (but cf. Great Amwell).
The apse has small roundheaded windows in the deep
inner splays, the nave has one such window on the N side.
On the S side the windows have been enlarged and altered
in the C14 and C15. The brick S porch dates from the C18,
the timber bell-cote from the C19. The S and N doorways
are original, and the chancel arch has an order of colonnettes with one scroll capital and the other with the face of
a man. The chancel and apse are surprisingly roomy. – S
DOOR. Probably C14. – COMMUNION RAILS. C18. –
PAINTING. On the nave E wall a C13 Deposition from the
Cross and indications of quatrefoil patterns. In the chancel painted ashlaring and a later, superimposed red
lozenge pattern. – TILES. Some of the C14 below the
Communion Table (cf. Much Hadham). – PLATE.
Chalice and Paten, 1626. – MONUMENTS. John Ryde,
mural tablet of 1665, by *William Stanton*. – Humphrey
Hall, 1742, by *Thos. Adey*, profile medallion held by
two putti with rather vacant faces. The background the
usual obelisk. – Daniel Minet † 1790, a modest tablet by
Nollekens.

BENGEO HALL. E front of 1745 with two canted bay windows, and a late C18 doorway to which a staircase with
handsome mid C18 iron railings leads up. The third floor
of the front hides three earlier gables.

BENINGTON

ST PETER. Essentially a late C13 to early C14 church, although the W tower with angle buttresses and a Herts
spike belong to the C15, as do the clerestory with big two-
light windows and the chancel S windows. The Sedilia in
the chancel are the earliest pieces in the church, much restored, but certainly made some time before 1300: stiff-
leaf, and crocket capitals and cusped pointed arches. The

Piscina is a little later; it has an ogee arch. Its style goes with that of the nave N windows. The N chancel chapel was added yet later, say about 1320–30. It is the most important part of the church. The windows have modest flowing tracery, the arcade to the chancel quatrefoil piers with thin shafts in the diagonals and simple moulded capitals (cf. Ashwell and Baldock). The labels rest on excellent corbels (head of a woman wearing a wimple, man piercing his body with a sword, etc.). The arches are of finely moulded sections. Under one of the two arches stands a MONUMENT with two more than lifesize effigies, a cross-legged Knight and a Lady wearing a wimple. The figures are defaced. On the sides of the tomb-chest mourners in arcades with triangular heads. The arch above is surrounded by a big crocketed ogee canopy flanked by thin buttresses on which some tracery is exactly identical with that of the windows. The style seems to exclude a date later than *c.* 1330; yet the heraldry is supposed to point to 1358. To the E of this chantry a smaller opening with a four-centred arch was pierced through early in the C15 for the placing of another MONUMENT with two effigies. The heraldry here indicates the date 1432. Ogee niches on the tomb-chest. The arch is panelled inside and has in the centre of the panelling the figure of an angel holding the little souls of the deceased in a cloth. Between the two openings BRASS of a priest, upper half only, C15. – FONT. Octagonal, with projecting, coarsely moulded shafts in the diagonals (cf. Walkern). – BENCHES. Simple C15. – PLATE. Chalice and Paten, 1639.

The VILLAGE GREEN is almost perfect, with individual scattered cottages, showing their timber-framing, or plastered and with overhangs and gables (BELL INN). Benington possesses besides several bigger houses of interest.

THE LORDSHIP, a Georgian house converted into a Neo-Norman fantasy to match the scanty remains of the KEEP of Benington Castle. This was a structure of flint with stone dressings 44 by 41 ft in size with thick walls and flat pilaster strips. The wall fragments stand to the height of 9 ft and are ivy-clad and adorned with Neo-Norman doorways, etc. A Neo-Norman gatehouse was also added between house and keep. This was designed, we are told, by a landscape gardener, *Pulham* of Broxbourne, not by an architect, a fact eminently characteristic of the age of the Picturesque.

OLD RECTORY. 1637. Brick front with three gables and a two-storeyed porch with Tuscan pilasters and a simple pediment. The windows all altered. Originally they were no doubt mullioned and had hood-moulds (*see* the windows in the gables).

BERKHAMPSTEAD, GREAT, *see* BERKHAMSTED

BERKHAMSTED

In contrast to the neighbouring Hemel Hempstead the church at Berkhamsted lies right along the High Street, more or less in line with the houses on the N side. This gives the church a decidedly urban character.

ST PETER. The result of much adding and enlarging. At least five periods can be distinguished (apart from *Butterfield's* restoration in 1871): chancel *c.* 1200 (lancet windows with nook shafts); crossing piers and N transept walls of the same date; nave with both arcades of seven bays (not at all in line with the chancel) late C13 (begun from the E with quatrefoil piers on the S, an alternation of circular and quatrefoil piers on the N side, and continued to the W with circular piers only; simple moulded capitals, double-chamfered arches); N transept E aisle with rib-vaults *c.* 1300; S chancel chapel early C14 (ogee reticulation in the window tracery; ogee-headed Piscina; two tomb-recesses, the E one with a renewed arch), outer S aisle mid C14 (with a wooden post separating it from the inner aisle); S aisle, W part of outer aisle (originally a porch), and clerestory C15; upper parts of the crossing tower 1535–6. The crossing tower dominates the external appearance of the large flint-built church. It is big and powerful with a NE stair-turret rising higher than its battlements. The body of the building spreads broadly along the street and faces on the other side across the churchyard the old Grammar School. – SCREEN. In W tower arch; C15, much renewed. – STAINED GLASS. Some C14 glass in chancel N widows. – S aisle window with three Saints, by *Kempe* 1880. – PLATE. Chalice, 1629; Almsdish, 1637; Paten, 1706. – BRASSES. Richard Torrington (?) † 1356 and wife (N aisle). – Demi-figure of Priest, *c.* 1400 (chancel). – Woman, *c.* 1360 (N aisle). – Richard Westbroke † 1485 (N aisle). – Thomas Humfre, *c.* 1470, shrouded, with wife and children, and figure of St Michael; re-used on the reverse for John Water-house † 1559 and wife (N transept aisle). – John Raven † 1395 (St John's Chapel). – Katherine Incent † 1520, shrouded (St John's Chapel). – MONUMENTS. Knight and Lady, late C14, defaced stone figures on tomb-chest with ogee-headed niches and shields. – James and John Murray † 1627 and 1634, epitaph with busts of the two brothers in a circle. They died young and are here seen holding hands. One of them reads in a book. Good quality (chancel). – Thomas Baldwin, 1642, by *Nicholas Stone*, large tablet without figures (S aisle near W end). – Elizabeth Cradock † 1704, standing wall monument of shallow relief; no figures; by *F. Hardy* (S transept). – Mary Isabella Smith † 1834, with large kneeling figure, apparently unsigned.

CASTLE. Large but only very fragmentarily preserved. The situation is unimpressive. The remains consist of an outer and an inner moat surrounding an area of *c.* 450 by 300 ft. In the NE corner is the motte or mount, *c.* 45 ft high, on which originally stood a shell-keep. The bailey was surrounded by a wall with some semicircular projections. Living quarters were on the W side and in the NE corner. From here two bridges crossed the narrow ditch between bailey and mount and a staircase led up to the keep. All that remains of stonework are stretches of flint walling nowhere more than 15 or 20 ft high. The castle was probably first erected with earth walling and stockades late in the C11 (William's half-brother, Robert of Mortain) and rebuilt in stone during the ten years when Thomas Becket held it in his quality of Chancellor. Documents refer to building work between c. 1160 and c. 1180. In 1216 the castle was besieged by King Louis of France. Later it became an appendage of the Dukes of Cornwall.

The Castle lies on the N bank of the river Bulbourne (and the N side of the railway), the HIGH STREET runs parallel with the river some distance to the S. Its centre is the church and the houses surrounding it. To the SW of the church COURT HOUSE, C16, timber-framed, very renewed, with a projecting upper storey. To the N of the church across the churchyard the GRAMMAR SCHOOL. Its nucleus is the building erected c. 1544 from the endowment of John Incent, Dean of St Paul's. It consists of a long brick-built room with kingpost roof and six three-light windows with four-centred heads. Gabled additions to E and W as houses for schoolmaster and usher, and large more recent additions behind to the N. – E of the church in CASTLE STREET nice quiet terraces of houses, Nos 1–4 brick and timber-framing, Nos 5–9 early C19 purple and red brick.* Finally, S of the church, that is in the HIGH STREET proper, the best house of Berkhamsted, INCENT'S HOUSE, half-timbered with overhanging upper floor, carefully restored. This is followed to the E, still facing the church, by Nos 117–121, three quiet houses of c. 1800.

The HIGH STREET is best visited from its W end. It begins in an informal villagey way with only a few individual houses worth noting. BOXWELL HOUSE (S), broad three-bay design of c. 1700, cemented front with quoins and quoins to the middle bay. A pediment over this. Doorcase with Ionic columns. – Then SAYER ALMSHOUSES (S), 1684, one storeyed row of six brick houses with big segmental pediment in the centre. – Opposite several nice Early Victorian villas with trellis porches, etc. – No. 189 (S), early C18, blue and red brick chequer. –

* Beyond the Grammar School in Castle Street a pretty, irregular group of timber-framed cottages, Nos 49–57.

No. 222, 1737, former Bourne Charity School, brick. –
By the War Memorial the street narrows on the N side
forming a very effective angle, where the BELL INN with
plastered gabled side appears behind some trees planted
with discrimination. – Opposite the KING'S ARMS,
three-bay red brick, with three oriels on the first floor;
the second floor is an addition. – Then the SWAN INN,
C17, with two symmetrical plastered gables, and close to
it Nos 135–137, early C18 with quoins and dressings
painted black in the early C19 way. – Past the church the
RED HOUSE HOTEL, the most ambitious C18 house in
the town: seven bays with a fine porch with Ionic
columns and pediment; big Venetian window above. –
Then Nos 103–109, an urban terrace of early C19 yellow
brick houses with pretty iron balconies. – After that the
architectural interest lessens.

On the other side the High Street is continued in GOS-
SOM'S END, first with solid rows of early C19 cottages,
then with individual houses. Gossom's Lodge (with
Gothick windows) and Gossom's Cottage, both of three-
bay width; Nos 77–80, a half-timbered group; and Edge-
worth House, three-bay, cemented C18 house, with tall
pilasters, lying isolated under old trees.

BAPTIST CHURCH, High Street, 1864. Yellow and red
brick, with an ugly, asymmetrically placed turret.
Typical of its date.

FRIENDS MEETING HOUSE, High Street, 1818. Simple
pedimented brick structure with arched door and two
arched windows.

THOMAS CORAM (FOUNDLING HOSPITAL) SCHOOL,
1933–5, by *J. H. Sheppard & Partners*. The statue of
Coram by *W. Calder Marshall*. A large axial composition
of pale brick buildings connected by colonnades. The
detail restrainedly Neo-Classical.

BERKHAMSTED PLACE. Gabled, symmetrical Elizabethan
house with central hall and central entrance. The wings
project in two steps. All this is only the remains of a
courtyard house of *c.* 1580, altered in 1610–11, and again
in 1662 after a fire had destroyed two-thirds of the house.

Original C16 work on the NW side, stone and flint chequer
pattern. At the NE end an original oriel window. Inside a
large original fireplace with late C17 alterations and a good
plaster ceiling on the first floor.

ASHLYNS, 1 m. s. *c.* 1800 with bow-fronted centre with iron
verandah. 'The whole building, gracefully set on the top
of a slope, has a light and easy air' (MHLG).

HARESFOOT, 2 m. s. Late Georgian five-bay two-storey
house with stuccoed frontages.

GRIMS DYKE. Traces of this Saxon boundary line can be
followed near Berkhamsted. They are on the opposite side
of the Bulbourne valley in the parishes of Northchurch
and Wigginton. Grims Dyke is a ditch of *c.* 35 ft across
and a bank of which two stretches survive, one 800, the
other 500 yds long. Its purpose was probably rather pro-
tection against cattle raids than against strictly military
aggression.

BISHOPS STORTFORD

Visually Bishops Stortford has little to compare with, say,
Hitchin or Hertford, let alone St Albans. It does not give
one the impression of the wealthy late medieval or Georgian
town which one might expect. The town consists chiefly of
the crossing of four main streets with the market square and
the Corn Exchange in the centre and the church along the
side of one of the four.

ST MICHAEL. A big, low, embattled Perp town church
with a W tower and tall spire, prominent for a long distance around, not owing to the early C15 which built it
(set-back buttresses, low stair turret) but to the year 1812
when a tall, slim upper stage of light brick was added,
with buttresses at the angles and pinnacles above and a
lead spire. The contrast between the business-like sturdi-
ness below and the fragility above is that between Gothic
and Gothick. The whole church is otherwise of the C15
(except for the C19 N chancel chapel and tall S vestry)
with typical Late Perp windows, with depressed segmental or depressed pointed arches (the latter with almost

straight sides), with a N porch two bays deep and a s porch. The chancel clerestory and chancel E window belong to the C19. The original E window of three lights is now in the s wall. The interior is big and airy. Tall [19] tower arch on thin responds, six-bay arcade with thin piers (four main shafts and four hollows in the diagonals) and two-centred arches, two-light clerestory windows, lower chancel. The roofs of nave, chancel, and aisles are original. In the nave the arched braces are traceried, and they rest on stone corbels with the figures of the Apostles. In the aisles instead of these there are grotesques and also such genre figures as a gardener with pruning knife, a cook with ladle, a woodman with bill-hook, etc. – FONT. C12, square, of Purbeck marble, with shallow blank arches; on five supports. – ALTAR AND SURROUND. 1885, by *Sir A. Blomfield*. – PULPIT. Locally made for £5 in 1658, an extremely late date for so purely Elizabethan a piece. The angles have termini pilasters decorated with raised ovals and diamonds. This and the decoration of the main panels with arches in feigned perspective probably comes straight from some pattern book. – SCREEN. C15; big, with two tall four-light sections on each side of the entrance. – CHANCEL STALLS. C15, with poppy-heads at the ends of the front stalls and MISERICORDS for the [31a] back seats. They represent *inter alia* heads of human figures and animals, very well carved, an angel, a swan, an owl, a dragon. – DOORS. Original, both in N and s porches. – STAINED GLASS. Chancel s window, by *Powell*, 1853 (TK), still in the painting tradition of the C18; not yet medievalizing. – w window, by *Kempe*, 1877, a very characteristic example of his early manner. – PLATE. Paten, 1563; Chalice, 1597; Chalice, 1683; two Flagons, 1721; Almsdish, 1741. – No monuments of any importance.

ALL SAINTS, Stanstead Road, Hockerill. 1937, by *S. E. Dykes Bower*. In a position overlooking the whole town. Big square tower with hipped roof and three excessively elongated lancet windows. The two entrances into the aisles with curiously lobed arches. Interior with tall circular piers, a long aisleless chancel and a rose E window with C20 flowing tracery.

CONGREGATIONAL CHURCH, Water Lane, 1860. Said to be by *W. F. Poulton.* Stock-brick on an elongated central plan with two façade towers. The trim is Italianate.

WAYTEMORE CASTLE, Bridge Street, on the other side of the river from the town, that is in a position just like Berkhamsted Castle. Of the rectangular shell-keep only foundations remain. It was on a narrow mount, 40 ft high. To the s was the bailey (now pleasure grounds).

CORN EXCHANGE. The secular centre of the town, built 1828 in a self-confident Neo-Greek style. Ground floor with Tuscan piers in the accentuated places, upper floors with a giant Ionic portico to the N, a portico *in antis* to the w. Architect: *G. Perry* of Bishop Stortford.

BISHOPS STORTFORD COLLEGE. The original buildings in the Gothic style 1867 by *J. Clarke,* boarding houses of 1914, etc. The Memorial Hall by *Clough William Ellis* (1921–2) in a 'Colonial' Georgian much more elegant than most of the Neo-Georgian work of the period.

HOCKERILL TRAINING COLLEGE. Red brick with diaper pattern and stone trim. By *J. Clarke,* 1852. Later additions.

PERAMBULATION

The corner of High Street and North Street is the GEORGE HOTEL. With its two-storeyed gabled and pargetted old part and its three-storeyed completely urban Early Victorian E part it marks the span of the building history of the town. HIGH STREET has the church on one side, on the other houses mostly of no special merit. But No. 10 (C17, gabled with second floor overhang) and especially No. 30 (broad, with three irregular gables; the overhangs rest on canted ground floor bays; central entrance arch, half bows to connect it with the projecting bays, a pretty C18 adaptation of the C17) are worth a look. The High Street is continued in the wider, more suburban WIND HILL. The houses here are more loosely placed and mostly early C19. An eminently picturesque group is No.

15B, C17 cottages with malthouse and granary. – NORTH STREET has a good assortment of houses on the W side, ranging from the HALF MOON INN (No. 31) to the tall early C19 CHEQUERS HOTEL with its two three-storeyed bay windows, and to Nos 7 and 9, both Victorian business Gothic of stock brick with stone and red brick trim, No. 7 Northern (*c.* 1868), No. 9 Tuscan in design.* Facing the N end of North Street THE CHANTRY, an irregular group of mainly C18 buildings and a glaring example of how a shop and a bit of showy sham-half-timbering can ruin an important vista. To the r., down NORTHGATE END, again bigger suburban houses, the best BROOKE HOUSE, white brick, three storeys, with Roman Doric doorcase and lower wings. The approximate date can be guessed from some cottages opposite called Waterloo Place.

Parallel with North Street runs WATER LANE with large detached houses whose gardens look towards the river (e.g. the house facing Barrett Lane). Water Lane runs into BRIDGE STREET. Here first a group of C17 plastered houses (Nos 2–6), and then the BLACK LION, a C16 57a building with exposed timbers, overhang and gables, very picturesque, although rather over-restored. Opposite No. 11, early C17, with nice interiors. Across the bridge and past the Castle DANE STREET turns S. Here and in DELL LANE pargetted houses mixed up with industrial building. From the Castle HOCKERILL STREET runs up the hill. No. 29 is nice Late Georgian, Nos 37–41 a specially hand-some group of the C17. At the top, facing Hockerill Street, is the COCK INN, early C17. Turning N a good way out in PARSONAGE LANE CHURCH MANOR, C18 brick frontages and fine early C18 gables with a cupola, blank oval and circular windows in the front and a large blank Venetian window on the side. Farther out on the DUNMOW ROAD the NAG'S HEAD, 1936, by *E. B. Musman*, once famous as one of the few architecturally modern pubs, now rather dated with its exact symmetry.

* The change of taste was contagious. The shop front opposite at No. 14 was also remodelled in Tuscan Trecento.

The Public Bar and the Saloon Bar are in their shapes and positions absolutely one the echo of the other. No distinctions of character, no use made of the capabilities of the corner position.

s of the centre the main streets are more thoroughly modernized. Only farther out a few things of interest. At the beginning of SOUTHMILL ROAD as the MHLG has rightly emphasized, some excellent examples of late C18 and early C19 malthouses, etc. (N earlier than S). At the beginning of SOUTH ROAD the house where Cecil Rhodes was born, typical, dignified, semi-detached, early C19 house with heavy Tuscan porch-pillars.

Two FARMHOUSES in the neighbourhood may be singled out as specially handsome: WICKHAM HALL, 1¼ m. NW, and STORTFORD PARK, 1½ m. W.

BLAKESWARE see WIDFORD

BOREHAM WOOD

ALL SAINTS, 1910, by *Francis & Minty* (GR). Arty-crafty and not good of the kind.

Some nice houses along the road W of the town, both Georgian residences and a farm (NICOLL FARM) with outbuildings.

64 COWLEY HILL COUNTY PRIMARY SCHOOL, see Introduction, p. 28.

BOVINGDON

ST LAWRENCE. 1845, by *Talbot Bury*, to whose memory (he died in 1877) a stained-glass window was put up in the church (N aisle). *Bury's* building is flint, clearly in the Herts style, no longer with the freedom (and ignorance) of the earlier C19. Only the aisle windows have a tracery design not historically documented. – STAINED GLASS. E window by *Lavers*, 1856 (TK). – MONUMENT. Tomb-chest with stone effigy of an unknown Knight in armour of *c.* 1400 (pointed bascinet).

RENTSTREET FARM, ½ m. SE. Brick and timber-framing.

The ground floor probably C16, the upper floor C17; *see* the closer spacing of the uprights below.

BOXMOOR

ST JOHN, 1874, by *Norman Shaw*. Surprisingly uninteresting compared with Shaw's later churches. Nave, aisles, chancel, and chancel aisles, turret on the nave away from the w end. Simple, small, mostly two-light windows in the style of *c*. 1300. Inside, quatrefoil piers.

CONGREGATIONAL CHAPEL, Box Lane. Built in 1690, but the outside now of an appearance as if re-done early in the C19.

WESTBROOK HAY. Large, stuccoed early C19 façades with curved and shallow rectangular bay windows. A rustic entrance lodge at the N gates.

BRAMFIELD

ST ANDREW. So much restored in 1840 that it appears an Early Victorian building. The w tower is hardly taller than the nave roof and has a spire. The tower arch is characteristically thin and bodyless. – PLATE. Chalice, 1562; Paten, 1617; Breadholder, 1757. – MONUMENTS. Two epitaphs to George Viscount Grandison † 1699 and the Rev. Edward Bourchier † 1775, of identical design.

QUEEN HOO *see* p. 188.

BRAUGHING

A compact village with the church in the centre. The main village street E of the church. The churchyard is surrounded by houses to the W, S, and E. To the W behind them a stream, which can only be crossed by footbridges and fords, and on the other bank another street higher up parallel to the main street.

ST MARY. With the exception of the chancel (N lancets) entirely early C15.* w tower tall, of three stages, with setback buttresses and a recessed spire rather than a spike.

* In 1416 John Kyllan of London left £5 for the work on the church.

W door with ornamented spandrels and niches to the l. and r. Two-storeyed S porch with ornamented spandrels to the doorways, large two-light side windows, a two-light upper S window with niches. Battlements and angle pinnacles (that is, everywhere a show of a little more money spent than by most of the neighbouring churches). Embattled clerestory with three-light windows, rood loft turret at the SE end of the nave. Late Perp N and S aisle windows. Tall W tower arch, arcades of four bays with piers of four main shafts and four hollows in the diagonals, the latter without capitals. The arches are re-used from an earlier arcade. Fine nave roof with the sub-principals carried on angels and the E bays panelled and decorated with bosses. – BENCHES. A few C15, buttressed. – STAINED GLASS. E window of 1916–17, just going C20 in style, that is with the leading getting heavier and more severe. (By whom?) – PLATE. Chalice, Paten, and Flagon, 1718. – MONUMENTS. Brass to man and woman, c. 1480, much rubbed off, 18 in. figures (S aisle). – Brass to Barbara Hauchett † 1561. – Tablet to Sir John Brograve † 1593, without figure. – Epitaph to Augustin Steward † 1597, frontal bust, very stiff. – Large standing wall monument to John Brograve † 1625 and his younger brother, two stiffly reclining figures, their heads propped up on their elbows, in a reredos framing with big columns and arch between them; in the spandrels the figure of an angel blowing soap bubbles (Vanity) and Father Time. – Large monument to Ralph Freman, D.D., of Hamels, † 1772 and his wife as well as two other Freemans and their wives. The portraits are in three medallions, each with two profiles, the main one on the severe sarcophagus which forms the centre of the composition. Two putti lie a little awkwardly on their bellies on the volutes of the curved top, Michelangelo's Medici allegories in reverse; the other medallions are on the sides outside the monument proper. The monument was designed by *James Stuart* (Athenian Stuart) and carved by the younger *Scheemakers*.

W of the church a handsome cottage with pargetted upper

floor, S of the church one with exposed timbers and brick nogging. In a kind of square E of the church a late C17 three-bay brick house and a C17 overhang house with two gables. THE BURY, NW of the church, the older manor house, also C17, with gables, quite extensive.

HAMELS *see* p. 104.

BRENT PELHAM

ST MARY. Essentially mid C14, save the C15 W tower (with diagonal buttresses and Herts spike). The restoration of 1861 added the S porch and renewed the S, N, and chancel E windows. In the chancel the N and S windows are original. But the most interesting tracery is that of the preserved S DOOR: early C14. The interior is wide, tall, and bare. Tall tower arch with big shafts with capitals and thin diagonal shafts without. – SCREEN. Some of the tracery of the C15 rood screen used in the tower screen. – PLATE. Chalice, 1628. – MONUMENTS. C13 black marble slab with foliated cross, angel above it holding a soul in a cloth and around him the symbols of the four Evangelists; a very remarkable work. – Brass to the two wives of F. Rowley † 1625 and 1627, two seemingly identical women with ruffs and hats.

BRENT PELHAM HALL. E of the church, a fine, broad, late C17 brick front of nine bays with slightly projecting pedimented three-bay centre and two-bay outer wings. Modillion frieze, hipped roof. Some of the chimney-stacks behind this front prove that the structure is earlier. A date-stone marked 1608 indeed remains.

THE BURY, ¼ m. N of the church. Farmhouse dated 1677 yet still with overhang and diagonally set 'Tudor' chimney-stacks.

BEECHES, 1 m. ESE of the church. Early C17 house with big outer chimneys with fine octagonal shafts and moulded capitals. In two of the chimneys are two-light mullioned brick windows. The main front altered in the C18.

BRICKENDON BURY
1¼ m. ssw of Hertford

Connected with Hertford by Morgan's Walk, an avenue ¾ m. long. The house seems to be Georgian, with giant pilasters on the entrance front, but redone in 1885–6, when an Italianate tower was added, and again in 1898, when the other fronts were made pretty with half-timbering and ornamental plasterwork.

BRICKHOUSE *see* GREAT HORMHEAD

BRIDE HALL *see* AYOT ST LAWRENCE

BRIDGEWATER MONUMENT *see* ALDBURY

BRIGGENS *see* STANSTEAD ABBOTTS

BROCKET HALL

A big square red brick mansion by *James Paine*, in a large park. The main vista from the house is the river Lea converted into an undulating lake with a bridge by *Paine* at the s end. The landscaping of the grounds is the work of *Mr Wood* of Essex. As for the house, which was begun about 1755 and completed externally in 1775 and internally about 1780, the most surprising thing about it is its utilitarian exterior as compared with its generous size and its magnificent interiors. It is a square block with no stone facings, no stone window trim, no portico. To relieve uniformity, no more is done than to give the saloon unusually large arched windows (the basement below them was only created when a formal garden was laid out in front of this façade), to add canted bay windows on the saloon (w) side and the E side, to give the main entrance (s side) attached columns and a pediment, and to enlarge some windows to the Venetian triple-window pattern. That is not much; it leaves the three-storeyed house a big structure inspiring more respect than affection. But inside splendid things were done. The plain Entrance Hall is connected with the central staircase, which starts with one arm and continues in two at right angles. On the first floor level a gallery runs round three sides of the staircase with fluted columns (the lower part spiral-fluted) and little circular and oval saucer domes. The centre above the staircase itself has a large glazed oval dome. The iron railing is of a delightfully lively honeysuckle pattern. Of the other rooms a few (the Billiard Room and the Study, the latter an asymmetrically shaped room cleverly balanced by the insertion of two columns to divide it into a main part and, as it were, an alcove) have Palladian mid C18 decoration, the others are frankly in the more fashionable taste of *Robert Adam*, with exquisite daintily detailed plaster ceilings. Most of the stucco work is white, but in the Saloon, a room of remarkable size, the coved ceiling is gilt, with paintings, on a scale very different from the dainty, playful, a little finicky scale of the Adam circle. These paintings were indeed designed and begun by *John Hamilton Mortimer*, an artist of genius who was capable occasionally of real Sturm und Drang savageries, and completed by *Wheatley* after Mortimer's early death in 1779. The Saloon is undoubtedly the climax of the house; and that is as it should be.

BROOM HALL *see* WATTON-AT-STONE

BROOKMANS *see* GOBIONS

BROXBOURNE

ST AUGUSTINE. A large church, entirely of the C15–C16.ᵃ Tall w tower with angle buttresses and a sw stair-turret higher than the tower. Decorated w door and four-light w window. Nave and two aisles, chancel, and two chancel chapels. The whole church is embattled, except for the N chancel chapel or Saye Chapel which has a parapet with an inscription recording its erection in 1522. The chapel is stone-faced, as is also the s chapel, whereas the rest of the church is flint. The s chapel was built before the N chapel, in 1476, by *Robert Stowell* who later built St Margaret's church by the side of Westminster Abbey. All the windows of Broxbourne church are Perp. Of post medieval only the s porch doorway, semicircular with complex classical surround. It may be *c.* 1650. There is no chancel arch, so that the arcades run through from w to e. Tall thin piers of four shafts and four hollows in the diagonals. The same design appears in the taller tower arch. The roof of the nave is original, so is the handsome panelled ceiling of the chancel, adorned with bosses. – FONT. Octagonal, Norman, with shallow blank arcading, two arches per panel. – STAINED GLASS. In the N chancel chapel, by *Willement*, 1857 (TK), with medallions containing scenes in strong colours. – PLATE. Chalice and Paten, 1606; Paten, 1633; Chalice and Paten, 1824. – MONUMENTS. Between chancel and s chancel chapel Sir John Say † 1474 and wife, tomb-chest with shields in blank arcades. On the lid good brass effigies of Knight and Lady, the figures *c.* 3½ ft long. – Between chancel and N chancel chapel tomb-chest with canopy to Sir William Say and family: early C16. Plain chest; the supports of the canopy polygonal, the canopy with depressed arches, quatrefoil frieze and cresting. The effigies were of brass and let into the E wall. They have disappeared. Brasses in the chancel to a priest, late C15; to another priest, early C16; in the nave to a knight carrying a mace (Sir John Borrell?), early C16. – Standing wall monument to Sir Henry Cock † 1609 with wife and children. Stiff effigies, she recumbent, he semi-reclining behind and above her. The children as usual kneeling against the front of the base. Coffered arch on solid side supports. Achievements and obelisks on top. Not of high quality. – Sir William Monson and wife † 1734, two busts above a long inscription tablet. – G. P. Williams † 1736 and wife; big epitaph.

MONSON ALMSHOUSES, High Street, 1728. Red brick, of four bays and two storeys, with widely spaced windows. Simple doorcase; above it a recess like a blank window, with a cartouche and inscription.

The church is quite a distance from the High Street, to be reached from it by an avenue. The High Street is part of that long ribbon of houses, C17–C20, timber-framed and plastered or of Georgian brick outer-suburban-London-types which stretches N all the way from the Middlesex border to Hoddesdon. The nicest houses on the Broxbourne stretch are by the bridge across the New River.

BUCKLAND

St Andrew. Nave, chancel, and s transept C14. An inscription in some stained glass is recorded giving the date 1348 for the construction of the church. W tower c. 1400, s aisle and s porch later C15. The W tower has diagonal buttresses. The nave and chancel have windows typical of the mid C14, the s aisle and s porch (depressed arch, two-light windows) belong to the late C15 or even early C16. The s aisle arcade has odd and very pretty piers consisting of shafts with capitals only for the inner order of the arches themselves. Towards the nave and aisle there are no capitals. Demi-figure of an angel on the W impost. Head-stops on the labels of the nave windows. – STAINED GLASS. C15 canopies in N windows. – MONUMENTS. Brasses to Alice Boteler † 1451; to William Langley, Rector of Buckland, † 1478; and to John Gyll † 1499 with children (chancel). – Susan Clarke † 1634, epitaph with bust and small Mannerist figures on the l. and r. – John Clare † 1772, big epitaph with bust above an asymmetrical Rococo cartouche with inscription. By *John Richards* of Bishopsgate.

In the village street BUCKLAND HOUSE, a fine Early Georgian house of chequered brick: seven bays, with projecting centre and a doorcase with attached fluted Ionic columns. A Venetian window above; the side parts filled in with Gothick timber panels.

BUCKSHILL
2¼ m. SW of Kings Langley

Buckshill Bottom. Two fine farmhouses. One of them, of brick and timber-framing with projecting porch, is in its unrestored state a perfect example of rural C17

building in West Herts. The setting also helps, in a dip
with no other houses in the neighbourhood.

GREAT WESTWOOD FARM. Good house of *c.* 1740. Brick,
five bays by three, and hipped roof. Nothing ornamental.
More attractive farmhouses on the road to Chandler's
Cross.

BUNTINGFORD

The little town possesses an enjoyable High Street, one
architecturally very remarkable church, and the stateliest
Almshouses in the county.

14a ST PETER. Built in 1614–26 as a chapel-of-ease to Layston.
Brick, on the Greek cross plan to which in 1899 a porch
and apse were added. The windows were also altered.
Kept in the church is a C17 BRASS PLATE showing the
interior of the church.

60a WARD'S HOSPITAL. Immediately N of the church, two-
storeyed, ashlar-faced along three sides of a courtyard
open to the street. The wings are two bays wide and five
bays deep, the centre bay is crowned by a pediment and
the doorcase by a scrolly open pediment. The windows
are low, of two lights with stone mullions. The hospital
was endowed by Bishop Seth Ward in 1684. Seth Ward,
the mathematician and astronomer, Bishop of Exeter and
(1667) of Salisbury, friend of Christopher Wren and
Chancellor of the Order of the Garter had, as the inscription in the centre of the hospital says, been 'born in
y[is] town W[th]in the parrish of Aspden & education in y[e]
free-school of Buntingford'.

LAYSTON COURT, near the S end of the High Street, that
is a little farther N than the hospital and on the other side
of the street, is the former Buntingford Grammar School.
It dates from the early C17 and consisted originally of one
room with open timber roof. The roof is now sub-divided
into two storeys and several rooms. At right angles to it
towards the street is the late C17 schoolmaster's house.

The HIGH STREET is long and straight, part of the Roman
Ermine Street. The houses, especially those of the C18,
look remarkably wealthy. They stand right at the S end.

No. 19, for example, is only three bays wide, yet has giant angle pilasters. No. 21 is detached and lies back, five bays, two storeys, with an Ionic doorcase. Opposite a small early C18 five-bay house with lively keystones and a door surround with alternating rustication. A similar doorcase was inserted at No. 41 (opposite), a C17 house with overhanging upper storey. The overhang rests on late C17 brackets. More overhang (e.g. No. 22) and more red brick houses follow. No. 46 is early C19, Nos 65 and 71 are Georgian. Opposite TUDOR HOUSE, with overhang and some fancy pargetting, then No. 66 also C17 overhang, and finally Nos 84–86, the most ambitious C18 house: five bays plus addition on the l., probably originally seven bays. Doorcase with scrolly carved brackets which may have carried a hood.

GREENWAYS ESTATE, on the road to Baldock. *c*. 70 houses by *P. Mauger & Partners*.

HARE STREET *see* p. 104.

LAYSTON *see* p. 153.

BUSHEY

Bushey, including Bushey Heath, extends along the A41 road to Watford for over two miles in a NW direction. At the NW end it merges into Watford. There is a nucleus of the village still by the church; the rest is hard to define: outer London suburban, Watford suburban, and in addition several large schools in their grounds.

ST JAMES. In a neatly kept churchyard at an equally well kept widening of the High Street. Flint, with a C13 chancel, a higher C15 nave and W tower with big diagonal buttresses and a NE stair-turret, and C19 aisles and N porch. On the inner N and S walls of the chancel tall wide blank arcading with Purbeck marble shafts and moulded capitals. The N and S lancet windows are also original. The chancel is separated from the nave by that rare feature a 'tympanum', that is a plastered partition with the Royal Arms (of Queen Anne), resting on a big beam. The nave roof is of the C15. – PULPIT. Jacobean with strapwork motifs; the tester is preserved. – CHANDELIER. Brass, C17 or C18, in the chancel. – PLATE. Cup and

Paten, 1633; Flagon, 1634; Salver, 1671; Almsdish, Wafer Box and Wine Strainer presented in 1754; Set presented in 1887.

RECTORY, E of the church. C17 but externally much altered in the C19. Two fireplaces and other details inside are original.

COTTAGES to the E and across the High Street to the N of the church. A pretty group.

High up the High Street to the SE more old houses; none of special merit. Some are wealthy (BUSHEY HOUSE with six-column Greek Doric portico; *c.* 1825, heightened *c.* 1900–10; BOURNE HALL opposite, eight-bay three-storey, Georgian, plastered white), some humbler. Of these some are weatherboarded (Fishmongers' Arms), some Georgian red brick (Ivy House), some whitewashed (No. 75). A number, including some higher up in Bushey Heath HIGH ROAD and SPARROWS HERNE, are early C19 Gothic villas. In the same taste, but larger and much later (after 1870), THE CLOISTERS in the High Street.

This lies next to the CONGREGATIONAL CHURCH, 1904, by *Morley Horder*, in the pretty playful style of the Nonconformist chapels of that moment; red brick with an asymmetrically placed tower. The METHODIST CHURCH, London Road, of 1904 by *Bell & Meredith*, is similar, but less well done.

Schools :

ROYAL MASONIC SENIOR SCHOOL, The Avenue. Very large group of red brick buildings by *Gordon & Gunton*, 1902. Tudor style. Facing the entrance a centrally placed tall tower in Gothic forms but with an odd Art Nouveau pavilion roof. The big courtyard in the middle turfed, closed to the S only by a cloister. Large hall with louvre in axis with the entrance tower. Chapel by *E. D. Webb*.

ROYAL MASONIC JUNIOR SCHOOL, London Road, 1926–9. By *H. C. Smart*, in a much more chastened Neo-Tudor. The main buildings on the sides of a central quadrangle. Behind this four double dormitory blocks of identical design.

St Margaret's Clergy Orphan Schools, Merry Hill Road; 1897, by *Alfred & Paul Waterhouse*. Yellow brick, with Waterhouse's typical abundance of smooth red indelible terra-cotta slabs; Gothic.

Royal Caledonian Asylum, Aldenham Road; 1902, by *Sir William Emerson*. Free Neo-Georgian. The central Neo-Gothic hall recently damaged by fire.

Highwood Mixed Junior School, Bushey Mill Lane. One of the new H.C.C. schools (*see* Introduction, p. 28).

C19 *and* C20 *houses in the centre :*

Lululand, Melbourne Road. Of Sir Hubert van Her-61 komer's, the celebrated portrait-painter's house, only the entrance survives. It must at all costs be preserved, as it is the only European work by the best American later C19 architect *H. H. Richardson*. It was built *c.* 1885. The entrance is eminently typical of Richardson: a big heavy archway with free acanthus foliage in the door lintel and tympanum, and two corner turrets. Good solid stone, white and red.

Bournemead, Herkomer Road; 1892, by *J. M. Brydon*. A good example of the picturesque brick and half-timber villa of that date.

Tilehurst, Grange Road; 1903, by *Voysey*. This and Myholme, Merry Hill Road, 1911, and also, in all probability, the house at the corner of Grange Road and Highfield Road, are characteristic examples of *Voysey's* work on the least ambitious suburban scale (very suitable for imitation by anonymous builders). The style has indeed had most undesirable consequences all over Britain. Yet Voysey's own houses are happily designed, unpretentious, unrhetorical, and fitting. Note the batter of the buttresses, the roughcast, the horizontal windows, and the irregular stone window surrounds.

Houses farther out (clockwise, starting N*) :*

Bushey Hall, Aldenham Road, *c.* 1880. Large symmetrical Neo-Jacobean brick and stone mansion, with tower on the l., away from the main structure. Built as a private house at a cost of £150,000, but soon converted into that incarnation of Victorianism, a hydrotherapeutic establishment.

HILFIELD, Hilfield Lane, *c.* 1795, by *Sir Jeffry Wyatville*. Originally known as Sly's Castle. Castellated, turreted, and cemented house with a gatehouse, complete with portcullis. Entrance and s sides both symmetrical. Outbuildings attached to the w.

CALDECOTE TOWERS (Rosary Priory School), Elstree Road. Obviously Mid-Victorian. A crazy display of commercial success with a big asymmetrical square tower. Much like a hotel at Harrogate or some such spa.

SPARROWS HERNE HOUSE, Elstree Road. C18 with long early C19 Roman Doric colonnade on the s front and wing added in 1938.

HARTSBOURNE LODGE, Hartsbourne Avenue. Early Victorian lodge with fanciful timber trim including a date plate 1517.

BYGRAVE

ST MARGARET. Nave and chancel only, with a polygonal w turret to give access to the bells. Norman s doorway with one order of colonnettes and one fat roll-moulding in the arch. The nave E angles are strengthened by Roman bricks. The chancel with the chancel arch seems late C14. – FONT. Octagonal with rectangular panels showing the Instruments of the Passion. – PULPIT. With an attached C17 iron hour-glass and bits of re-used C15 panelling. – BENCHES. Some with poppyheads. – SCREEN. C15 with simple Perp tracery. – COMMUNION RAILS. C17 with long sausage-shaped balusters.

CADDINGTON HALL
1 m. NE of Markyate

House of 1804, built of light and dark chequer brickwork; seven bays, two and a half storeys, with semicircular entrance porch on Tuscan columns. Early Victorian roof.

CALDECOTE

St Mary Magdalene. The stone-built church stands like a miniature model on the grass, N of the barns of a big farm. The W tower starts broad and then, by means of hips, goes narrower. The tower windows seem to be of the late C14. The nave and chancel windows are Perp and of modest dimensions. There is inside no structural division between the two parts. The only more ornamental part of the church is the S porch, embattled and with a unique canopied and crocketed STOUP inside. – FONT. Perp, octagonal, with traceried and cusped panels. – BENCHES. Some in the nave C15, with little decorative buttresses. – STAINED GLASS. In a S window fragment of a kneeling figure. – PLATE. Chalice, 1569; Paten, 1696.

CALDECOTE TOWERS see BUSHEY

CHANDLERS CROSS
2½ m. NW of Watford

Chandlers Farm. Pretty brick and timber-framed farmhouse with outbuildings. Restored.

CHESHUNT

St Mary. Built between 1418 and 1448 by the then Rector of Cheshunt (who was also a Baron of the Exchequer), and important as a dated example of the Perp style in Herts. All-embattled. W tower of ashlar stone with taller SE stair-turret and low buttresses, W door with spandrels decorated with shields and three-light W window. The aisle windows have depressed arches, three lights, and elementary panel tracery. The five-bay arcade inside on piers consisting of four shafts and four hollows in the diagonals. Broad two-centred arches. Two-light clerestory windows. The stencilled and painted decoration of the nave belongs probably to the restoration of 1874 under *Bodley*. – PLATE. Chalice, 1638; Flagon, 1638; Paten, 1672. – MONUMENTS. Unimportant Brasses E end of N aisle and E end of nave, C15, 1609, and 1449. – Robert Dacres † 1543, tomb-chest in recess in the chancel, the superstructure remodelled by Sir Thomas Dacres in 1643. – Henry Atkins † 1638, physician to James I and Charles I, under arch similar to the previous one, but with draperies tied round the flanking columns. – Margaret Watton † 1675, small standing wall monument crowned by an urn. At the foot an inscription in Greek. – Daniel Dodson † 1747, life-size figure nonchalantly leaning on an urn, back wall with garlands hanging down to the l. and r. By the younger *W. Woodman*.

The old village lies close to the church. In CHURCHGATE and CHURCHFIELD some of the village character is still preserved, though badly interfered with by CHESHUNT COLLEGE almost opposite the E side of the graveyard. The College was founded by Selina Countess of Huntingdon and transferred to Cheshunt in 1792. When it moved to Cambridge the premises were taken over by the Church of England. They consist of two earlier Georgian red brick houses by the street, the modest original College building of stock brick, and the big and self-assured new buildings of 1870–1 (by *Lander & Bedells*). They are of stock brick in the E.E. style with a tall tower of typically High Victorian outline, and detail all kinds of excrescences, even bargeboarding. At the E end of Churchfield stands another educational building, three hundred years older and correspondingly modest, the DEWHURST CHARITY SCHOOL of 1640, of brick with mullioned brick windows and three gables.

Half a mile to the E of the old village a new development took place along the main road from London, the usual ribbon development (which came as natural to the C17 and C18 as it comes to ours). The High Street (or combined Crossbrook Street, Turners Hill, and High Street, the latter also known as Cheshunt Street) stretches for over a mile. In TURNER'S HILL near the S end of Cheshunt, where it merges into Waltham Cross, a first group consisting of Nos 75 (standing with its gable to the street), 77–79 (a fine pair of five-bay brick houses), 88 (early C19,

yellow brick with a gently projecting bow window), THE
GRANGE (also yellow brick, also early C19), Springfield,
and Nos 102–104 (with a date-plate 1698). Then, in
Turner's Hill, past the Public Library, the so-called
MANOR HOUSE, early C18, of four bays and three
storeys with two-bay lower wings. The doorcase has
rusticated pilasters; the windows are segmentheaded. A
little to the N on the W side the DEWHURST ALMS-
HOUSES founded in 1642, a row of ten plain one-storeyed
brick cottages. Off Turners Hill lanes lead down on the
E side towards the river Lea. Much of the area is now
covered by the glasshouses of market gardeners and
nurserymen, the dominant motif of the scenery around
Cheshunt.

To the W occasional large individual houses remain along
such streets as COLLEGE ROAD (BROOKSIDE HOUSE
and CHESHUNT COTTAGE, large, early C19, with many
bargeboarded gables and with hood-moulds above the
windows; GROVE HOUSE, C18 brick), CHURCH LANE
(one castellated Late Georgian house with Venetian windows), BLIND MAN'S LANE (CLOCK HOUSE, seven-
bay, two-storey, red brick, C18). Also in Blind Man's
Lane the new JUNIOR MIXED INFANTS SCHOOL (*see*
Introduction, p. 28).

CHESHUNT GREAT HOUSE lies ½ m. NW of the church. It
is the still impressive remains of a much larger moated
house. What remains is no more than one wing of a courtyard house. The wing incorporates the Great Hall, a hall
40 ft long and still preserving its timber roof with wind-
braces. The roof is now plastered. The date of the hall is
probably late C15. Of the exterior architecture nothing
survives earlier than *c.* 1600 (the N gable with its blocked
mullioned window). The rest was converted into a house
of more comfort about 1700. Of that time the blocked
segmentheaded hall windows, the plain ten-bay E front,
and the S entrance front which, however, was again
altered later, probably in 1801, when the other ranges of
the house were pulled down. The four-centred entrance
arch and the window above would go well with a date *c.*

1800. The finest C18 piece in the house is the large stair-case with slim balusters of three alternating shapes, broad spiral, narrow spiral, and columns.

CHILDWICKBURY
2 m. NW of St Albans

Large and well-kept mansion. Supposed to contain later C17 work incorporated in what was done in 1854 and about 1900. The building history of the house has not yet been elucidated. (Good Rococo overmantels inside.)

Close to Childwick Green, just S of the E end of the church, a miniature Jacobean house. Central doorway with four-centred arch at the top. Canted bays l. and r.; mullioned and transomed windows.

CHIPPERFIELD

ST PAUL, 1837, by *Talbot Bury*. Flint, aisleless nave, transepts and chancel; lancet windows. The only remarkable feature the timber roof forming a proper crossing with diagonal beams at the meeting of nave, transepts, and chancel.

MANOR HOUSE. C17 brick and half-timbering and a modern extension at the back; the front an extremely handsome addition of 1716 (date on a cistern); eleven bays wide, two-storeyed, of red brick, with parapet. Fine iron gates to the Common.

LITTLE WINCH. On the S side of the Common, close to the SW corner. 1935, by *Maxwell Fry*. A brick and a weather-boarded part, of different heights. The two parts and the fenestration show an admirable sense of proportion. The result, though entirely of the C20, is as restful as Herts C17 or C18 farm architecture. It should, however, be added in fairness that the architect had intended a concrete house and that the use of local materials was an afterthought, caused by objections from the Council. The large living room is on the ground floor on the E (r.) side, the studio on the upper floor on the W (l.) side.

CHIPPING BARNET

Barnet, although the one town in Herts which is not at all separated from London by open country, yet keeps some of an urban individuality of its own. This is to a large extent due to the position and personality of the parish church.

St John the Baptist. The church points with its E end towards the High Street which comes up the hill from London. To its l. and r. the main roads fork to Watford and to St Albans and Hatfield. The architecture of the church, which is largely Victorian, makes the most of this position, more than the medieval church had done. This was built at the expense of John Beauchamp who died in 1453.* When *William Butterfield* was commissioned in 1875 to enlarge the old building, he decided to keep the medieval nave and N aisle and to add to it a new higher nave with its own aisle to the S. He also removed the old chancel and tower. So the present church seems to have two naves and two aisles. From the N you see a low aisle and a nave with a clerestory of three-light windows. These clerestory windows on the S side look into Butterfield's nave. His own clerestory has somewhat perverse alternating three-light and circular cinquefoil windows. The old church was of flint with sparing stone dressings; Butterfield's has plenty of stone-bands and chequerwork to enrich the rhythm of the flint work. His W tower is most impressive, big and broad, a beacon when you come up from London, and a dominant accent for the town. Inside, the mid C15 church has an arcade with piers with four attached shafts, four hollows in the diagonals, and complex mouldings in the two-centred arches. Butterfield's piers and arches are much more robust. – STAINED GLASS. N and S windows of the aisles, good Arts and Crafts style of the 1880s. – PLATE. Small Cup, 1679; Cup and Paten, 1706. – MONUMENTS. Thomas Ravenscroft 36a † 1630, excellent recumbent alabaster effigy under canopy. The details of the canopy an interesting example of

* *See* the inscription in the spandrel of one of the arcade arches.

Gothic Survival: cusped arches, rib-vault, quatrefoil frieze of the top cornice. – James Ravenscroft † 1680 and his wife † 1689, two fine small marble busts in an altered, Neo-Gothic surround.

CHRIST CHURCH, New Road.* Flint with stone dressings, 1845–52, by *G. G. Scott*. N aisle 1855. The pretty CHURCH HALL (brick, flint, and stone) in a fancy Tudor style, 1907, by *L. W. Ridge & Waymouth*.

The town itself has little of pre-Victorian date. The only Georgian stretch is w of the church in WOOD STREET: a row of varied cottages (Nos 10–16) on one side of the street, mostly of brick, and one or two opposite; farther out a few individual houses, not specially noteworthy.

In addition the following buildings:

QUEEN ELIZABETH GRAMMAR SCHOOL, Wood Street, opposite the s side of the church. Later c 16. Tudor brick-work, with diapers of vitrified headers, three-window front, the windows with wooden mullions, at the angles two polygonal towers.

RAVENSCROFT ALMSHOUSES, Wood Street, 1679. But of that date now only the central archway and gable.

GARRETT'S ALMSHOUSES, Wood Street, 1731. Very simple one-storey row of six cottages.

LEATHERSELLERS' ALMSHOUSES, N end of Union Street, 1843 plus addition of a further eight houses 1865. Three ranges; white brick in the typical timid Tudor style of so many early c 19 almshouses.

CHORLEYWOOD

CHRIST CHURCH, 1870, by *Street*. Flint, with low shingled w spire. The only other feature of interest is the triple traceried opening from the chancel into the s chapel.

The architectural significance of Chorleywood is connected with the name of *Charles F. A. Voysey* who built himself a house here in 1900–1. It is called THE ORCHARD and situated in SHIRE LANE. The garden front is espe-

63a

* Administratively in South Mimms, Middlesex.

cially characteristic, with two identical gables (with *Voysey's* typical tiny ventilation slits), but a gentle, carefully balanced asymmetry in the centre. Some of the trees in conjunction with which the house was meant to be seen have been replaced. Inside, the Hall with the staircase and fireplace is one of the best Voysey designed. The metalwork such as door-hinges is also in the daintiest Voysey fashion.

HOLLYBANK, the neighbour of The Orchard, also by *Voysey*, was built in 1903–4. It is as good in most respects as The Orchard.

A smaller job of *Voysey's* was the r.-hand-side addition to HILL COTTAGE farther N in Shire Lane.

CLOTHALL

ST MARY. The church has a SW tower in which is the porch. This is C14; so is the S chapel. The latter is the most interesting part, with an arcade to the nave on unusual piers with semi-octagonal members and a Piscina characteristic of the period. – FONT. C12, of the table-top type, Purbeck marble, square with shallow blank round-headed arches. – BENCHES. Some bench-ends with poppyheads. – DOOR. In the S doorway, with long iron hinges, probably C14. – STAINED GLASS. Christ, the Virgin, and Saints in medallions, only fragmentarily C15, ornamental quoins with flowers and delightfully drawn birds; thick canopies above; hardly before 1400 and perhaps later. – BRASSES (in the chancel). Early C16 priest, *c.* 3 ft long; John Vynter † 1404, Rector of Clothall, *c.* 3 ft long; John Wryght † 1519, Rector of Clothall, with scrolls and the Trinity above the figure; two more brasses covered by the chancel stalls.

N of the church a nice Georgian brick house of the usual five-bay, two-storey type.

CODICOTE

ST GILES. Mostly 1853, but the S aisle has C13 bases to its arcade, the nave N wall has a C13 lancet window, and the tower arch is of the C15. – PULPIT. Jacobean. – PLATE. Small engraved Chalice, 1558; Paten, 1568; large Standing Paten, 1772.

At the triangular village centre some pretty half-timbered (George & Dragon Inn) as well as chequerwork brick houses.

CODICOTE LODGE. Mainly late C18. Seven bays with recessed three-bay centre. Doorway with Ionic columns, bulging frieze, and segmental pediment. A specially rich contemporary fireplace inside.

CODICOTE BURY. Red brick, built c. 1655. Good staircase with spread tapering banisters, leading up through all storeys.

NODE DAIRY AND STUD, 1927, by *Maurice Chesterton*. An extremely odd design. Circular with a circular courtyard, thatched, and with a very fantastically detailed entrance arch. The tower top is no less surprising.

COKENACH *see* BARKWAY

COLNEY HEATH

ST MARK, 1845, in the Transitional Norman style. Of yellow brick. N porch with fat columns and from it an outer staircase *à la* King's School, Canterbury, leads up to the starved NW tower. Apsed E end with roundheaded lancet windows. Thin W gallery inside.

CORNEY BURY
1 m. N of Buntingford

Early C17 brick manor house with three straight gables on the W side, one over the centre, the others over unequally projecting wings. The porch and the whole S and E sides remodelled later in the C17. A rainwater head gives the date: 1681.

COTTERED

ST JOHN THE BAPTIST. The outstanding feature is the spacious aisleless nave with large three-light transomed Perp windows with four-centred heads. It makes the church appear a palatial Hall. The masonry of the nave is older (*see* the C14 doorways). Of the C14 also the W tower (*see* the W window and tower arch). The tower is unbuttressed and has a lead spire. The chancel is lower than the nave. Its windows are Perp but the chancel arch looks early C14. – FONT. Early C18, of lovely grey Derbyshire marble, with baluster stem and fluted bowl. – DOORS. Nave, heavy oak, C15 (?). Vestry, with Late Medieval ironwork. – PAINTING. On the nave wall large figure of St Christopher with indications of river surroundings and much incidental drama of the medieval highway. – PLATE. Chalice and Paten, 1711.

LORDSHIP HOUSE. Large, irregularly gabled manor house, partly C15, partly C17. The house is surrounded by a moat.

ALMSHOUSES. Brick, mid C18, one-storeyed with quoins and three dormers. Altered lately.

SCHOOL. Built in 1825. Plain rectangle. Windows with hood-moulds.

CROMER *see* ARDELEY

CROXLEY GREEN
1 m. E of Rickmansworth

ALL SAINTS, 1872, by *J. Norton*. In 1907 *Temple Moore* added a new nave to the S of the old (GR). The difference in quality is remarkable. *Temple Moore's* design is original and interesting, with the lancet windows, and the wall-passage carried also along the straight E end. The arches towards the old building are roundheaded and rest on short heavy rectangular piers. Exterior of yellow brick with bands of stone.

The characteristic feature of Croxley Green is its long triangular Green with several pretty buildings, especially towards the N end.

E of the N end of the Green in LITTLE GREEN LANE one of the new H.C.C. schools (*see* Introduction).

At the S end of Croxley Green beyond the railway CROXLEY HALL FARM with a splendid late medieval barn,

101 by 38½ ft, and well preserved inside and out. Nave and aisles, one entrance transept, kingpost roof, amply strutted. At the Hall some C16 panelling and a brick chimney remain. The Hall belonged to Dr Caius.

DANE END

DANE END HOUSE. Handsome white early C19 house of five bays and three storeys with lower side wings. In front of the centre a one-storey porch of four coupled Ionic columns.

DANESBURY see WELWYN

DATCHWORTH

ALL SAINTS. Small flint church. Nave to which late in the C13 a N aisle was added (arcade of four bays on octagonal piers with slightly hollow-chamfered arches). W tower and chancel C15 (upper stage of the tower 1875, chancel remodelled C17). The plastered C15 nave roof looks rather domestic with its wind-braces. – FONT. Good C15 work with panelled stem and panelled octagonal bowl. – STAINED GLASS. E window early C19. – In the N aisle W window good c. 1875 glass in the style of *Walter Crane*. – PLATE. Chalice and Paten, 1569. – MONUMENT. Coffin lid with foliated cross; c. 1300.

HOPPERS HALL. Timber-framed and plastered gabled C17 building. The plan is L-shaped and the two wings differ a little in date.

DELAMERE HOUSE see GREAT WYMONDLEY

DELROW see ALDENHAM

DIGSWELL

The visual character of this leafy village of houses in their gardens is determined by the austere back screen of the RAILWAY VIADUCT. Forty brick arches (built by *Lewis Cubitt* in 1850).

ST JOHN THE EVANGELIST. A small church close to Digswell House. The external appearance much altered in

1811. Cemented. The NW tower small. Inside, a plain arch of *c.* 1200 between chancel and N chancel chapel. The Piscina in the chancel is of the C13. In the N aisle a very curious display of blank geometrical tracery of *c.* 1290, perhaps connected with a founder's monument. – SCREEN. Doors from a former rood screen, *c.* 1540, the earliest example in Herts of the new Renaissance fashions of ornamentation. – STAINED GLASS. Window s aisle (SS Michael and George) by *Kempe,* 1894. – PLATE. Engraved Chalice, 1563; Flagon, 1672; Paten, 1673. – MONUMENTS. Brasses in the chancel. Outstandingly fine brasses to John Peryent, Standard-Bearer to Richard II, and his wife † 1415, big frontal figures. – Small brasses to a Knight, *c.* 1430; to Thomas Hoore † 1495, wife and children; Robert Battyl † 1557, wife and children; to William Robert and wife, both figures in shrouds, *c.* 1480. – Epitaph to Richard Sedley † 1658, large and good, with oval inscription surrounded by a laurel garland, black columns, and fine ornament.

DIGSWELL HOUSE, by the church, good early C19 stone mansion of five bays, with a giant portico of unfluted Ionic columns and straight entablature to the garden and a plain Tuscan porch to the drive.

EASNEYE *see* WARE

EAST BARNET

ST MARY, Church Hill. Nave walls and three small win- 11a dows in the N wall, Norman. The rest C19. Tower of yellow brick in a Neo-Norman style, aisle 1868, chancel 1880. – PLATE. Cup of 1636. – Fine graveyard, with old cedar-tree s of the church tower. In the graveyard MONUMENT to John Sharpe † 1756, large urn on big base under heavy arched baldacchino.

BAPTIST CHURCH, Crescent Road, 1931, by *F. Goldsmith.* Red brick, with a front whose unmoulded verticals reach right up into the gable.

East Barnet is entirely Outer London, rural only in the immediate neighbourhood of the church. Of individual houses only two are remarkable: OAKHILL COLLEGE, long white mansion in ample grounds, five-bay centre, with lower two-bay wings and an outer four-bay wing on the s side. The house has an Early Georgian nucleus and was altered and enlarged in the early C19.

TREVOR HALL, Stuart Road, built for Colonel Gillum *c.* 1860 by *Philip Webb*, the architect of William Morris's Red House at Bexley Heath, Kent. Surprisingly fresh and un-Victorian in its plain gables and the broad coving on the w side. Originally called Church Hill House.

MONKFRITH AVENUE INFANTS SCHOOL (*see* Introduction, p. 28).

EASTBURY

1¼ m. sw of Oxhey Place

FRITHWOOD HOUSE and THE GLADES, both in Watford Road, are excellent examples of the two main types of English domestic architecture in *c.* 1900–5. Frithwood House is by *Mervyn Macartney*, The Glades probably by *Voysey* (no documentary evidence). The former is Neo-William-and-Mary, the latter Neo-Tudor; but both handled with personality and imagination. Frithwood House is brick, with brick quoins, white wooden mullioned and transomed window casements and far projecting roof. The Glades has *Voysey's* characteristic sloping buttresses, roughcast and irregular stone surrounds to the windows. It is a composition of great charm

EASTWICK

ST BOTOLPH. A short yew avenue leads to the church which was rebuilt in 1872 by *Blomfield*, except for the chancel arch and the w tower. Blomfield's church consists of nave and chancel only and is of no interest. The chancel arch is an astonishingly ambitious piece of C13 design with three orders of tall Purbeck shafts and a complexly moulded arch, as if for a cathedral (cf. Standon). – PLATE. Paten, 1705; Chalice, 1719; Paten, 1735. –
31b   MONUMENTS. Under the tower the best C13 effigy in the

county, a marble Knight in chain mail with long surcoat. His legs are crossed. – Brass to Joan Lee † 1564. – Epitaph to Mary Plummer † 1700, good, of diptych type, with three Corinthian columns. – Epitaph to Walter Plummer † 1746, so good that it may well be by *Rysbrack* (*see* the delightful cherubs' heads and the exquisitely carved classical details of frieze and pediment).

ELSTREE

ST NICHOLAS, 1853, by *P. C. Hardwick*, with the use of the short octagonal piers and capitals of the C15 church. The C19 building rather ugly outside with low SW spire. – FONT. Perp, octagonal, with little decoration. – SCREEN between nave and chancel, very pretty wrought metalwork, designed by *Sir Arthur Blomfield*, 1881. – The stencilling on the N side of the chancel is probably by *George Walton* (*see* below).

SCHOPWICK. House N of the church, Georgian, brick, five-bay, two-storeyed house.

COTTAGES S of the church, thoroughly beautified by sham half-timbering about 1920, yet no doubt decidedly pretty.

HILL HOUSE (former Elstree School), farther S. The main school buildings consist of a long, low, whitewashed house to which is added a red brick C18 house with two symmetrical polygonal bay windows and a central Venetian window. Across the road the chapel with a number of *Kempe* windows. The STAINED GLASS dates from 1877 to 1906. The oldest windows are in the apse and the Nativity in the nave. The Angels and Shepherds are 1878, the Charge to St Peter, 1879, etc.

THE LEYS (Middlesex C.C. Home) in Barnet Lane to the E of Elstree was built in 1901 by *George Walton*, a Glasgow architect, friend of Charles Rennie Mackintosh, and one of the most interesting domestic architects of Britain about 1900. The detail betrays the Glasgow Art Nouveau, but the composition is symmetrical and quiet, without the high tensions and *outré* expression of Mackintosh's work. The interior has been altered by the M.C.C., but

enough of the original woodwork remains to give the
South Englander a whiff of Scottish air.

ESSENDON

St Mary, 1883, by *W. White*. Essendon is worth a special
visit if only to see the FONT in the church. It is of Wedg-
wood's Black Basalt ware, an exquisitely beautiful clas-
sical shape and with all the appealing matt sheen of the
Wedgwood body. It was given to the church in 1780. –
PLATE. Chalice and Paten, 1569; large Paten, 1692;
Flagon, 1769; Baptismal Dish, 1778. – MONUMENTS.
Brass to W. Tooke † 1588 with wife and children (s aisle).
– Large Epitaph to W. Prestley † 1664.

Essendon Place. Probably early C19.

Church of England School (*see* Introduction, p. 28).

FANHAM'S HALL *see* WARE

FLAMSTEAD

St Leonard. Low w tower of flint and random stone,
patched up with brick, also Roman brick. High up traces
of two-light Norman windows. No battlements; thin
spike. The body of the church flint; nave with clerestory,
aisles, heavily buttressed s porch, unbuttressed N porch,
low much restored C14 chancel, C14 NE vestry. Most windows are simple Perp, but the N aisle has one which is Dec
(ogee reticulated tracery). The interior confirms that the
w tower is Norman. The tower arch is depressed roundheaded on the simplest of imposts. Into it, during the C13,
a smaller arch was inserted, treble-chamfered on imposts
with typical capitals of that century. The Norman nave
was aisleless of the same width as the present nave. The
six-bay arcades show that aisles were added in the early
C13. Octagonal piers, the w and E responds (except for
one) slimmer attached circular shafts. The capitals are
stiff-leaf, much renewed; the capitals of the responds
have the leaves composed in two tiers. The chancel arch
and the Piscina in the chancel are C14, but one N lancet

window goes back to C13. – C15 nave roof on carved stone corbels. – PULPIT. 1698; just framed panels with very little inlay. – COMMUNION RAILS. *c.* 1700 with twisted balusters. – SCREEN. Well preserved C15 work; tall arcades, each division of six lights, with the central mullion running up to the apex of the arch; the individual lights end in round arches, the tracery is elementary Perp. – WALL PAINTINGS. Apart from St Albans the most important series in the county, all revealed only in 1930–2. None well preserved. Between the spandrels of the nave arches lower parts of four Apostles, large figures, C13. – Nave upper wall even larger C15 figure of St Christopher. – Above the chancel arch Christ in Glory C13, with Doomsday scenes C15. In the NE chapel mid C14 series of stories of the Passion in two tiers. Last Supper, Crucifixion, Mocking of Christ, Entombment (the best preserved and hence most readily appreciated scene), Crowning with Thorns, Resurrection. – PLATE. C17 Chalice and Paten; Pewter Flagon, 1675; Flagon, 1690; Breadholder given in 1700. – MONUMENTS. Brass to John Oudeby, Rector, † 1414, with indent above showing that there was a demi-figure of Virgin and Child under a canopy. – Tomb-chest with stone effigies of man and woman under one ogee canopy; early C15, the figures badly preserved. – Sir Bartholomew Fouke † 1604, the usual kneeling figure. – Saunders Children, erected about 1690, large altar tomb 36b of black marble with the figures of five deceased young children in contemporary dress and with praying hands placed on a ledge which could be used as the S aisle altar. The surviving sixth child kneeling on the floor, no doubt not in the original position. The monument is by *William Stanton* and cost £1,500. – Sir Edward Sedbright, by 39a *Flaxman*, 1762. Nobly carved composition with Hope and Faith reclining to the l. and r. of a slender fluted urn.

To the N of the church the SAUNDERS ALMSHOUSES, 1669, of brick, one-storeyed with roundheaded entrances and plain two-light windows. – VINE COTTAGE to their E, a handsome house, timber-framed with brick infilling.

FLAUNDEN

OLD CHURCH, just E of Latimer village in Bucks, in a spinney, completely hidden. Only a few crumbling walls remain now amidst the trees and undergrowth. The Royal Commission on Historical Monuments could still in 1910 draw a plan and describe the building which dated chiefly from the C13 and had the interesting peculiarity of a Greek cross plan. Traces of C13 wall paintings had also survived until then.

ST MARY MAGDALENE, in Flaunden village; 1838. *Sir George Gilbert Scott's* first building, described by him in his Memoirs as 'the poor barn designed for my uncle King' who was then vicar of Latimer (GR). Flint and brick dressings. Lancet windows in the Commissioners' tradition, timber bellcote. – FONT. Octagonal bowl, Perp, with quatrefoil decoration. – PLATE. Chalice and Paten, 1576; Salver, 1731.

FROGMORE

2 m. S of St Albans

HOLY TRINITY, 1842. Norman, of flint, with red brick dressings and stone details: singularly violent and raw contrast. Bellcote, E apse, nave, and aisles; no galleries. The interest of the church is the name of its architect: *Sir George Gilbert Scott*. He cannot in later life have thought with much pleasure of this youthful effort.

FROGMORE HALL *see* ASTON

FURNEAUX PELHAM

ST MARY. A big church, Perp except for the long chancel whose lancet windows (two with inner nook-shafts) and Sedilia and Piscina arrangement and details (stiff-leaf capitals) date it as middle of the C13. Tall unbuttressed W tower with Herts spike. The nave aisles frame the tower. Two-storeyed embattled S porch with two-light windows, markedly higher than the unembattled aisle. Big S chapel

coming forward as far as the s porch. The windows Late
Perp. As the chapel was built (by Robert Newport) about
1518 and the N and S aisle windows are of the same shape
as those of the chapel, the same late date may be assumed
for the former as well. Two-light clerestory windows. The
N and S aisle arcades are of a late type too, with semi-
octagonal shafts and hollows (without capitals) in the
diagonals. Low-pitched nave roof with tie-beams, high-
pitched chancel roof with struts and collar-beams. In the
nave the sub-principals are carried on angels. – FONT.
Octagonal, C13, of Purbeck marble with shallow blank
pointed arches. – STAINED GLASS. In the s chapel *Morris*
and *Burne-Jones* windows for the Calvert family, that on
the s with four figures of angels 1866, that on the E with
the Virgin, Gabriel (by *Morris*), and Michael 1873. The
quality is outstanding, especially if compared with other
Victorian glass. – MONUMENTS. Tomb-chest in the s aisle
at the w end with cusped quatrefoils and shields. On it the
exquisite, *c.* 3 ft long brass figures of a man and woman of
the early C15. They lie under a cusped double ogee canopy
with pinnacles to the l. and r. – Brass plate to R. Newport
with kneeling figures, dated 1518, on a marble slab. –
Tomb-chest of Edward Cason † 1624, with black marble
pilasters and top slab. Against the back wall inscription
tablet.

FURNEAUX PELHAM HALL. C16 brick manor house with
stepped gables (cf. e.g. Great Hormead). Mid C17 alterations of those on the w have given them a curved shape.
(Good panelling inside.)

GADEBRIDGE *see* HEMEL HEMPSTEAD

GARSTON

ALL SAINTS, 1853, by *Sir G. G. Scott.*
LONDON TRANSPORT GARAGE, 1951–2, by *T. Bilbow.*
KYTES. An Early Victorian red brick house forms the centre
of the recent Colony for men with spine injuries: one-
storey brick cottages, ingeniously equipped; a friendly
group round the lawn; by *Norman & Dawbarn.*

GILSTON

ST MARY. Basically C 13; *see* the W doorway of three orders, the chancel lancets, and the N doorway and one N window of the nave, the latter with elementary plate tracery. The upper parts of the tower probably late C 16 (brick with S stair-turret; cf. Sawbridgeworth). The N aisle is old, the S aisle C 19. The arcades are low and have quatrefoil piers with later arches. – FONT. Hexagonal, C 12, of Purbeck marble, with shallow blank arches. – SCREEN. A survival of first-rate importance. Evidently late C 13 and well enough preserved to have made reconstruction possible. Tall dado, shafts thin and only 2 ft long, trefoiled pointed arches and stylized flowers in the spandrels. Straight top. – PLATE. Chalice and Paten, 1562; Paten, C 17; Flagon, 1697. – MONUMENTS. Two good big mid C 17 epitaphs: Bridget Gore † 1659, white standing figure in shroud in front of an oval black niche, drapes l. and r., and weeping putti wiping their eyes with them. The type had been made popular by John Donne's tomb in St Paul's Cathedral. – Sir John Gore † 1659, black and white, with long inscription flanked by blank columns; thin curly broken pediment with small figures on it; signed by *Joshua Marshall*.

GILSTON PARK. Large asymmetrical mansion of random rubble in the Early Tudor style with Gothic detail in the tower and entrance. Mullioned and transomed windows, stepped gables. 1852, by *Philip Hardwick*.

GOBIONS
1½ m. NW of Northaw, 2¼ m. SE of North Mimms

The house belonged to the More family, including Sir Thomas More, in the C 16. It was pulled down in 1836 by the owner of BROOKMANS who wanted to add the grounds to his own estate. All that remains of it is the FOLLY ARCH, a large sham-medieval entrance gate at the S end, by Hawkstead Road. It was erected by Sir Jeremy Sambrooke († 1754), owner of Gobions. It has a large roundheaded arch and rectangular thin turrets with rectangular windows. Centre and turrets are castellated. Sir Jeremy also erected the Battle of Barnet Memorial at Hadley. The Folly Arch is a very early example of medieval revival, contemporary with *Kent's* and earlier than Walpole's Gothicism. The designer seems to have been *James Gibbs* (Manuscript life of Gibbs, perhaps an autobiography, at the Sir John Soane Museum). Sir Jeremy's grounds also belonged to the early examples of the new picturesque taste. They were laid out by *Bridgeman* (who also planned the grounds of Stowe).

Brookmans was built *c.* 1680 in the plain sound style of that date, but destroyed by fire in 1891. Only the stables survive, with an upper storey added and the carriageway through the centre blocked up.

GOLDEN PARSONAGE *see* GREAT GADDESDEN

GOLDINGS

By *Devey*, one of the most successful and least known Victorian domestic architects, *c.* 1870. A vast Neo-Tudor mansion of red brick with diapers. The principal front is broadly symmetrical and of moderate size, but to its r. is a wing attached at an angle which has a turret and a big tall square tower and no symmetry at all. The whole is successful, though undeniably a piece of presumptuous display.

GORHAMBURY

Of Sir Nicholas Bacon's mansion of 1568 the porch and masonry of the Hall and one projecting wing survive. The porch is a would-be classical composition with Tuscan attached columns flanking the entrance arch on the ground floor, and Ionic columns and niches flanking the two-light upper windows. It led to the screens passage. The dais end of the Hall is marked by a large window.

In 1777 a new house was begun by the third Viscount Grimston. The architect was *Sir Robert Taylor*. The house is ashlar-faced and has a grand Corinthian portico raised on a plinth with broad outer staircase and three

H.—4

windows on each side. On the garden site the portico is of attached columns. Originally the house had low wings connecting the main building with side blocks. The low N wing was replaced by a two-storeyed building in 1816–17, and the outer N block by a more substantial one in 1826 (*W. Atkinson*). In the same year the old S wing and S block were pulled down.

The interiors have as their most beautiful adornment several magnificent fireplaces attributed to *Piranesi* who illustrated in his engravings two superb Roman urns belonging to the house. Many family and other portraits of value. Terracotta busts of Sir Nicholas Bacon, his wife, and their little son, the famous Francis. Stained glass from the old Bacon mansion made up into two large screens.

GRAVELEY

ST MARY. Small flint church. W tower with diagonal buttresses, nave and long chancel. The latter dates from the C13 (*see* the windows on the N and S sides, the fragments of E windows replaced by a Perp window, and especially the double Piscina with pointed arches formed by the intersection of semicircular ones just as at Jesus College, Cambridge). The chancel N doorway was originally in the nave. Its date is C12, a date which is borne out by the nave Double Piscina. The windows of the nave C14– C15. The N aisle 1887. – SCREEN. C15; nothing special. – MONUMENT. Big epitaph to Mary Sparhauke † 1770, by *B. Palmer* (classical with a crowning completely smooth and unadorned urn against a black obelisk).

GRAVELEY HALL, W of the church. C17 brick house.

GREAT AMWELL

The space N of the church is one of the most delightful spots in Herts, thanks no doubt to *Robert Mylne*, architect to the New River Company and a man eager to perpetuate his own and others' fame. The New River was begun by Sir Hugh Myddelton in 1609 to give London better water. He completed the great enterprise after only four years in 1613. To

commemorate this great feat which was indeed after two
hundred years still of some importance to London, *Robert
Mylne* erected a MONUMENT TO MYDDELTON, an urn [40a]
of *Coade* stone on a pedestal on which we read in pretty
letters : 'From the Spring at Chadwell 2 miles west and from
this source of Amwell the Aqueduct meanders for the space
of XL miles conveying health, pleasure, and convenience to
the metropolis of Great Britain . . . an immortal work since
man cannot more nearly imitate the Deity than by bestow-
ing health.' Then it goes on to say that the monument was
dedicated by 'Robert Mylne, Architect, Engineer etc. in
1800'. It stands on an island in the New River with four
weeping willows and a yew tree and smoothly cut lawn.
Close to it is the source, also embellished by a stone with a
poem ('O'erhung with shrubs, that fringe the chalky rock /
A little fount pur'd forth its gurgling rill', etc.), and another
yet smaller island has a second monument to Myddelton
('AMWELL, perpetuated be thy stream / Nor e'er thy
spring be less / which thousands drink who never dream /
whence flow the streams they bless'). The whole is a perfect
picture with the church up the hill, standing in its GRAVE-
YARD, uncommonly well provided with memorials larger
than tombstones. The most striking of these is that built by
Mylne in 1800 for himself and his family, a white brick
cube, crowned by an urn. Others are the Cathrow Monument with four short baseless Tuscan columns and a big
Grecian sarcophagus, and the Plomer Monument of 1728,
an obelisk.

ST JOHN THE BAPTIST. A small church of great antiquity,
   distinguished by its Norman apse, a feature very rare
   amongst Herts parish churches (cf. Bengeo). Of the same
   period the low roundheaded chancel arch, of two orders
   on the simplest imposts and one window whose equal
   splays outside and inside suggest an C11 date. The other
   architectural features are of less interest. C15 W tower
   with diagonal buttresses and pyramid roof behind the
   battlements. The W DOOR is of the same date as the
   tower. – PULPIT. Mid C17 with termini caryatids at the
   angles. – PLATE. Chalice and Paten, 1620; Paten, 1786. –

BRASSES to a priest (nave), and to a man with two wives
and children (nave), both C15.

GREAT BERKHAMSTED *see* BERKHAMSTED

GREAT GADDESDEN

ST JOHN THE BAPTIST. On the hillside in a not very attractive village, but well placed against a screen of beech trees
with the E end facing the valley. The E end is the chief interest of the church. The visitor sees two gables, the r.
one of the brick-built NE Halsey Chapel of 1730, the l. one
of the C12 chancel (window C19) with quoins and shallow
buttresses strengthened with Roman bricks. In the S wall
of the chancel is a small C13 lancet window. The nave has
arcades of four bays, that on the S side with octagonal
piers carrying big stiff-leaf capitals said to be original
early C13 work, but drastically re-tooled if not new. The
arches are hollow-chamfered. The N arcade has the same
arches and moulded capitals. The N aisle E window late
C13. The building needs renewed study to clarify its
history. S porch, clerestory, tower and nave and aisle
roofs are all C15 (tower rebuilt 1861). – PLATE. Chalice,
1637.

MONUMENTS. Brass to William Croke † 1506 and wife
(chancel). – Brass to an unknown woman, *c.* 1520 (N aisle).
– John Halsey † 1670, exceptionally good Italian-looking
epitaph with finely designed cartouche and, on top, a
Berninesque bust (chancel). – Thomas H. † 1715, Anne
† 1719, Jane H. † 1725, Henshaw H. † 1739, all four the
same dignified design with busts under drapery baldacchinos between pilasters and below open segmental
pediments. The sculptor is not recorded. – Charles H.
† 1748, white epitaph with bust against obelisk. –
Frederick H. † 1762, white epitaph with profile medallion
against obelisk. – Agatha H. † 1782, small epitaph with
large angel holding a book. By *Flaxman*, and the only
signed monument of this important series. – Thomas H.
† 1788 and wife, with obelisk and on it oval medallion
with Mrs H. taken up to heaven.

GOLDEN PARSONAGE, 2 m. NE. The original house of the Halseys. This C16 house was probably enlarged in 1705 and then, when the family moved away to Gaddesden Place, the out-of-date old house was pulled down and only the more modern wing left standing. The wing is of five by four bays, red-brick-built with angle pilasters and a plain parapet. The windows are segmentheaded. The doorway has a fine segmental pediment on richly carved corbels and between these a frieze rising from both sides to a point in the centre (a typical early C18 motif). Pretty staircase with finely twisted banisters.

GADDESDEN PLACE. Built by *James Wyatt* for the Halsey family in 1768–73 (the earlier date scratched into a wall on the ground floor, very early, it will be noticed, for *James Wyatt*). Five-bay centre with portico (rebuilt after a fire of 1905) with one-storeyed semicircular galleries and outer two-storey wings with central Venetian windows.

GREAT HORMEAD

ST NICHOLAS. Away from the village street, on a hill behind Great Hormead Bury. The church is much restored (1874), the chancel rebuilt, and the S porch an addition. W tower with diagonal buttresses (late C14 to late C15), nave, and two aisles. Three bays with octagonal piers, moulded capitals, and double-chamfered arches. The date may be c. 1300. The last much shorter arcade bays were added, probably later in the C14. The W tower arch still later, say c. 1400 (shafts with capitals and, in the diagonals, hollows without capitals). – FONT. Norman, undecorated, on thick circular stem and eight shafts set around. – PLATE. Two Chalices, 1740, 1748. – MONUMENT. Lt-Col. Stables, killed at Waterloo 1815, Grecian sarcophagus with the word Waterloo on it in an oval laurel wreath. By *Kendrick*.

The VILLAGE STREET is uncommonly charming. No house of special importance, but thatched cottages with narrowly spaced exposed upright timbers and with Gothick windows (in chronological order: Tudor Cottage, Judds, Milburns, The Cottage).

GREAT HORMEAD BURY. Simple Georgian but with a
Tudor centre still recognizable.

BRICK HOUSE, 1½ m. NE of the church. Quite on its own
and at the time of writing in a neglected state. An interesting rather tall and gaunt early C16 small manor house,
with stepped gables and some brick mullioned windows
under brick hood-moulds.

GREAT MUNDEN

ST NICHOLAS. Unbuttressed W tower of the C15 with
spike. The body of the church with much restored walls
and windows. The masonry goes back originally to the
C12: see the simple Norman N doorway (an order of colonnettes, and roll moulding in the arch) and one small Norman N window in the chancel. At the E end of the S aisle
one fine Dec three-light window, at the W end a similar
one of two lights. The interior bears out the exterior impression. Of the Norman chancel arch the N side survives
with one primitive volute or rather spiral capital and one
with a face either with fingers pulling the mouth open or
with sprays of foliage growing out of the mouth.* The S
side of the Norman chancel arch was destroyed when the
arch was widened in the C15. The S arcade is of three bays
and has C14 detail, and there are besides in the aisle two
ogee-headed recesses and a fine stone reredos at the S end,
also with little ogee niches. The top is castellated. –
PULPIT. Jacobean, with two tiers of the usual blank
arcades. – CHANCEL STALLS with a few rather starved
poppy-heads. – PLATE. Chalice of 1696.

HIGH TREES see p.

GREAT WYMONDLEY

ST MARY. Small flint and stone church. Its most remarkable feature is its apsidal chancel. Nave and chancel are
Norman as proved by the S doorway (colonnettes with
rudely carved faces on capitals, star ornament of the abaci,

* A Norman arch in the N side of the chancel was found at the restoration in 1865 but not left exposed.

and star ornament all over the tympanum) and the chancel arch (shafts with primitive volutes at the angle of the capitals). The Double Piscina also has waterleaf capitals. The windows are C13 lancets (chancel) and C14 and C15 designs in the nave. The W tower with diagonal buttresses and a pyramid roof behind the battlements is C15. The nave roof also belongs to the C15. It rests on primitive head corbels.

DELAMERE HOUSE. The three-storeyed brick building of c. 1600. The N front has two straight gables, the E and S fronts curved gables of the later C17. Good staircase of c. 1600 and some contemporary fireplaces.

GRIMS DYKE see BERKHAMSTED

GROVE, THE, see WATFORD

GUBBINS see GOBIONS

HADHAM HALL see LITTLE HADHAM

HADLEY see MONKEN HADLEY

HAILEYBURY COLLEGE
1 m. SE of Little Amwell

The college was opened in 1809 as a training school for the 59a East India Company. The original buildings were designed by *William Wilkins*, the architect of Downing College, Cambridge, begun in 1807, and of University College, London. The arrangement chosen for the buildings is a representational stone-faced façade to the S and behind it a quadrangle of yellow brick ranges. The façade is one-storeyed and has a central six-column portico, intermediate accents of four columns, and outer accents of pilasters. The whole is of forty-two bays and (Wilkins's usual fault) not sufficiently pulled together. In the quad also the individual parts appear somewhat scattered. Access from the S front is through the intermediate porticos which were originally open towards the quad. The E one still is. The main *point de vue* in the quad was the N side with a pediment and cupola. But even that is no more representational than, say, the Barracks of Woolwich at the same time. The appearance of the quad was rudely dramatized with the erection of a big new chapel in 1876. Until then the chapel had been the present library with its gently coved ceiling, and there had been no dome pressing on Wilkins's long horizontal façade. The new chapel, designed by *Sir Arthur Blomfield*, is a hefty building in a kind of Byzantine or some such *Rundbogen* style, and stretches out arched cloisters to the l. and r. The style did not suit the elder Blomfield who was a Gothicist by conviction. Its coarseness was mitigated in 1936 when *Sir Herbert Baker* added an impressive apse extending very sheer into the quadrangle. The interior also was chastely classicized. Other additions to the original scheme are, in chronological order: Bradby Hall, 1887, by young *Reginald Blomfield*. He cannot in his later Franco-Classical manner have looked back with approval to this gabled Neo-Jacobean design with its red brick walls, thick wooden galleries, and open timber roof. *Reginald Blomfield* also designed the African War Memorial (1903), an obelisk on a scrolly Baroque base. The Lodge and Form Rooms facing the memorial are by *Sir J. W. Simpson & Maxwell Ayrton* (1905–8) who are also responsible for the Big School (New Hall) with its Ionic façade on the E side of the quadrangle.

HAMELS
1½m. wsw of Braughing

A Late Elizabethan mansion of some fame was replaced about 1720 by a big plain Early Georgian one. This in its turn was made sham Elizabethan in the C19. Of the later C18 a number of exquisite fireplaces, one having as its central relief a representation of Shakespeare and his Muse.

HARE STREET
2 m. E of Buntingford

Typical of many hamlets in Herts. Developed along a main road with notable houses, both of the C16–C17 timber-framed overhang type (e.g. former SWAN INN near S end) and the more formal Georgian brick type (HARE STREET HOUSE, five bays, two storeys, parapet and hipped roof. Doorcase with pediment on Roman Doric pilasters. Nice iron gates to the street. The chimney stacks show that the structure of the house is older and the front a later re-modelling.)

HARESFOOT *see* BERKHAMSTED

HARPENDEN

The chief attraction of Harpenden is the way in which the High Street has a broad, turfed and sloping, tree-planted band in the middle, with the houses standing higher on one side than the other, and the way in which at the E end the High Street opens out funnel-wise into the Common. Otherwise there is not much of interest, only a few old houses of note as against the hundreds of phoney half-timbered residences of well-to-do Londoners which have grown up in the last thirty years.

ST NICHOLAS, 1862 by *W. Slater*, except for the w tower (flint and stone, diagonal buttresses, sw stair-turret, spike). In the N aisle on window ledges C12 scalloped capital from the former chancel arch and C12 capital with upright stylized leaves. – FONT. *c.* 1200, polygonal bowl of Purbeck marble with two blank pointed arches on each panel. – MONUMENTS. Brass to William Anabull † 1456 and wife, very decayed figures (close to pulpit). – Brass to William Cressye † 1559 and wife, kneeling figures in stone surround (N transept wall; cf. Wheathampstead, Heyworth). – Godman Jenkyn † 1746, standing wall monument with bulgy sarcophagus and obelisk with scrolly shield.

OUR LADY OF LOURDES, Rothamsted Avenue, 1905, by *F. A. Walters.*

METHODIST CHURCH, High Street, 1929, by *A. Brace.* Broad, symmetrical, free Neo-Tudor stone front.

In the village proper just one house: BOWERS HOUSE, early C18, two-storeyed, eleven-bay, grey brick with vertical strips of rubbed bricks and aprons to the upper windows. Older parts behind. The whole house is now hidden by a new parade of shops.

Towards the Common on the W side the former BULL INN, an excellent C15 half-timbered house with the original Hall, half-timbered additions of the Tudor age, especially a barn at the back, and a Late Georgian bow-fronted addition at the front next to the C15 gable. – Opposite on the E side two good houses: HARPENDEN HALL, the l. side early C17 with porch, some brick and flint chequer, and a brick cornice on the ground floor, the r. side of *c.* 1700 with six bays (originally seven?) and a doorway with curving up cornice and broken segmental pediment. Corinthian pilasters and a charmingly carved vase with garlands under the pediment. C18 red brick also Nos 15 and 17–18.

The ROTHAMSTED EXPERIMENTAL STATION has its Neo-Georgian main building of 1914–16 on the W side of the Common (by *Freeman & Hodgson*).

CROSS FARM, 1 m. SE. C17 gabled brick front and an attached timber and brick block.

48a MACKERY END, 1½ m. NE. Fine stately symmetrical brick front dated 1665, still with 'Dutch' gables with pedimented tops. Central porch with brick pilasters and segmental pediment. The back proves that the body of the house goes back to *c.* 1600 or earlier.

LAWRENCE END *see* p. 153.

HATFIELD

About the year 970 Edgar, King of Mercia, gave Hatfield to the Benedictine monks of Ely. In 1109 the monastery of Ely was converted into a bishopric, and Hatfield became Bishop's Hatfield which is its administrative name to this day. The bishops had a residence at Hatfield which was re-
41 built on a palatial scale by Bishop Morton towards the end of the C15. Of this Bishop's Palace substantial remains survive, close to the parish church, which is dedicated to St Etheldreda, the patron saint of Ely. The palace became Crown property after the dissolution, and in it Mary Tudor and Queen Elizabeth I spent years of their childhood, both

under conditions close to imprisonment. King James I, much impressed by Robert Cecil's palace of Theobalds on the occasion of a visit suggested he should exchange it for Hatfield, and Robert Cecil hastened to accept and took over Hatfield in 1607. However, the old palace was gloomy and out of date, and so Robert Cecil also hastened to pull down most of it and use the materials to build for himself a new house as palatial as Bishop Morton's had been four generations before. This is how Hatfield came to possess its two palaces and its church of St Etheldreda.

The church lies on a hill which, though not high, rises sufficiently above the Great North Road to give shape to the whole cluster of houses which forms the old town. A new Hatfield has grown up within the last fifty years or less on the other side of the railway. It has been known as the New Town long before the Ministry of Town and Country Planning (now of Housing and Local Government) decided to make it the site of one of its projected 'new towns' or satellite towns of London. Its planning is now a joint enterprise with that of Welwyn Garden City.

ST ETHELDREDA. The parish church and its churchyard lie on the top of an eminence. Down the hill run the main streets. Behind the church to the E is the entrance to Hatfield Palace and one of the entrances to Hatfield House. The W tower makes an impressive show from the high road below. It is of four stages, with set-back buttresses, a broad W door with quatrefoil decoration in the spandrels, and a four-light W window. The exterior of the nave is a disappointment after this first impression. It looks strikingly Victorian and was indeed rebuilt by *David Brandon* in 1872. He changed the windows from Perp to Dec, raised the roof, removed box pews and three-decker pulpit, and (strangest alteration of all) narrowed the chancel arch. In spite of all this the general impression of the interior is interesting, with its broad nave and the vistas through into the various openings of the E parts. These are in a more genuine condition and architecturally very remarkable. The church possesses a transept with the unusual adjuncts of two W chapels, and a chancel with a C15 S and a C17 N chapel. The chancel, transepts, and W transept chapels are the oldest surviving portions. They date from the C13, as can be seen from the inner jambs of the chancel E window with nook-shafts, the chancel Piscina, the blocked E lancet window in the S transept, and the blocked trefoil-headed larger opening to its N, and the surprisingly splendid arch between S transept and W chapel. This has trefoil responds with big dogtooth decoration between the shafts, large stiff-leaf capitals, and a complex arch section. The C15 added the W tower and the S chapel. Its arcade towards the chancel is unusually ornate. Instead of the customary four-shaft-four-hollow section the pier has four triple-shafts and above the hollows of the diagonals demi-figures of angels holding shields. The arch from the S chapel to the transept (which cuts into the C13 trefoil opening) is triple-chamfered and has no capitals between jambs and voussoirs. It looks as if it belonged to the C14, in which case a S chapel prior to the one now existing must be presumed.

Finally in 1618 William, Second Earl of Salisbury, built the N chapel as a mortuary chapel to hold his father's tomb. The SALISBURY CHAPEL is the only part of the church which is stone-faced. Its windows are still entirely in the Perp tradition, but the three-bay arcade to the chancel has tall Tuscan columns (cf. Watford, 1595). Two bays are original, the third was added in the C19. The columns are of Shap granite, a material which was only coming into favour at the end of the Tudor era. The interior of the Salisbury Chapel was lavishly adorned by the third Marquis in 1871. The artists employed were Italians (cf. Hatfield House). There is plenty of Salviati mosaic and of alabaster used (the latter notably for the blind arcading of the N and E walls). The W and S openings are filled by exquisite iron gates of early C18 Flemish work which were brought by the third Marquis from Amiens Cathedral. In the chapel stands the MONUMENT TO ROBERT CECIL, First Earl of Salisbury, † 1612. It was ordered by the second Earl from *Simon Basyll*, and the sculptures on it are by *Maximilian Colt*. The monument is entirely in the Dutch tradition, established by *Tommaso Vincidor* in the Nassau Monument at Breda. The Earl lies on a black marble slab supported by four kneeling allegorical figures: Faith, Justice, Fortitude, and Prudence. One of these has her breasts bare, a reminder of the distance which European civilization had travelled between the time when the church and when the chapel was built. But behind the four Virtues, below the effigy of the Earl in his full State dress, lies a skeleton on a rough straw mat, and that rude reminder of the vanity of worldly glory takes one back to the late Middle Ages. – In the same chapel are, moreover, the following MONUMENTS: A knight in armour, his chest covered by his shield, C13. – A body in a shroud on the floor; he lies relaxed, the attitude and the mastery of handling might be Italian. It is the effigy of Sir Richard Curle, by *Nicholas Stone*, 1617. Stone wrote in his notebook: 'I mad a pector lieng on a grave ston of gre marbell for Mr Corell of Hatfield for which I had £20.' – The Third Marquis of Salisbury † 1903, Prime Minister to Queen Victoria, bronze by *Sir William Goscombe John*, replica of the monument in Westminster Abbey.

OTHER FURNISHINGS. PULPIT. By *A. E. Richardson*, 1947. Polygonal, with plain wooden panels with coloured shields. – ORGAN GALLERY. By *W. H. R. Blacking*, 1927. On Tuscan columns, arranged so as to let the light from the W window come in unimpeded. – COMMUNION RAILS. C17 with broadly twisted balusters. – CHANDELIER. Brass, given in 1733 (S chapel). – STAINED GLASS. Nothing medieval, but a good cross-section though Late Victorian glass. Infinitely the best the S transept window by *Morris & Co.*, designed by *Burne-Jones*, 1894. It has a purity of glow, with its typical prevalent green and its peacock blue and rose-colour, never achieved by any other glass before the early C20. – Chancel E window and N chapel E window by *Clayton & Bell*, c. 1870–2. – The N windows of the N chapel and the E window of the S chapel by *Burlison & Grylls*, the former

1881, 1894, 1899, the latter, to the design of *Temple Moore*, 1902. – PLATE. Two Chalices and Patens, two Flagons, two Almsdishes, and a Spoon, all dated 1684 and all made for the Coronation of James II. – Cross and Candlesticks in the S chapel, designed by *Temple Moore*. – Processional Cross in the same chapel designed by *A. E. Richardson*. – MONUMENTS (other than those in Salisbury Chapel). Brass to Fulke Onslowe † 1602, inscription on stone tablet (chancel, N wall). – Sir John Brocket † 1598, very simple standing wall monument, without figures. Sir John was a merchant; yet his helmet is suspended above the tomb. – Dame Elizabeth Brocket † 1612 and his mother. Big standing wall monument with the two ladies stiffly reclining, propped up on their elbows, one behind and above the other. The background architecture flat and not too costly. – Sir James Reade and his son John, by *Rysbrack*, 1760. Two busts, and above a portrait medallion against the usual obelisk. By the sides two big beautifully carved adult cherubs with large wings. – Thomas Fuller † 1712, standing wall monument with inscription on drapery and two putti l. and r.; not of high quality. – Several late C18 to early C19 epitaphs high up in the nave, particularly fine the Heaviside Monument by *Thomas Banks*, 1787, the side pieces later. In the centre two female allegories of Death (a reversed torch) and the Caduceus, the symbol of Medicine.

39b

CHURCHYARD GATES. Magnificent ironwork taken to Hatfield from St Paul's Cathedral. They were made about 1710.

41 BISHOP'S PALACE. What remains of Bishop Morton's Palace is the foremost monument of medieval domestic architecture in the county and one of the foremost monuments of medieval brickwork in the country. It is no more than one wing of a palace built round a courtyard and in addition the gatehouse range to its W. The palace was built in this form *c.* 1480–90. It is known in the form it had immediately before its destruction from a drawing of *c.* 1608. It had then the surviving hall range as its W range, and N, S, and E ranges with exterior details and internal

arrangements clearly no earlier than the Elizabethan age. The hall range is a brick building *c.* 230 by 40 ft with projecting porches on the W and E near the centres of the sides and buttresses of the C19. The windows are of two lights under hood-moulds; not large. The original tall bay window at the dais end is blocked up. The dais was at the S end of what now appears to be the Hall. This went originally only as far as the porches. To the N of these were the Kitchens and Offices. The porches have four-centred entrances, and that of the W front a stair-turret rising higher than the porch itself. At the top of the porches are parapets on brick corbel-tables. The roof of the hall is a splendid specimen of late medieval timber construction, with the principals resting on carved stone corbels, the arched braces moulded, the collar-beams cross-trussed, and with ogee-shaped wind-braces in two tiers between the principals. The rooms adjoining the Hall on the N and S are gathered under large cross-gables. The gatehouse range is simpler, with stepped end-gables and brick windows similar to those of the hall range.

The hall range was converted into stables in 1628 and remained in use for that purpose until the C20. To its N an early C19 Gothick range, similar in style to the contemporary work at Hertford Castle.

HATFIELD HOUSE. Hatfield House was built by Robert Cecil, first Earl of Salisbury in 1608–12. The W wing was gutted by fire in 1835 and redecorated by the second Marquis († 1868). He also did much redecoration in other parts of the house and was followed in this by the third Marquis (the Prime Minister, † 1903). The house is the most important mansion in the county and one of the four or five most important Jacobean mansions in England.

In plan Hatfield House does not at first sight seem to be anything out of the ordinary. It keeps to the Elizabethan tradition of the E-shape. In size, however, it is unusually large for that plan type (*c.* 300 by 150 ft). The wings are thus designed to have a thickness of two and at their ends even of three rooms. These ends are emphasized by square angle turrets. The wings face what was originally the approach road from London. Recessed between them along the front of the main range lay an open loggia, closed by the second Marquis in 1846 and converted into an Armoury. Such loggias were becoming fashionable in England just in those years in which Robert Cecil built Hatfield. Other examples are at Cranborne in Dorset and Holland House in London. Neville's Court at Trinity College, Cambridge, can also be regarded as a parallel. There is in fact documentary evidence to suggest that the loggia was an afterthought conceived while construction of the house went on. The loggia has round-headed arches separated by Roman Doric pilasters busily decorated with strapwork as are also the spandrels. Above it runs the Great Gallery with mullioned and transomed windows separated by pilasters and a crowning strapwork balustrade. In the centre of the loggia rises the three-storeyed porch with coupled free-standing superimposed columns of the Roman Doric, Ionic, and Corinthian orders. There is again a lavish display of strapwork and similar fanciful decoration, finishing on the top with a balustrade with squashed bulgy pilasters and a large carved date, 1611. The wings have larger mullioned and transomed windows for their various bays. Entrances into the wings are also roundheaded, though those to the turrets and some in the loggia still use the four-centred form (one of the few survivals of Perp traditions).

In contrast to the sumptuous display on the S side, the N side is surprisingly bare and matter-of-fact. Save for the central doorway and the fine, tall, square, stone cupola above the centre there is practically no decoration, just the smooth brick walls with large many-mullioned and transomed windows on two floors and an attic floor above with small low windows. The squareness and horizontalism of all this strikes one as curiously modern in the C20. While the N and S fronts are not strictly symmetrical, in the E and W sides the designer has made an attempt at compositions complete in themselves.

We are in the fortunate position at Hatfield to know who the designer was. His name is *Robert Lyminge*. He

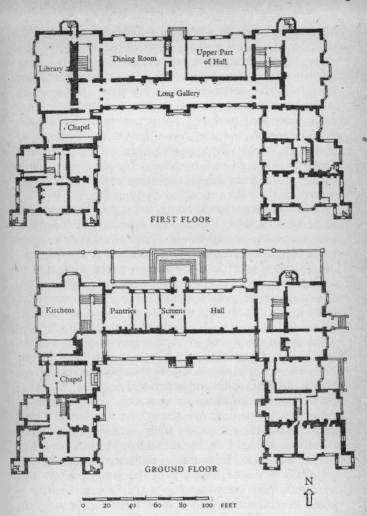

FIRST FLOOR

GROUND FLOOR

N

0   20   40   60   80   100 FEET

HATFIELD HOUSE

was by trade a carpenter, and he went from Hatfield to
Blickling in Norfolk, where he died and was buried in
1628. In the parish register he is called 'architect and
builder' of Blickling Hall, and as according to the Hatfield records he also provided drawings there apart from
supervising the workmen and giving orders to them, his
was in all probability the creative work on the elevations.
Others may well have had something to do with more
general decisions too, e.g. *Simon Basyll*, the Surveyor of
the King's Works who appears several times, and divers
friends of Robert Cecil, especially *Thomas Wilson*, later
Keeper of the State Papers. Building began in 1608 and
was complete by the time Cecil died in 1612.

Across the centre of the house on the ground floor runs
the Screens Passage. This and the adjoining Hall are still
in the traditional medieval and Tudor position. The open
arcade from the Screens Passage to the l. is not original.
46a The SCREEN itself is a spectacular piece of Jacobean
carving, immensely skilful and of barbaric profusion. Its
projecting upper gallery towards the HALL was only
closed in the C19. Facing it, at the other end of the Hall,
is a second gallery, a very unusual feature. This is corbelled out of the E wall which has here two stone doorways to the Great Staircase. In one of them still an
original door. Original woodwork also, besides screen and
gallery, the long tables, and benches. The ceiling is coved,
not, as was still customary about 1600, of the hammer-
beam type. The main cross-beams have fine fretwork and
pendants, but the panels and their painting are the work
of Italians brought in by the third Marquis in 1878
(painter *Taldini*). The fireplaces also date from that time.
45b The GREAT STAIRCASE is of the same richness and
the same superb craftsmanship as the Screen. In style it
should be compared with that at Blickling. It runs up
on three sides of a narrow rectangular open well and has
elaborate tapering banisters and newel posts covered
with strapwork and pretty figure decoration (one whole
post has trophies with garden tools and a little figure of a
gardener in relief). The posts are crowned by lion sup-

porters and naked putti carrying musical instruments and
other objects. The staircase ceiling belongs to the remodelling campaign of the second Marquis. E of the
Staircase is the SUMMER DRAWING ROOM, specially
well preserved, except for the C19 fireplace. The Organ
was bought for the Chapel from a Dutchman in 1609 at
the enormous price of £1,084. S of the Drawing Room are
the YEW ROOM and the MORNING ROOM with an
original fireplace. The ARMOURY, originally open to the
S (*see* above), has a set of important tapestries not belonging to the Jacobean house. It represents the four seasons
and was made by *Sheldon* in 1611. The ceiling is C19 but
the stately stone doorway to the Screens Passage is
original. – At the other end of the Armoury lies the
CHAPEL facing the courtyard with a large E window with
two transomes, the only one which has still rounded heads
to its individual lights. The window is filled with the
original Flemish stained glass; and the biblical pictures
presented by Sir Henry Wotton to Cecil are also original.
They are of the Venetian school. As for the rest, only the
arcading of the Chapel Gallery is Jacobean, everything
else was redone by the third Marquis and his Italian men
between 1869 and 1880.

The W part of the main range contains serveries and
gives access to the KITCHENS which are in the basement,
not a unique but an unusual position in Elizabethan and
Jacobean times. The secondary staircase here, called the
ADAM AND EVE STAIRCASE, was remodelled in the C19
but retains a fine door surround of *c.* 1700 on the first
floor. The largest room on the first floor is the LONG
GALLERY, about 180 ft long. Halfway down a branch
leads off at right angles running across the centre of the
house and opening towards the Hall. It is doubtful
whether this has always been part of the Long Gallery or
whether it was not originally divided off, as were indeed
the two ends of the Gallery which are now marked by
columns. It is also not certain, it seems, how far the ceiling and the fireplaces are original. The rooms to the W of
the S–N branch of the Gallery are the DINING ROOM

(C19, with a C17 big fireplace brought to Hatfield from Quickswood, another Cecil house) and then, beyond the Adam and Eve Staircase, the LIBRARY (very restrained marble fireplace with a mosaic portrait of the first Earl, made in Venice, 1608). At the E end beyond the Great Staircase is KING JAMES'S DRAWING ROOM, with a new or much renewed ceiling and a magnificient fireplace no doubt by *Colt*. The large figure of the King is not of bronze; it is painted to look bronze. The idea of such a standing figure above a fireplace is taken from Blondeel's grander composition at the Greffe at Bruges. The fireplace from the Summer Dining Room on the ground floor is now in KING JAMES'S BEDROOM. There are several more original fireplaces in other rooms.

The gardens were begun at the same time as the house, and that to the E, though completely redone in the C19, conveys a good idea of the design of a Jacobean garden. The original fountains were devised by the celebrated *Solomon de Caus*, and plants were bought by the equally celebrated *John Tradescant*. The terrace on the S side has a handsome brick balustrade. To the W of the house in the gardens is a large C18 RELIEF of Queen Elizabeth I and her Courtiers which comes from the Royal Exchange. To the N the C19 approach drive connects the house with the railway station. At the station end is a decorative GATE of terracotta and wrought iron and a seated STATUE of the third Marquis († 1903) by *Frampton*.

Farther away in the Home Park is the RANGER'S COTTAGE, timber-framed, early C17, but refaced with brick later in the century. The whole of the park is 530 acres in size, the largest in the county.

THE TOWN

From the churchyard start the main streets down the hill towards the Great North Road: Church Street and Fore Street. At the beginning of CHURCH STREET, overlooking the churchyard, Nos 2–4, a group of half-timbered late C16 houses with the upright timbers exposed. The other houses in the street are of minor interest. FORE

STREET is a perfect example of the self-respecting street 6b
in a small Georgian town, with its visual charm considerably increased by the stepping down of the houses to
follow the descent of the street. Nos 2–4 are one mid C18
composition of fifteen bays, almost entirely plain and thus
ideal as a foil to the church which it faces. Then a gap and
at the corner THE EAST INDIAN CHIEF, five-bay,
earlier C18. After that the Georgian procession marches
on without a hitch: No. 12, late C18, with an Adamish
doorcase, and so on to No. 20. Nos 16 and 18 are of
chequered purple and red brick. Meanwhile an accom-
paniment has set in on the opposite side: No. 3 with a
door-hood on lushly carved brackets; No. 7, still entirely
in the same tradition yet dated 1826, etc. Towards the
foot of the hill the houses are smaller and humbler, and at
the corner of PARK STREET appears the first of the
timber-framed and gabled type of the C17, the EIGHT
BELLS INN. In Park Street are more early houses, e.g.
Nos 9–11 with overhanging upper floor and symmetrical
outer gables. The old street ends soon, and the C19 sealed
it first by the fine Late Georgian house No. 38 which is
entirely in the country, not in the town style, and then by
the Viaduct arches of the third Marquis's station approach
to Hatfield House (with its Neo-Jacobean balustrade).
Little else of interest in the old town. In the GREAT
NORTH ROAD No. 52, Late Georgian, of five bays and
two storeys with a porch displaying clustered Gothic
shafts, and No. 69, Late Georgian, with a door surround
in *Coade* stone *à la* Bedford Square, London. Off the
Great North Road in BATTERDALE the COLONELS'
HOUSE (the colonels of the Herts Regiment), late C17
brick, and the cottage at the back (in FRENCH HORN
LANE) which was the Herts Regiment's Armoury.
NAST HYDE *see* p. 175.

THE NEW TOWN

Hatfield New Town had already developed to the NW,
before it was established as one of the 'New Towns' in
the sense of to-day. It had first grown in conjunction

with the de Havilland Factory (1935, by *J. M. Munro*). A little earlier still, the COMET, by *E. B. Musman*, 1933, one of the earliest inns in England, built in the style of the C20, without borrowings from the past. Of the new New Town one neighbourhood is growing up in 1951–2: ROE GREEN, just S of the Comet. The plans and most houses by *Lionel Brett* and *Kenneth Boyd*. So far about one-third of the new population lives in four-storey flats, the rest in terrace houses. Density *c.* 16 dwellings to the acre. Well calculated vistas, and nice contrasts of yellow and red brick with a certain amount of white plastering. May it stay white. Also flats by *Hening & Chitty*.

H.C.C. TECHNICAL COLLEGE, Roe Green Lane. By *Howard Robertson*, 1951–2. A large group of buildings, facing the Barnet by-pass road. The main block, incorporating Hall, offices, and library is at the NW corner. This has a tall entrance motif to the W with the fashionable projected and canted-out frame, which gives the general view from the S an odd outline. The block has a pitched roof and a large S window running with a triangular head right up to the roof-pitch. The roof of the canted porch is continued into the roof-pitch without any break. The classroom wings are arranged round courtyards with an attractive connexion between them by a long straight N–S promenade across the courtyards and below the crosswings. Construction was with the aid of prefabricated units with hardly any wet processes on the site. A large extension is going up to the S of the main group. This will be a Secondary Modern School. A piece of sculpture by *Barbara Hepworth* at the SW angle of the completed buildings. Inside two decorative panels by *Ben Nicholson*.

HEMEL HEMPSTEAD

One of the most attractive towns of Herts, with its High Street running up along a hillside so that on part of its course one side lies several steps lower than the other, and the church appears at a broad opening considerably below the street level. It is to be hoped that the development of the satellite town (*see* below) will be carried out so that this specific character of the town and its many good Georgian houses will be preserved, as was indeed intended by the planning consultant *G. A. Jellicoe.*

ST MARY. A large church essentially Norman, the only one [10] in the county with the exception of St Albans. Nave and aisles, transepts, crossing tower, chancel, and a small room N of the chancel. The outer walls of flint are all C12, though windows have in the C14 and C15 been enlarged. The earliest part is the relatively low chancel. This seems [16b] to date from *c.* 1150 and is (a rarity in England) rib-vaulted. The ribs and transverse arches have the simplest roll mouldings and rest on wall shafts with scalloped capitals. The narrow room to the N (had it originally an apsidal E end, or was it a sacristy?) is also rib-vaulted. The chancel N window is Norman with double nook-shafts. The transepts and nave were built after the chancel. The nave can hardly be earlier than *c.* 1175. It has six bays with circular piers with shallow bases and capitals of many varieties or ornamented scalloping. Little stylized leaves occur and also the so-called water-leaf motif. The arches are simply of two steps. The clerestory is contemporary, a rarity. The windows have nook-shafts inside, and a billet-frieze runs all along the outside and around the window arches. The W end of the nave has a doorway of two orders with zigzag and leaf motifs in the voussoirs. The crossing tower is extremely simple on the lower stage, but opens in large shafted twin windows on the upper stage with decorated voussoirs. The staircase turret on the SE is circular in its upper stages. The tower is crowned by a fine big leaded spire rising to nearly 200 ft. In the S transept the W window is also Norman. Otherwise the windows are mostly Perp, except for those in the S wall of the chancel which are Dec.

On its W side the church faces scenery still completely rural. The E end lies below the High Street.

The interior of the chancel was repainted in 1888 to

Bodley's designs. – The only early roofs are those of the transepts. They are C15 and have arched braces with traceried spandrels. – STAINED GLASS. S chancel windows, 1858, by *Clayton & Bell*; S aisle, 1870, by *A. Gibbs*. – PLATE. Covered Chalice, 1563. – MONUMENTS. Brass (W end S aisle) to Robert Albyn and wife, very good work of the late C14. – Sir Astley Paston Cooper † 1841, Neo-Gothic epitaph by *S. Manning*.

FRIENDS MEETING HOUSE, St Mary's Road, off the High Street. Early C19; plain rectangle of purple and red brick. The front half domestic, the back with arched windows for worship. The burial ground lies by the side.

TOWN HALL, High Street. Neo-Jacobean, red brick with stone dressings. The centre 1851 by *George Low*, additions of 1861 and 1868.

SOUTH HILL JUNIOR MIXED AND INFANTS SCHOOL (*see* Introduction, p. 28).

The HIGH STREET is one of the most agreeable streets of Herts. It rises in a gentle curve, skirting the hillside and opens about halfway to reveal the churchyard and church with its spire. The most characteristic element of the street is its early C18 houses with their typical segment-headed windows. Most of these houses are of purple brick with red dressings, but some are whitewashed. The best examples are on the E side: Nos 33–39, dated 1728 on a rainwater head; No. 51, dated 1725; Nos 65–69, dated 1714; No. 71, dated 1730; and No. 81 (The Sun), dated 1726. Earlier buildings are the group of rambling cottages on the W side (Nos 60–68), and lower down No. 41, the King's Arms, with half-timbered premises going far back into the side alley. These side alleys running up the hill to the E are characteristic of Hemel Hempstead High Street. To follow them means to realize how near the countryside still is to the town. Of houses of later Georgian date the best is No. 1 with stone façade and an Adamish door surround.

To the N the town comes to an abrupt end at the N end of the High Street. Big trees to the l. and r. indicate a change of scene, and the best houses farther N are indeed right out in the country: MARCHMONT HOUSE on the road to Piccotts End and the Gaddesdens (early C19 with Greek Doric doorway *in antis*, and four pediments to street and garden sides), and GADEBRIDGE in its own grounds off Gadebridge Lane (*c.* 1800 with portico of giant Ionic pilasters; the whole front is eleven bays wide). s of Gadebridge, i.e. to the W of Hemel Hempstead in Bury Hill, LOCKERS COTTAGE (pretty, of timber-framing, brick, and plaster, with a weatherboarded extension) and LOCKERS (of two parts, the l. one C16 with gables, the r. one C18 with fine doorway). In Bury Road s of Bury Hill a late C16 two-storeyed stone porch with columns, known as CHARTER TOWER, is attached to a C19 building.

Only to the s does the High Street continue in an urban way. The MARLOWES running parallel with Bury Road is a street proper. Its architecture is chiefly early C19. The best individual houses are a little earlier: LITTLE MARLOWES HOUSE and OLD MARLOWES HOUSE, both three-bay, two-storey cottages. The rich doorcase of the latter is, however, Early Georgian. Near the s end of the Marlowes is CORNER HALL, a good timber-framed house with close-set uprights in the overhanging upper storeys; C15 or C16.

Further s, the new OFFICES for SIR ROBERT McALPINE & SONS, by *H. J. Bebb*, 1951–2, are the first introduction to the New Town. They stand close to what is going to be the Town Centre; but of that not an indication can yet be seen. That is a matter for regret, here and in other New Towns; for only the urban character of a centre would endow the housing with a corresponding urban character. Without such a centre it tends to look suburban and indeed to be suburban. The office building for McAlpine's is an interesting, if a little mannered design, with a display of just too many unexpected motifs. Parallelogram of light brick. Three storeys with a recessed and shorter fourth ending to the s in a deep sun canopy with concave south edge. The s side of the storeys below with large window strips with concrete mullions and transomes. In contrast to this the long (w) entrance side has lower window strips and above each of them slanting panes of a different shape related to curiously sloping ceilings inside. Concrete porch with canted supports.

Of the domestic quarters of the New Town one has so far been specially developed: ADEYFIELD. The architect is *H. Kellett Ablett*. First house April 1949, thousandth April 1952, not a spectacular rate of growth. Density intended to be 20 persons to the acre, but still considerably less. The terrace houses are nothing special. The most remarkable thing is the Shopping Centre. It is crossed diagonally by a road with large pedestrian spaces in the angles. Arcaded shop-fronts of simple design and flats above. The E side is broken up into smaller detached buildings which so far seems no advantage. But the Social Centre which is going up in 1952 to close the square to the S may alter that impression. S of it one long, taller block of flats with weird, somewhat perverse details, a low zigzag parapet wall in the front, pram sheds with pebbled or cobbled fronts between this and the main doorways, and a centre balcony – just one – in the middle of the whole composition, very Tecton in style. E of this group is the future recreation ground, and E of this a two-storeyed H.C.C. SECONDARY SCHOOL (*see* Introduction, p. 28). A PRIMARY SCHOOL a little way to the S of the Shopping Centre.

The beginnings of an INDUSTRIAL AREA (Addressograph-Multigraph, Ltd., by *Fuller, Hall, & Foulsham*, Alford & Alder, by *W. Leslie Jones*, etc.). $1\frac{1}{2}$ m. E of the old church and $\frac{3}{4}$ m. E of Adeyfield, extending northward.

LEVERSTOCK GREEN *see* p. 155.

HERTFORD *

The county town, and all that the centre of a predominantly rural county should be, not too big (14,000 inhabitants in 1951), with much of its visual traditions left and yet not at all a museum piece. The only architecturally unfortunate thing is that of the five medieval parish churches of Hert-

* I have to thank Mr G. E. Moodey for many valuable contributions.

ford, three have completely disappeared, and the other two are without medieval remains.

ST ANDREW, St Andrew's Street, 1869, by *J. Johnson*; the steeple 1876. The style is, according to Kelly, 'transitional between Early English and Decorated with some intermixture of French Gothic'. Of the church preceding *Johnson's* only the N doorway survives: C15, with hoodmould on demi-figures of angels and the usual quatrefoil decoration of the spandrels. – PLATE. Elaborately chased C16 Chalice (Spanish?); C18 Chalice and Paten.

ALL SAINTS. Off Fore Street to the S. To the S of the church the open country seems to begin, with plenty of fine trees. The church was designed by *Paley, Austin, & Paley* of Lancaster in 1895, and completed in 1905. The penalty of going to a Northerner for the design is that the church, built of red Runcorn stone, is completely alien in Herts. It is of good conscientious design and impressive size, with Perp detail, a tall tower with taller stair-turret, and some original features such as the hexagonal NW porch. – STAINED GLASS. A vast seven-light E window by *Kempe*, 1900 ('I am the vine, ye are the branches'). – PLATE. Flagon, 1680; Chalice and Paten, 1696; Paten, 1725.

BAPTIST CHURCH, Cowbridge, 1906, by *G. Baines & Son*. Nco-Perp with Art Nouveau licences.

FRIENDS' MEETING HOUSE, Railway Street, 1670. Red brick with two front gables and originally no doubt mullioned windows. On the ground floor there seem to have been two doors towards the street. Well preserved woodwork inside.

SHIRE HALL, 1768–9, by *James Adam*, Robert Adam's brother. Large yellow brick block in the middle of the town completely unadorned, unless the two curved projections on the N and S are accepted as ornamental. The arcades at the back were originally open and gave access to a covered market. Plain three-bay entrance on the E, above which there was originally a grand Venetian window. Fine top-lit rotunda on the upper floor in the centre.

COUNTY HALL, 1939, by *James & Bywaters* and *Rowland Pearce*. Large group of Neo-Georgian buildings, the detail with the freedom which England learned from Scandinavia about 1930. Scandinavian are the precedents of the slender cupola, the portico of fluted, not pilasters but pilaster strips, the ornamental motifs sparingly used and the cloister arcading to the r. of the portico.

CORN EXCHANGE AND PUBLIC HALL, Fore Street, 1857, by *Hill* of Leeds. The stone-faced front is like that of an ambitious Methodist Chapel: three bays with giant Corinthian pilasters, large, tripartite, and arched, debased Cinquecento window between, and a big pediment. Immediately behind it the

COVERED MARKET, Market Street, 1889, by young *Reginald* (later Sir R.) *Blomfield*. That is the only remarkable fact about it. One-storeyed, red brick with arcading and glazed, raised centre.

CASTLE. Not much is left of the once renowned castle: the mount, about 22 ft high, some of the C12 flint curtain-wall of the Bailey with a postern gate and octagonal tower at the SW angle, and on the N side of it a late C15 gatehouse of brick with angle turrets on both sides. Its only decoration is friezes of round arches on corbels, subdivided into twin arches. The gatehouse was much altered about 1800, when the gateway was blocked, a porch made, a S wing added, and the fenestration regularized. So the building is now typical Gothicism of that date. Moreover the lawns and nice sited trees stretch down to the river to make a picture of gentle arcadian charm.

HALE'S GRAMMAR SCHOOL, NE of All Saints. Early C17 building of brick with a porch on one front and a projecting staircase opposite on the other. Gabled and with brick windows under hood-moulds originally no doubt with brick mullions.

CHRIST'S HOSPITAL SCHOOL FOR GIRLS, Fore Street. Founded as a school for the younger children of Christ's Hospital, Newgate Street, London, in 1683. The original buildings were completed in 1695. Of these the following remain: The Gateway in Fore Street with lead figures of

Bluecoat boys, given in 1721, and at the N end of an avenue
of trees the Steward's House and attached to it on the W
the School Hall, formerly the Writing School, refaced
and embellished in the C20 but inside still with its original
coved ceiling.* Originally cottages or wards ran along the
l. and r. sides of the avenue, but these have been replaced
by larger buildings of 1900–2, at the time when the school
was converted into a school for girls. A hundred years
before (in 1800) an addition had been built to the W of the
School Hall, the Dining Hall, also much altered. It is a
large room on the upper floor with arched windows, and
in it are the wooden corbels and frieze from the Hall of
the original London Christ's Hospital which was pulled
down in 1902. The words and figures date from 1829. By
the entrance a fine Rococo bust of Thomas Lockington,
Treasurer of Christ's Hospital in 1707–16. It was brought
to Hertford from St Mary Magdalene, Great Fish Street,
London. More recent new ranges towards the NW: 1901
and 1906 by *A. R. Stenning*. The new library was built by
S. Tatchell in 1935. Facing Fore Street a long range of
red brick with pediment and niches containing figures of
Blue-girls. This is the original girls' school of 1778. To
the r. of the Entrance Gates the Grammar School and
Schoolmaster's house, both of 1783.

MORGANS ROAD JUNIOR MIXED AND INFANTS
SCHOOL (*see* Introduction, p. 28).

HERTS COUNTY HOSPITAL, North Road. The centre,
1833, by *Mr Smith* (probably Thomas). Stuccoed front of
seven bays and two and a half storeys with a three-bay
pediment embellished with carved statuary.

PERAMBULATION

The centre of the town is now Parliament Square, an open
space made only in 1821. From here streets run in three
directions: Fore Street E, the Wash, leading to Mill
Bridge, and St Andrew's Street N, Castle Street S and
then W. In PARLIAMENT SQUARE, as a characteristic

* The Bluecoat boy in the niche over the entrance comes from the
former Bluecoat School at Ware.

beginning, side by side Nos 12 and 14, the former C17, plastered with a big twin gable, the latter early C19, severely classical with good bold capital lettering in an Egyptian type. FORE STREET, the main street of Hertford, carries on this contrast. At its start, No. 1, three-storeyed and stuccoed, with Italian Renaissance trim, c. 1850, like London city buildings of the same date. Then at once Nos 3–13, a long C17 house with an exceptionally richly pargetted façade, the motifs chiefly thick foliage scrolls. Some of it redone skilfully in the C20. Opposite, BELL LANE leads past an overhang storey on the l. and a 'manufactory' of the early C19 on the r., to BAILEY HALL, a stately early C18 mansion of five bays and two and a half storeys with parapet and giant angle pilasters. The three middle bays slightly projected and also flanked by giant pilasters. Originally there was a big curved pediment on top. Pedimented doorcase with Tuscan columns against a rusticated background. An arched window above. The entrance side has a doorcase with a segmental pediment on fluted Corinthian pilasters, and inside a staircase with delicate twisted and columnar balusters. E of all All Saints churchyard the BRITISH SCHOOL OF INDUSTRY and the HARRISON ALMSHOUSES of 1850 and 1854, both red brick, in a villa Tudor style. Also the ABEL SMITH MEMORIAL SCHOOL, of yellow brick, with red brick and stone, 1861, and the COWPER MEMORIAL SCHOOL, red brick Tudor of 1841. Back in Fore Street, at the corner of Church Street, the SALISBURY ARMS, late C16 to early C17, much restored and wholly re-pargetted, but with a good original Jacobean staircase and an overhanging upper floor towards Church Street. At the s end of Church Street, on the r., the OLD VICARAGE, timber-framed and plastered, the front-door dated 1631. The Shire Hall faces the small MARKET PLACE: this, Salisbury Square, and another street widening to the N of the Shire Hall form a pretty, varied group of squares. Off Salisbury Square to the N, the short BULL PLAIN leads to the gates of LOMBARD HOUSE, the house of Chauncy, the Herts historian of c. 1700, with an irregular, roughcast C17 back overlooking the river and weatherboarded storehouses, barns, and cottages, and an early C18 brick façade. A Jacobean overmantel in the Hall. On the way to Lombard House on the r. Nos 16–20 also of the late C17 and early C18. – Back to Fore Street and on the E. The keynote is plastered early C19 fronts, little (except the Post Office) jars acutely. The most interesting houses No. 42, an Egyptian front of 1825 with Egyptian shop window, Nos 76–78 of *c*. 1830, Nos 88–96, a typical early C18 brick house of six bays, and the Regal Café which looks Early Victorian but has original Jacobean panelling inside. The continuation of the Christ's Hospital buildings in Fore Street comprises the Blue Boy Inn on the corner of South Street and the former Brewery adjoining it. This has a semi-hexagonal front with a semi-hexagonal porch, rising to a height of 3 storeys; tiny flanking wings.

CASTLE STREET has a number of worthwhile timber-framed and plastered cottages, e.g. Nos 14–18, then No. 20, Georgian brick, and then LONGMORE'S of yellow and red brick, castellated, built probably *c*. 1840–50 (w half 1904). Opposite THE WALNUTS, mid C17 with C18 alterations. At the end facing us Nos 55–61, one composition with Nos 1–3 WEST STREET. Also one composition Nos 4–16 WATER LANE, off Castle Street, formerly, the MHLG suggests, outbuildings of the Castle. The N front of this group is Gothick of *c*. 1800, like the remodelled Castle gatehouse. Castle Street is continued by WEST STREET. Here No. 6, one of the usual two-storey, five-bay brick houses. The second and fourth upper windows have brick aprons. The house is dated 1719. It was the Brewer's house of a Brewery still operating behind. Next to it the weatherboarded maltings and then, No. 10, the maltster's house, reported late C18. No. 17 West Street has a carved door dated 1654 in the yard, No. 37 a Jacobean porch and door.

ST ANDREW'S STREET runs to the w. It begins with Nos 2–6, Georgian brick of different heights and designs, then cottages with overhangs, No. 22 with Early Victorian bargeboarding, and No. 28, an ambitious design dated 1726: five bays, with giant Ionic angle pilasters and above the cornice an attic storey. The broad doorway has Ionic brick pilasters, the window above a segmental pediment reaching up into the cornice. This and the houses in the immediate neighbourhood of St Andrew's Church are the best of Hertford. To the w No. 51 of the later C17, timber-framed with broad plaster panels. Modillion frieze; late C18 doorcase with pediment. To the E of the church the OLD VERGER'S HOUSE, No. 43, with overhanging upper floor and broad narrowly spaced vertical timbers. To the N CECIL HOUSE, No. 52, with a charming elaborate C18 Gothic porch. Off St Andrew's Street to the N OLD CROSS with a FOUNTAIN composed of fragments of the demolished church of St Mary the Less. The central motif is a C13 lancet window with two nook-shafts and dog-tooth ornamentation. The continuation of Old Cross is COW BRIDGE, where on the l. is a Neo-Jacobean cottage with a middle loggia. This is a replica of one designed by *H. Roberts* for the 1851 Exhibition as an example of the improved working-class housing developed at the request of Prince Albert (cf. Abbots Langley). At the corner of Cow Bridge and PORT HILL a group of early C19 yellow brick houses designed as one composition, with central pediment and raised angle blocks. Another such example of early C19 planning is NORTH CRESCENT, or North Road, the N continuation of St Andrew's Street. This is a row of semi-detached houses, the whole row connected by lower links. At the beginning, opposite, stands NORTH ROAD HOUSE, with a Greek Doric porch, which dates the composition as *c.* 1825.

HERTINGFORDBURY

ST MARY. All 1890 in outer and largely C19 even in inner appearance. w tower with diagonal buttresses and recessed spire. Chancel, nave, and N aisle, C19 N chapel. The chancel actually dates from the C13, and the group of three lancets with the middle one higher than the others, nook shafts and elaborate inner arches is the best piece of

Roman Remains: St Albans, Sea-God mosaic

Scenery: Broxbourne and the river Lea

(a) *Scenery:* Ashridge Woods

(b) *Scenery:* The village green at Westmill

Scenery: Village street at Ashwell (*Copyright Country Life*)

4

Scenery: Village street at Much Hadham

5

(a) *Town Scenery:* St Michael's Street, St Albans

(b) *Town Scenery:* Fore Street, Hatfield

(a) *Scenery:* Gazebos, Ware, overlooking the river Lea

(b) *Scenery:* Burton's Mill, Sawbridgeworth

Scenery: The railway viaduct, Welwyn

8

Church Exteriors: St Albans Cathedral; Norman transept and crossing tower, Early English Chancel, Decorated Lady Chapel

Church Exteriors: Hemel Hempstead, Norman crossing;
the spire later

(a) *Church Exteriors:* East Barnet, a Norman village church

(b) *Church Exteriors:* Ware, a prosperous Perpendicular town church

Church Exteriors: Aldenham, a Perpendicular village church

Church Exteriors: Ashwell, an exceptionally ambitious Perpendicular village church (*Copyright Country Life*).

(a) *Church Exteriors:* Buntingford, 1614–26, the apse of 1899

(b) *Church Exteriors:* Ayot St Lawrence, 1778–9, by Nicholas Revett

(a) *Church Interiors:* St Albans, St Michael's church,
tenth and early twelfth centuries

(b) *Church Interiors:* St Albans Cathedral, Transept triforium,
late eleventh century

(b) *Church Interiors:* Hemel Hempstead, Chancel, twelfth century.

(a) *Church Interiors:* Weston, Crossing, twelfth century

16

Church Interiors: St Albans Cathedral, Nave, late eleventh century and *c.* 1220–30

(b) *Church Interiors*: Baldock, early
fourteenth century

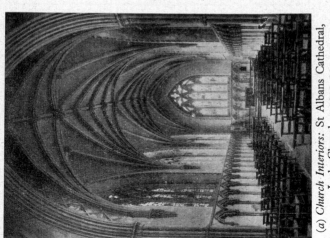

(a) *Church Interiors*: St Albans Cathedral,
Lady Chapel, c. 1300–20

18

Church Interiors: Bishops Stortford, fifteenth century

(a) *Church Interiors:* Wyddial, Chancel chapel, 1532

(b) *Church Interiors:* St Paul's Walden, Chancel, 1727

(a) *Church Details:* Offley, thirteenth century capital

(b) *Church Details:* Ippollitts, Corbel head, probably
early fourteenth century

(a) *Church Details:* Stanstead Abbots, Porch, fifteenth century

(b) *Church Furnishings:* Gilston, Screen, late thirteenth century

Church Furnishings: Sandridge, Chancel arch and screen, *c.* 1100, late fourteenth century, and 1886

Church Furnishings: St Albans Cathedral, Iron Grille of the chantry
chapel of Humphrey, Duke of Gloucester,
late thirteenth century

Church Furnishings: St Albans Cathedral, Vault of the chantry chapel of Humphrey, Duke of Gloucester, † 1447

Church Furnishings: St Albans Cathedral,
Ramryge chantry chapel, *c.* 1515–20

Church Furnishings: Wyddial, Screen, early seventeenth century

Church Furnishings: Essendon, Font, of Wedgwood's
Black Basalt ware, 1780

Church Painting: St Albans Cathedral, Crucifixion, thirteenth century

(a) *Church Sculpture:* Sandridge, Reclining figure from the chancel screen, late fourteenth century

(b) *Church Sculpture:* Ware, St John the Baptist, from the Font, fifteenth century

(a) *Church Carving:* Bishops Stortford, Misericord, fifteenth century

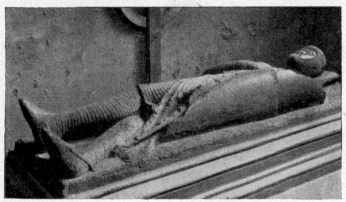

(b) *Church Monuments:* Eastwick, thirteenth century

(a) *Monuments:* Waltham Cross, 1291, by Nicholas Dyminge, Roger Crundale, and Alexander of Abingdon

(b) *Church Monuments:* Sawbridge-worth, John Chauncy † 1479

Church Monuments: Hatfield, Robert Cecil, first Earl of Salisbury
† 1612, by Maximilian Colt (*Copyright Country Life*)

Church Monuments: Watford, Sir Charles Morrison, by Nicholas Stone, *c.* 1630

Church Monuments: Knebworth, Judith Strode, † 1660

(a) *Church Monuments*: Chipping Barnet
Sir James Ravenscroft, † 1680

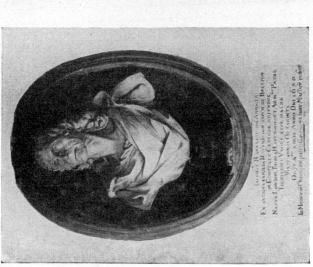

(b) *Church Monuments*: Flamstead, Saunders
Children, † 1690, by William Stanton

(a) *Church Monuments*: Knebworth,
Lytton Lytton, † 1710

(b) *Church Monuments*: Offley, Sir Henry Penrice
† 1752, by Sir Robert Taylor

37

Church Monuments: Abbots Langley, Lord Raymond † 1732,
by Sir Henry Cheere

(a) *Church Monuments:* Flamstead, Sir Edward Sedbright † 1782
by John Flaxman

(b) *Church Monuments:* Hatfield, John Heaviside † 1787, by Thomas
Banks ; the side pieces are later

(a) *Monuments:* Great Amwell, Memorial to Sir Hugh Myddleton, 1800, by Robert Mylne

(b) *Church Monuments:* Little Gaddesden, John William seventh Earl of Bridgewater † 1823, by Sir Richard Westmacott

Country Houses: Hatfield, Bishop Morton's Palace, *c.* 1480–90.
(*Copyright Country Life*)

(a) *Country Houses:* Shenley, Salisbury Hall, *c.* 1540–5

(b) *Country Houses:* Little Hadham, Hadham Hall *c.* 1575

(a) *Country Houses:* North Mimms House, *c.* 1600
(*Copyright Country Life*)

(b) *Country Houses:* Hatfield House, 1608–12
(*Copyright Country Life*)

43

Country Houses: Hatfield House, Frontispiece of the former entrance front, 1611 (*Copyright Country Life*)

Country Houses: Hatfield House, Staircase, *c.* 1612

(a) *Country Houses*: Hatfield House, Screen, *c.* 1612
(*Copyright Country Life*)

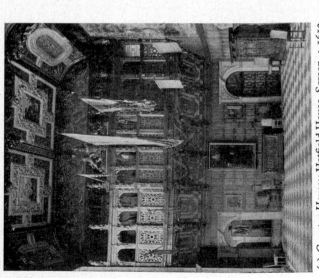

(b) *Country Houses*: Balls Park, *c.* 1640–5,
Porch *c.* 1720

Country Houses: Balls Park, Plaster ceiling, *c.* 1650 (*Copyright Country Life*)

(a) *Country Houses:* Mackery End near Wheathampstead, front 1665

(b) *Country Houses:* Tyttenhanger, *c.* 1655–60
(*Copyright Country Life*)

Country Houses: Tyttenhanger, Staircase, *c.* 1660
(Copyright Country Life)

(a) *Country Houses:* Beechwood, 1702 (*Copyright Country Life*)

(b) *Country Houses:* Gobions, Folly Gate, *c.* 1730, by James Gibbs

Country Houses: Moor Park, 1720, by Giacomo Leoni or Sir James Thornhill (*Copyright Country Life*)

Country Houses: Wormleybury, Drawing Room, 1777-9, by Robert Adam
(Copyright Country Life)

Country Houses: Woodhall Park, 1777, by Thomas Leverton
(Copyright Country Life)

Country Houses: Ashridge, 1808–19, by James Wyatt and Sir Jeffry Wyatville

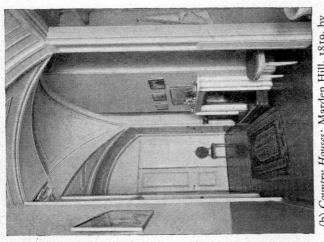

(b) *Country Houses:* Marden Hill, 1819, by Sir John Soane (*Copyright Country Life*)

(a) *Country Houses:* Ashridge, Chapel

Town Buildings: Theobalds Park, Temple Bar, 1672, by Sir Christopher Wren

(b) *Town Houses*: St Albans, Ivy House, early eighteenth century

(a) *Town Houses*: Bishops Stortford, the Black Lion

57

(a) *Town Houses:* St Albans, Romeland House, *c.* 1710

(b) *Schools:* Berkhamsted, *c.* 1544

(a) *Schools:* Haileybury College, 1809 by William Wilkins, the dome by Sir Arthur Blomfield, 1876

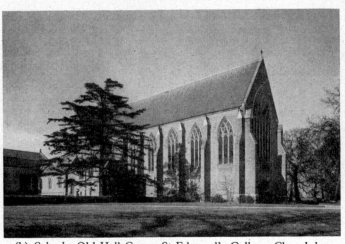

(b) *Schools:* Old Hall Green, St Edmund's College, Chapel, by A. W. N. Pugin, 1845

(a) *Almshouses:* Buntingford, Bishop Ward's Hospital, 1684

(b) *Almshouses:* St. Albans, Duchess of Marlborough's
Almshouses, 1736

Late Victorian and Edwardian Architecture: Bushey, entrance to
'Lululand', 1885 by H. H. Richardson

Late Victorian Architecture: London Colney, All Saints Convent, 1899 by Leonard Stokes

(a) *Late Victorian Architecture:* Chorleywood, The Orchard, 1900, by C. F. A. Voysey

(b) *The twentieth century:* Welwyn Garden City, begun *c.* 1920, by Louis de Soissons and A. W. Kenyon

The twentieth century: Primary School at Boreham Wood
by the Hertfordshire County Architect's Department

medieval architecture the interior has preserved. – BENCHES with carved ends in the Rococo taste by the celebrated *Joseph Mayer* of Oberammergau. – PLATE. Covered Cup, standing Paten and Flagon, 1675; Cup and Paten. 1706. — MONUMENTS. Lady Calvert † 1622, standing wall monument with recumbent effigy and a kind of overmantel back. – Sir William † probably 1637, and Lady Harrington, both recumbent, in shrouds. One daughter kneels at their feet turned towards the altar. Attributed to *E. Evesham*, but not of any striking quality. – Spencer Cowper, a judge of the Common Pleas, † 1727, an early work by *Roubiliac*; only a smallish epitaph but the relief with Cowper in his judge's robes and the graceful figures of Faith and Justice standing to his l. and r. are of great fluency and charm. – William Early Cowper † 1764. A seated life-size allegorical figure with wings, dull in her face and classical in her draperies, points to cherubs and rays up against a pink marble obelisk. To the r. a putto holds the Earl's portrait on an oval medallion. – Thomas Francis de Grey Earl Cowper † 1905. Tombchest with recumbent effigy, by *Henry Poole*, 1909. – The high iron railings of the Cowper (N) Chapel are dated 1891. – In the churchyard big plain raised sarcophagus to Sarah Lady Cowper † 1719.

WOOLMERS or WOOLMER PARK *see* p. 279.

HEXTON

ST FAITH. Early C19, except for some details of nave and w tower. The latter has recently partly collapsed. The nave piers are circular on the S, quatrefoil on the N side. Can that be a capricious C19 invention, as the Royal Commission seems to believe, or must one assume a nave and aisles of *c*. 1300? Box pews and a reading desk placed symmetrically. The S chancel chapel is nice pre-archaeological Neo-Gothic, complete with vault and the Commandment Boards, etc. – PLATE. Pieces of 1818–27. which probably dates the restoration of the church. – MONUMENTS. Plain tablet to Peter Taverner † 1601 and his wife, who 'was a grave, prudent, provident, above her

H—7

sexe learned, and religious matron'. – One epitaph of 1845 by *Gaffin*.

RAVENSBURGH CASTLE, 1 m. SW, on Barton Hills. Iron Age hill-fort on the summit of the Chilterns, naturally cut off on three sides by steep slopes. It is oval, 22 acres in extent, 1,435 by 695 ft. The ditch around the camp measures 40 to 60 ft, while the bank is 16 to 18 ft high. On the W side is a double ditch, and in the NW corner is an entrance, marked by the bank on one side curving inwards, on the other outwards.

HIGH BARNET *see* CHIPPING BARNET

HIGH CANONS *see* SHENLEY

HIGH CROSS

ST JOHN THE EVANGELIST, 1846, by *Salvin*. Grey stone with a SE steeple and a red brick Vicarage behind. Architecturally not specially interesting, but exhibiting an interesting contrast between the STAINED GLASS of the E and W windows. That in the E by *Kempe*, an early work of 1876, with his typical full forms and rather overdone yellows. That on the W was designed by *Selwyn Image* and dates from *c.* 1893. It is most extraordinary for that date, evidently with knowledge of what Burne-Jones had done for Morris & Co. windows, but entirely original in the sombre glowing colours and the rather mannered, Ravennesque central figure of Christ. The diagonal trails of leaves above and below the figures are charming, as are all the decorative features. The window might easily be mis-dated as modern English work of *c.* 1930.

HIGH DOWN *see* PIRTON

HIGH TREES
1½ m. s of Great Munden

HIGH TREES FARM. Timber-framed and plastered house of two storeys, probably of *c.* 1600. Inside the Hall Screen is preserved, not a frequent thing in Herts. Its approximate date is 1650.

HIGH WYCH

St James, 1861, by *Pritchett* (GR). A perversely ugly church, but as original in its handling of Gothic forms as anything in the Art Nouveau of forty years later. Flint, with red brick and stone dressings. Asymmetrical circular turret, polygonal above and ending in a spirelet. Very big, low-starting roof. s porch with an apsidal w bulge. Interior of yellow brick with red brick trim and much surface decoration at the E end. Thin circular aisle piers with big, square, richly and naturalistically foliated capitals. Pointed arches. The School next door also by *Pritchett*. Even the churchyard wall rises oddly at the gates.

HILFIELD see BUSHEY

HINXWORTH

St Nicholas. Nave without aisles, low w tower with angle buttresses, chancel of C18 brick. The rest is mixed stone and flint. s porch with three-light windows as at Ashwell. Inside the church two niches for statues, one on the E side of a N window, the other in the SE corner of the nave. – BRASSES. Man and woman, mid C15 (chancel N wall). – Man and woman, nearly 4 ft long with, below, individually cut and mounted figures of six children. Late C15, unusually good, believed to be John Lambard † 1487, Alderman of London.

Hinxworth Place. One of the best preserved C15–C16 stone (clunch) manor houses of Herts. Rectangular block with sw wing. Originally perhaps H-shaped. Several C15 doorways and two to four-light straightheaded windows with the individual lights pointed and cusped at the top. In addition later mullioned and transomed three-light and four-light windows. – Elizabethan improvements.

HITCHIN

Hitchin is without doubt, next to St Albans, the most interesting and visually most satisfying town of Herts. It has not only plenty of good timber-framed and gabled as well as

c 18 brick houses, but very little to spoil the harmony of
these two types. There is indeed not a shop nor an office
building in the centre of the town which seriously jars, especially nothing on a wrong scale. Moreover the town has kept
its medieval plan virtually without interference, a real market square (rare in the county) with parallel streets running
off at the angles to the N and S. The church lies back with its
E end to the river, and one street runs parallel with the others
on the other side of the river terminating the town on that
side.

ST MARY. The church is different from all other Herts
parish churches in that it is evidently a building representing the commercial wealth of a late medieval town. As in
most English towns the source of the wealth was wool.
The building has a nave and aisles of five windows and a
chancel and chancel chapels of five windows, the chancel
chapels projecting exactly as far as the chancel. Thus the
E view, from where the town has opened it up to the nicely
landscaped river, is of three parts with their large 5-light
windows, the aisles low-pitched with battlements, the
chancel flat-topped with angle pinnacles and battlements.
The church is in fact embattled all round, one of the usual
ways to express importance and money spent. The most
spectacular piece is the S porch, two-storeyed with an E
staircase turret, two bays, window openings on the W and
E sides, an elaborate lierne-vault inside, an inner doorway
of six orders of thin colonnettes, and an outer doorway
with above it a three-light window and four niches with
brackets for statues and a relief of the Trinity in the central battlement. The arms of the Staple of Calais promi-
nently displayed on the S wall. This porch was probably
paid for by Nicholas Mattock, a rich merchant of Hitchin.
The N porch is also two-storeyed. The N and S windows
of aisles and chancel chapels are all Perp, large, and of
three lights. There are, however, other differences between nave and chancel. The nave is flint, the chancel
chapels stone, the nave battlements are flint, those of the
chancel renewed in brick. Much brick has also gone into
repair work of the relatively low W tower (with spike) which,

in spite of its angle buttresses, was begun in the C12 and completed in the C13. Under the angle buttresses early flat buttresses have been found. The W door is obviously E.E. (two orders of shafts with moulded capitals and voussoirs of complex section), the windows on the bell-stage are also E.E., the stair-turret starts rectangular, before it becomes polygonal, and the treble-chamfered tower arch towards the nave can well be of the C13 too.

The general impression of the church from outside is one of comfortable spaciousness, an impression which the interior bears out. Nave arcades of octagonal piers with double-chamfered arches, early C14, with a clerestory irregularly added in the C15, four-centred chancel arch erected at that time above the responds of an earlier one, and chancel of four bays with stone piers with shafts in the main axes and hollows in the diagonals. Irregularities at the E end of the chancel (where a charnel-house is built underneath) and at the junction of nave and chancel. Oddly enough the nave has four bays but the aisles four windows and the porches, that is five bays, and the chancel has also four bays and the chancel chapels five windows. No building dates are recorded.

Uncommonly fine series of ROOFS. The flat ceiling in the N aisle with its broadly and beautifully cusped panels looks early C14, the S aisle and S chapel, nave, and chancel roofs are all C15. That of the S chancel chapel has principals resting on stone angels and sub-principals with long wooden angel-figures at their feet.

Uncommonly fine series of SCREENS. N and S chancel chapel to N and S aisles and Parclose Screens to the chancel. The latter are, of course, simple, but the W screens are richer than any other in the county and differ from each other in design. No standardization of tracery design in the Parclose Screens either. – FONT. Stone, C15, with mutilated figures under ogee canopies. – PULPIT. With angle buttresses and restored C15 panels. – BENCHES. Some with poppy-heads in the chancel. – DOOR. Impressive S door with cusped panels, C15. – PAINTING. Adoration of the Magi, Flemish, C17. – PLATE. Patens, 1625 and 1634; Salver, 1635; two Chalices and two Flagons, 1705. – MONUMENTS. Many, but none of great importance. They will be given here topographically. Chancel: Brass to a priest, largish, late C15. – Brass to a man and woman in shrouds with children, late C15. – Brass to a man † 1452, wife and children, large frontal figures. – Brass to a woman, late C15, the figure much rubbed off. – Brass to a man with three wives, late C15. – N Chancel Chapel: Three C15 tomb-chests with quatrefoil and heraldic decoration, on two of these brasses (John Pulter † 1485; civilian and wife). – Brass to a shrouded young woman with hair let down. – N Aisle: On window sills three defaced stone effigies, one mid C13, the other two late C14. – Epitaph to Ralph Skinner † 1697, with scrolly pediment, flowers and garlands, but no figures (by *Stanton*, according to Mrs Esdaile). – s Chancel Chapel: Many epitaphs, notably to four Radcliffes, c. 1660. – s Aisle: Brass to a shrouded woman with children. – Brass to a man with indent of wife. – Nave, w end: Mid C15 brass to a civilian and wife. – s. Aisle: Epitaph to Robert Hinde † 1786, by *Chadwick* of Southwark, with a female standing under a palm tree.

HOLY SAVIOUR, Radcliffe Road, 1865, by *Butterfield*, and in every way a full-blooded example of his style: E.E. of red brick with stone and blue brick dressings; no tower; only a w bellcote, the w front with two windows and three buttresses so that one runs up the centre of the façade. Interior rather dark, as all windows have stained glass. Short rectangular piers without capitals, and walls decorated with sgraffito, white brick, red brick, and blue brick in complex diapers. Twice as many clerestory windows as arcade arches. Thin iron Screen with trefoil arched tops to the sections.

For NONCONFORMIST CHAPELS and PUBLIC BUILDINGS (Town Hall, Library), *see* Perambulation.

PERAMBULATION

The best plan will be to start at the MARKET SQUARE and fan out from there. The Square itself has no specially noteworthy old houses. The best are Nos 2–4, later c18 and three-storeyed. On the w side the former CORN EXCHANGE, Italianate of 1851, with big Venetian window and lantern turret and next to it one of the few houses at Hitchin which look somewhat out of place: Burton's, the Tailor of Taste, with a façade *à la* suburban shopping parade. The most interesting corner is at the NE end, where a street seems to start like the others but there is instead only a passage through to church and churchyard. Here lie Nos 10–12 Market Place, a c15 timber-framed house of eight windows width (with shop windows on the ground floor), with gables and originally a courtyard at the back. The CHURCHYARD is surrounded by modest two-storeyed houses, the prettiest being the Georgian terrace Nos 24–28. To the E of the church nicely kept lawn with willow trees, the river made into a rectangular pool and behind it a raised terrace and a square. All this was done in 1929 (architects *Bennett & Bidwell*). On the s side of this new square lies a long terrace of eight chequer-brick cottages, and behind this, by the river, are the BIGGIN ALMSHOUSES, early c17, on an unusual plan, round a narrow irregular courtyard with, on one side, a Tuscan colonnade. On the E side of the Square runs QUEEN STREET, the easternmost street of the pre-Victorian town. In it mostly Victorian houses (No. 40, a nice villa) and also two Nonconformist chapels and a school: BETHEL 1869 (style still like 1845), BRITISH SCHOOLS 1857, CONGREGATIONAL 1855 (yellow brick with alternatingly rusticated giant pilasters and pediment). At the s end, facing what used to be called The Triangle, the LISTER HOUSE HOTEL, a four-bay, three-storeyed, stuccoed Early Victorian building in the Georgian tradition (after 1845).

BRIDGE STREET leads towards it from the w. In it at the NE end Nos 20–21, a c15 house (altered) with overhangs continued into Queen Street, and original chimney-stacks. On the s side Nos 30–40 a completely preserved row of c15–c18 houses, with Nos 31–33 the best: timber-framed, with overhangs also towards the river, crossed here by a small bridge. The streets leaving the Market Place towards the s run into Bridge Street.

These are Bucklersbury and Sun Street. BUCKLERSBURY is on the whole of minor interest (Nos 29–31, the WHITE HART, C16, with overhang on the l. and carriageway, higher overhang, and gable on the r.), but SUN STREET has several houses of far more than local quality. On the E the ANGEL (overhang, renewed plastering between the timbers, carriageway on one side), then the SUN, an excellent three-storey, nine-bay front of blue brick with rubbed brick dressings with segmentheaded windows, and central carriageway. In the courtyard on the r. a low half-timbered range, on the l. the Assembly Room (with a Venetian E window) added in 1770. Between the two unfortunately rises the glass roof of the hotel garage. Next to the Sun follows the CONSERVATIVE CLUB, Later Georgian of dark and rubbed bricks with a three-bay pediment. Opposite this group on the other side Nos 30–25 of c. 1700 (central first floor window with ornamented brick lintel), c. 1800 (with very pretty two-window shop), and c. 1820 (stuccoed, with wreaths to decorate the frieze of the cornice). On the E side follows Roslyn House, an early C19 adaptation of an overhang house (below the overhang two bay windows on the ground floor). An annexe on the r. has an ogee-headed Gothick central window. The s end of Sun Street is on both sides of pleasant quiet brick terraces. At their s ends both Sun Street and Bucklersbury meet Bridge Street and its w continuation Tilehouse Street.

TILEHOUSE STREET again is worth careful study. Only the high lights can here be mentioned: No. 3 timber-framed with herringbone pargetting; Nos 4–5 early C19, stuccoed; Nos 8–10 C17, with a gabled l. end and the rest of the front recessed; Nos 11–12 C16 or C17, with a l. gable and an overhang raised above the carriageway; Nos 13–17 all later C18 brick, No. 19 C17, pargetted. Opposite No. 88, three-bay stuccoed early C19 house with doorcase with two wreaths in the frieze; Nos 83–84 Early Georgian; Nos 81–82, eminently interesting C15 survival. The l.

side had originally a canted bay window of three three-
light Perp windows with four-centred arches, and one-
light windows in the sides. The w end of the street is a
very good start for anybody coming from Luton into
Hitchin : Nos 70–75 on the l. (N) with a half-hipped end
to the long mansard roof of the low cottages, and No. 35
on the r. (s), Late Georgian brick of four bays. In fact
Tilehouse Street continues still a little into the Luton
Road, and here lie No. 42, a more ambitious Late Georgian house with five bays and Ionic doorcase, built when
there was no urban congestion, and then the BAPTIST
CHAPEL of 1844 with two giant angle pilasters and
four attached giant Tuscan columns. Metope frieze and
pediment.

From the Market Place to the N runs the HIGH STREET,
less attractive than the other principal streets of Hitchin.
It is more affected by C20 shop intrusions, and such
houses as Nos 22–23 of c. 1700 do not get their due. Nos
9–10 of the early C18 shows the coming of the three-
storeyed façade. But three-storeyed buildings remained
rare at Hitchin right down into the C19. The High Street
is continued into BANCROFT, an early ribbon development far out of the confusion of the medieval town. It is
one of the best streets of Herts, as wide as St Peter's
Street, St Albans, and the High Streets of Berkhamsted or
Stevenage. In it Nos 18–19 with a Late Georgian brick
front with unpedimented doorcase on Tuscan columns.
No. 21 a largish Late Georgian brick house of five bays
and three storeys, No. 22 of white brick, early C19, and
then Nos 26–27 of the early C18 (segmentheaded windows) with an amazingly grand doorcase displaying fluted
Corinthian pilasters, and a decorated segmental pediment.
The MHLG suggests convincingly that the doorcase may
come from a bigger house. No. 34 is mid C18, two-
storeyed, five bays. The doorway has a Gibbs-surround.
The front is finished by a one-bay pediment. Opposite,
Nos 114–116 are of the C15 or C16 with closely spaced
vertical timbers and two gables (ground floor shop window, alas!); No. 107, late C18 with doorcase with fluted

Ionic columns, and Nos 105–106 with carriageway and asymmetrical gables. Then Nos 99–100, early C19 white brick with Greek Doric porch, and Nos 68–83, the SKYNNER ALMSHOUSES of two one-storey ranges along the street. They are dated 1670 and 1698.

Off the N end of the High Street turns BRAND STREET with the dignified stuccoed front of the OLD TOWN HALL, 1840, by *Bellamy* (Italian Renaissance of the Barry brand), and adjoining it the SUBSCRIPTION LIBRARY (also 1840 with a small temple front and a closed Tuscan porch) Opposite the NEW TOWN HALL, 1900–1, by *Mountford* and *Geoffrey Lucas*, Neo-Georgian with lantern turret.

Individual houses: THE PRIORY, 1770–1. A mansion of stone with a noble Palladian S front with small central semicircular porch and two projecting wings, each turning a large Venetian window towards the garden. The N side looks on to a courtyard which represents, and incorporates fragments of, the cloisters of the Carmelite Priory of Hitchin, founded early in the C14. On the W side are two arches (without capitals to the piers) and on the upper floor three small cusped one-light windows and two C16 mullioned brick windows. On the N side four more cloister arches. The N front of this N range has an interesting façade of 1679, with a ground floor arcade on octagonal brick piers with round arches. The church lay probably where the S range of the house now is. The whole house is still surrounded by a moat.

About 1900 outer suburbs began to spread with well-to-do houses in gardens. They represent the usual Late Victorian and Edwardian styles. Two specially good examples of the red brick free Tudor version are by *Fred Rowntree*: WHITEHILL CLOSE, Whitehill, and LAVENDER CROFT, Wymondley Road, the latter of 1906.

STRATHMORE AVENUE PRIMARY SCHOOL (*see* Introduction, p. 28).

HODDESDON

ST PAUL. Of the building of 1732 nothing will be noticed externally. But the interior of the nave can still give an idea of it, a plain rectangle with flat ceiling and arched windows. The w front red brick with pediment. All the rest now appears in the form given to it in 1865 (chancel and chancel chapels) and 1888 (s steeple).

The centre of Hoddesdon is the triangle s of the church with the CLOCK TOWER of stock brick erected in 1835 (by *T. Smith*). From here streets run NW and NE (in the latter a five-bay, two-and-a-half-storey house of yellow brick, mid-Georgian with all the windows tripartite), and the High Street runs s towards London, part of that long ribbon which was already by about 1800 flanked by houses for a good deal of the way. The following deserve notice: the WHITE SWAN on the w side, long and low, with overhanging upper floor and a central bay resting on Tuscan columns to form a porch, and the BULL with a yet bolder overhang on pillars, and a big pediment. No. 76 opposite is a house of considerable historical importance, as its back wing is dated and shows the characteristic mid C17 motifs of one-storeyed pilasters along the whole front, and of a pedimented shaped gable. The date is 1637. On the same side No. 68 (MONTAGU HOUSE) is a big early C18 building. Five bays with quoins and the central three bays flanked by rusticated pilaster strips. No. 70 may have been part of the composition. HOGGIS HALL, No. 64, has remains inside of its C15 Hall (shaped beams, doorway). No. 56 is RATHMORE HOUSE, *c.* 1740, purple and red brick, of six bays, and with a doorcase on Roman Doric pilasters. The GOLDEN LION of *c.* 1600 has many exposed oak beams inside.

ST MONICA'S PRIORY a little farther s was originally no doubt outside the village. It was the manor house of Marmaduke Rawdon, built in 1622. It has tall and stately brick E and W fronts with shaped gables. Five gables face W; in the middle is a two-storeyed porch, and to its l. and r. are two-storeyed bays. On the E front the centre is a tower which used to carry a cupola. Of interiors the most important are the Hall with plaster ceiling and the large staircase. A wing was added in 1880 in the style of the original building by *George & Peto*.

More Georgian houses farther s (Nos 48–50) with Gibbs surrounds to the windows; THE GRANGE, early C18 but altered, with segmentheaded windows and a semicircular porch; YEW HOUSE with Cedar House and Brickwood House; LOWEWOOD (Public Library), mid C18 house of five bays and two storeys with pedimented doorcase and C17 remains at the back.

1 m. NE of Hoddesdon quite on its own and in neglected surroundings the remains of RYE HOUSE, famous from the Rye House Plot of 1683. What remains is the Gatehouse of c. 1443 : red brick with blue brick diapering. The doorway has a two-centred arch with quatrefoil decoration in the spandrels. The windows have brick hoodmoulds. Upper projections on a corbel-table of intersected arches and two corbelled out oriel windows. To the SW of the moat of Rye House the RYE HOUSE INN, with two bargeboarded gables and beneath them two completely glazed bow windows with extremely pretty Gothic glazing bars, part of a Victorian scheme of converting the whole neighbourhood into a pleasure garden à la Vauxhall and Ranelagh.

Close to Rye House a new POWER STATION is being built to the design of *Sir Giles Gilbert Scott* who established himself for that kind of work with his Battersea Power Station. It is large, of pale pink brick and a little busy in the details, of a style by now quite typical of English power stations.

HOLWELL

ST PETER. Mostly by *Ewan Christian*, 1877 (GR), but apparently with the use of old materials. – Brass to Robert Wodehouse † 1515 with no effigy but a chalice with wafer and at the top instead of a coat of arms two wodehouses or wild men.

OLD RAMERICK, 1 m. N. Handsome seven-bay, two-storey front of c. 1700 with parapet and hipped roof. The tiling in a zigzag pattern.

HOPPERS HALL *see* DATCHWORTH

HUNSDON

House and church lie close together and at some distance from the small village. For several reasons the church appears indeed an appendix of the house.

HUNSDON HOUSE. What remains, and is attractive neither in shape nor in decoration, is of the greatest historical interest. It is one-quarter or less of a great Tudor house. A house had in fact been built here by Sir John Oldhall about the middle of the C15; but of that no visible traces exist. Then, about 1525, Henry VIII owned it and apparently rebuilt it. Engravings show the prior extent of the buildings, and the Early Tudor brickwork in the present structure shows what is preserved of Henry VIII's time.* It is the following parts the: gatehouse at an odd angle and surprisingly close to the main building, some walls in the neighbourhood, and a small raised summer-house or plaisance (cf. Hampton Court), and of the house itself the V-shaped angle buttresses and much of the masonry. The house was the projecting N wing of a mansion of that E-plan so usual at the time of Queen Elizabeth I and later, but still very rare under Henry VIII. The main range ran N–S at the W end of the remaining wing, and at the S end another wing corresponded to it. The Engravings show the house with big scrolly end-gables and a cupola, so that one might say that perhaps the extension to E-shape was due only to the C17. But Barrington Court, Somerset and the outer front of Hampton Court are both pre-Elizabethan and yet of the same plan as the Hunsdon of the engravings. So Hunsdon must be added to these early attempts at getting away from the asymmetry of Perp house-planning. The central and S wing were pulled down in 1804. Since then the interior has been much altered, and the exterior also unfortunately has window surrounds, a new Jacobean veran-

* Mr Salzman quotes documents according to which bricks for the house were burnt in 1525 and the brick chimneys were completed in 1528.

dah, and other features which are evidently mid-Victorian.*

ST DUNSTAN. A small village church with interesting Tudor and later additions. The church has a small un-buttressed W tower (with recessed spire), and a nave and chancel. The windows are Late Perp, the tower arch is Perp too, though earlier. The best part of the church is the N porch, of heavy coarse timbers like a lychgate and with elementary bargeboarding (cusps ending in an ogee at the top). Of a pre-Perp building the re-used N chapel E window gives evidence. It is early C14. The N chapel is an addition of the C16, and a S chapel followed about 1600. Both chapels are brick-built, with all window details also of brick. – Not much need be said architecturally of the interior; but the furnishings deserve close notice. – PUL-PIT. Jacobean, with tester. – SCREEN. The rood screen was Perp but only the dado survives. But early in the C17 a bigger and more sumptuous screen was erected between the nave and the new S chapel. It is the best example in the county of a Jacobean screen: with a panelled dado with Roman Doric pilasters, sturdy baluster columns car-rying little arches, a broad cornice and a big pierced strap-work achievement on top. Behind the screen high FAMILY PEWS also with some Jacobean decoration. – COMMUNION RAILS, c. 1700, with twisted balusters. – STAINED GLASS. C15 bits in the tracery of the E window. – PLATE. Chalice and Paten, 1660. – MONUMENTS. Brass to Margaret Shelley † 1495, shrouded figure nearly 3 ft long, representation of the Trinity above (chancel). – Small recess with four-centred arch at top and canted panelled sides and arch. The top is straight and crested. It is the monument to Francis Poyntz † 1528. The inscrip-tion is in the newly revived Roman lettering, but the de-tail otherwise is still all Perp (chancel). – Brass plate to James Gray, park-keeper, † 1591, showing him aiming at a stag, while Death is aiming at him. Death says *Sic pergo*

* Mr W. Branch Johnson has drawn my attention to a diary entry of Mrs Calvert, wife of the then owner, who in April 1805 writes 'I hear there is hardly a bit of old Hunsdon House left standing'.

(So I proceed; i.e. I do as you do) (nave N wall). – Big standing wall monument of alabaster to Sir John Carey † 1617 and wife. Black double columns to the l. and r. of a coffered arch. Achievements on top. The effigies lie side by side with folded hands. The sculptural quality is of the highest then available in England. The work may well be by *Colt* (s chapel). – Equally outstanding the standing wall monument to Sir Thomas Forster † 1612 (chancel), recumbent in Judge's robes under a low six-poster with scale-adorned ogee-shaped cupola. The ornamental detail, especially ribbon-work, etc., is exquisite. – The C18 added some good epitaphs. Felix Calvert † 1713 (nave). The only figures are two small putti on the curves of the broken pediment and two brilliantly carved cherub's heads at the foot. – Opposite, Robert Chester † 1732. The same composition, also only with small figures. At the top what seems a fine relief. – Mrs Jane Chester † 1736 (chancel), medallion with lively head in semi-profile, the inscription below on a hung-up drapery.

HYDE HALL
1 m. NE of Sawbridgeworth

A remodelling of 1806 of a square Tudor courtyard house. The remodelling is said to be by the younger Wyatt, that is *Sir Jeffry Wyatville*. The present fronts show nothing older than the C18. The five-bay, two-storey centre of the garden side seems to be the core to which in 1806 stuccoed additions with their giant pilasters with palm capitals were made. This latter style is clearly that of the s and the entrance sides. The courtyard was roofed in in 1806 and a staircase hall built which belongs to the finest of the period in the country. Extremely delicate design clearly under some *Soane* influence. Who was the architect? The name *Wyatt* has been given, but does not seem convincing. The Entrance Hall has a semicircular end screened by Greek Doric columns (and few but Soane used these in England in 1806? They repeat in the gate lodges). The Hall is square. The staircase is an uncommonly excellent addition in the style of the original. It was done in 1920 by *H. S. East*. It goes up behind the Hall starting with one central flight, turning into two, and ending at right angles to the beginning on the gallery above the Hall. The gallery has sky-lit saucer domes and an arched opening into the Hall. The Hall itself has a sky-light balancing on flat thin Soanian arches which rest on pilaster strips (just as at Soane's Pitzhanger of 1805). The staircase continues with a second identical run from the first to the second floor and then is covered by a segmental tunnel-vault.

In the garden, used as flower pots, some of the original Ionic capitals from the portico of *Smirke's* old General Post Office in London.

ICKLEFORD

St Katherine. Nicely placed amid cedar trees. Not very attractive plastered exterior. The interesting history of the church becomes more evident as one enters. The s doorway and a blocked N doorway are C12 with inner zigzag arches. The s doorway has in addition three orders of scalloped columns outside and three orders of zigzag voussoirs. The w tower has one lancet window on the s side, the chancel one on the N side. The chancel arch is also clearly C13. Nave roof on stone corbels and s porch C15; s aisle and s chapel 1859 (by *Sir G. G. Scott*). – STAINED GLASS. w window, 1898, by *Kempe*. – PLATE. Cup, 1798. – BRASS. Thomas Somer and wife, late C14, demi-figures (nave, E end).

IPPOLLITTS

St Ippolyts. On an eminence above the houses of the village. Rebuilt in 1879 with careful re-use of the old materials. Low w tower with much set-off angle buttresses. Nave and aisles with gabled N porch with decorated outer doorway (niches to l. and r. and above) and s porch of brick and timber. Windows in the chancel and s aisle and a doorway in the N aisle are clearly of the early C14 (*see* the Dec window). The nave arcades belong

to the same date. They are cut into a much older wall*
and have double-chamfered arches. The inner voussoirs
rest on remarkable broad-faced, broad-haired C14 heads. 21
The chancel arch is C15, but the Piscina shows that the s
wall at least must be E.E. – SCREEN. Only bits are old. –
PLATE. Chalice, 1634; Paten, 1639. – MONUMENTS.
Brass of 1594 with small kneeling figures (chancel). –
Effigy of a priest, C14 (recess in s aisle).

A house to the w of the church with C17 gable and to the r.
of it a four-bay early C18 brick façade. The OLIVE
BRANCH INN has closely set timber uprights and an
overhanging upper floor.

(AVENUE FARM, Gosmore, ¾ m. w. five-bay brick front of
the C18.)

JULIANS see RUSHDEN

KELSHALL

ST FAITH. Perp, much restored in 1870. All embattled.
Quite a big w tower (diagonal buttresses, Early Perp w
window). Big two-storyed s porch with NW turret. Aisle
and largish clerestory windows of Late Perp shapes. The
arcades to the aisles (four bays) have their piers with four
main shafts and four hollows in the diagonals, the latter
without capitals. The arches are two-centred. The tower
arch has compound responds with semi-octagonal shafts
with concave panels. In the E wall modern window and
two old brackets l. and r., an angel and a bearded face. In
the NW corner of the N aisle a curious niche 12 ft high and
only 1½ ft wide with hinges for a door. What can it have
been? The nave and aisle roofs are old and painted. The
painting is supposed to be based on old traces and gives a
good indication of the colouring of such roofs. – SCREEN.
Only the dado survives with four painted figures of saints,
C15, poor quality. – DOOR. The s door is probably
original including its lock, key, etc. – STAINED GLASS. E
window, 1868, good, under *Morris* influence. – PLATE.

* An C11 window with stone surround has been exposed in the s
wall.

Paten, 1685. – MONUMENTS. Brasses to Richard Adam and wife, 1435; the figures *c.* 2 ft long (E end of nave). – Epitaph to E. Franklin † 1617, the usual kneeling figures, but to the l. and r.; instead of columns two figures of Faith and Charity; very Flemish.

RECTORY. Late Georgian five-bay front, stuccoed, added to an older house.

KENDAL'S HALL see RADLETT

KIMPTON

SS PETER AND PAUL. Large flint church standing to the NE of the village. The exterior seems Perp, the interior tells of earlier history. Low W tower with spike, nave with clerestory and hipped roof at the E end (when was this unusual feature introduced? In the C18?). N and S aisles, S porch of two storeys with outer stair-turret, S chancel chapel, and lower chancel. Of all this nothing reveals motifs earlier than the C15 except the chancel E window of three cusped lancet lights under one two-centred arch. This is a motif of *c.* 1300 (renewed). And the masonry of the chancel must date back further still in the C13; for inside, the E window can be seen to have replaced simpler lancet windows. Even they, however, are not the oldest evidence in the church. Directly one has entered, one sees that the whole of the long even N and S arcades of six bays are of Transitional or E.E. date. Which of the two is it? There is no answer to the question. The truth as proved by this village church is that the Transitional overlap into the E.E. style was more considerable and important than is realized. All piers are circular, all arches of the same complex moulding which must be later than 1200, but of the capitals of piers and responds eight are scalloped with little bits of abstract decoration in the individual flutings and six have fully developed stiff-leaf, ranging from upright to diagonal. – The S chancel chapel opens into the chancel with finely moulded arches and a slim pier with the usual C15 section of four shafts in the main axes and four hollows in the diagonals. The s aisle roof is also *c.* 1500. – SCREEN. C15, broad divisions of four lights each, with simple Perp tracery. The coving seems much renewed. – BENCHES. Some with poppy-heads. A few of them have little faces at the lower lobes of the poppy-head. – PAINTINGS. Remains of early C13 figures of angels in the jambs of the chancel lancets. – STAINED GLASS. S chancel chapel, Lord Chesham Memorial, 1885, with *Morris* influence. – PLATE. Chalice, 1635. – MONUMENTS. Brass to a woman with open hair, early C15 (chancel). – Thomas Brand, twentieth Baron Dacre, † 1851 : an E.E. blank arch with stiff-leaf and dog-tooth decoration; no doubt the design of a notable architect.

KINGS LANGLEY

The village owes its name to a ROYAL PALACE on the hill to the w, of which no more than a fragment of a flint wall with brick quoins remains. It was here that Edmund of Langley, fifth son of Edward III, was born in 1341. He was buried in the adjacent DOMINICAN FRIARY, founded *c.* 1312. It was Edward II's favourite friary, and in it Piers Gaveston was buried in 1315. Of the Friary a two-storeyed rectangular building 76½ by 18 ft survives, incorporated in a private school. It was divided into two rooms and possesses a number of plain original windows and doorways. The tomb of Edmund of Langley was, at the time of the dissolution, transferred to the parish church.

ALL SAINTS. Flint and stone dressings. Thick short w tower with diagonal buttresses, battlements, and a spike. Short nave with aisles and clerestory, lower chancel. C15 arcades with octagonal piers with finely moulded capitals and double-hollow-chamfered arches. C15 tower arch. The S chancel chapel has an arcade like the nave, the N chapel a somewhat later arcade with stone pier of four attached shafts with four hollows in the diagonals. The only indications of pre C15 architecture are the C13 Piscina in the chancel wall and the Dec two-light w window of the N aisle. – PULPIT. First half C17, with book rests on three sides of the hexagon and tester. Elaborately carved panels and even more elaborately carved back. – SCREEN. In the tower arch, C15, much renewed. – REREDOS. Alabaster, designed by *Joseph Clarke*, 1878. – STAINED GLASS. W window *Clayton & Bell*, 1894; N aisle Queen Victoria Memorial Window, 1901, *Clayton & Bell*; W window *Powell*, 1908; in the s aisle one window (Mary and Martha), *Ward & Hughes*, 1876. – MONUMENTS. Edmund of Langley, late C14 tomb-chest with a display of heraldry instead of artistic genius. There are thirteen alabaster shields in all. – Sir Ralph Verney and wife (?), c. 1500, recumbent effigies on a tomb-chest decorated with shields in richly cusped fields. – Brass to John Carter † 1508 with wives and children. – Unnamed Brasses to two ladies, c. 1500 and c. 1600. – Large epitaph to Mary Elizabeth Crawford † 1793, signed by *Bonomi* (*inv.*) and *Westmacott* (*sculp.*). Long inscription and above small medallion with weeping putto and garlands.

The High Street has a number of pleasant old brick houses, starting promisingly at the s end with the ROSE & CROWN INN on the one side, the BLUE COURT HOTEL on the other, the one brick with a pretty iron verandah, the other a neat symmetrical three-bay early C19 villa of stock brick.

BARNES LANE ESTATE. Cottages by *Yorke, Rosenberg, & Mardall*, 1950.

KINGS WALDEN

ST MARY. Flint with stone dressings. Externally, including the W tower with angle-buttresses and a SE stair-turret, mostly C15 and C19 restoration (by *Eden Nesfield & Norman Shaw*, 1868). The only remarkable exception is the NE vestry of brick with three-light Perp windows. This belongs to the early C17. But inside the N and S arcade reveal a much older age. They are of the early C13, proof (just like those at Kimpton) of the long survival of Transitional forms into the E.E. style. For the short circular piers have capitals with slightly decorated scallops as well as a variety of water-leaf and also with stiff-leaf in two tiers. The arches are double-chamfered. The chancel arch looks late C13. The chancel windows are all renewed. – SCREEN. Two two-light sections on each side of the entrance. Each light has as its tracery an ogee arch and tiny Perp panelling above. – STAINED GLASS, S window by *William Morris*, 1867. Three arch-angels, wonderfully clear and fresh in the design; none of the mannerism of most Burne-Jones figures yet. The memorial tablet which goes with the window also evidently by Morris. How noble and susceptible to the nature of the glass-painter's material does such a window appear, if one compares it with other Victorian stained glass, even the work of a man like *Kempe* (*see*, for example, his E window of 1901). – PLATE. Tankard, 1736.

KINGS WALDEN BURY. Neo-Elizabethan, chiefly 1889–90, by *Burmeister & Beeston*.

KNEBWORTH

ST MARY AND ST THOMAS. The church stands in the grounds of Knebworth House, everywhere surrounded by fields but within a stone's throw of the front terrace of the mansion. The exterior attractive owing to its position but architecturally insignificant: nave, chancel, C15 tower (diagonal buttresses, SE stair-turret higher than the tower, and spike), N chancel chapel (Lytton Chapel) added *c.* 1705 to house the new sumptuous family monuments. The interior has a low Norman chancel arch with one order of scalloped colonnettes and a blocked Norman chancel N window. – ALTAR TABLE. C18 on classical columns. – PULPIT. C18 with carved panels of Flemish origin; one of them dated 1567. – BENCHES. C15, of plain solid profile. – IRON GATES to the Lytton Chapel designed by *Lutyens*, also one of *c.* 1705 under the tower arch. This was originally in the arch between chancel and Lytton Chapel and is of excellent quality. – STAINED GLASS. Three-light window in S wall by *Clayton & Bell*, *c.* 1875. – PLATE. Chalice, C17; Paten, 1668. – MONUMENTS. The Lytton Chapel contains the most remarkable display of family pride in the county. The chapel is really far too small to hold the three marble tombs put up in it between 1705 and 1710. On the N and S walls Sir William Lytton † 1705 and Sir George Strode † 1707. These two are both by *Edward Stanton* whose signature on the former is almost too prominent. Both men are represented semi-reclining; they are stout and wear wigs, and their clothes are meticulously portrayed. They tell of much self-confidence and worldly success. Both monuments have reredos backgrounds, the former with detached columns, the latter with pilasters. The former, moreover, has life-size allegories standing outside the columns, which carry a coffered segmental arch. On the W wall is the monument to Lytton Lytton † 1710, obviously by a different hand and the sign of a change in taste (Mrs Esdaile suggests *Thomas Green*): more classical and a little less Baroque (e.g. fluted pilasters instead of columns). Mr Lytton stands in the centre, a more than life-size portly figure, against an arched niche. – In the same chapel are Brasses to Roland Lytton † 1582 and his two wives, a tablet to Anne Lytton † 1601, with pretty thin ribbon-work on pilasters and frieze, and the epitaph to William Robinson Lytton Strode † 1732 and his wife, two stiff kneeling figures facing a sarcophagus with a relief of allegorical putti, and another relief above. – This monument is signed by *John Annis*. – But the highest aesthetic quality and certainly the most discriminating taste is not to be found in the chapel but in the chancel: the epitaph to Judith Strode † 1662: a surprisingly Roman-looking frontal bust without any frills and furbeloes of dress, set against a background of black marble as noble in shape and sophisticated in detail as any by the Florentine Mannerists of the C16. – Also in the chancel Brass to Simon Bache † 1414, priest, frontal with figures of saints in the orphreys of his cope.

E of the church in rather neglected surroundings MAUSOLEUM erected by Mrs Bulwer Lytton in 1817. Chapel with curved pediment in the front and crowned by a big sarcophagus. The architect is unrecorded.

ST MARTIN. In New Knebworth, on the A1 road. One of

Lutyens's most remarkable churches. Red brick with stone dressings. No tower, but excessively far projecting roof eaves. So far of the three bays of the nave only one has been built. The aisle separated from the nave by little arches on Tuscan columns, three arches per bay. Big and high transepts, two bays deep. Between the two, separating the transepts from the crossing, one colossal Tuscan column on each side, deliberately dwarfing those of the arcades of the aisles. Similar small arcades on the outer sides of the transepts. Bare chancel and apse. The interior is all white with a timber ceiling supported by the walls and the two giant transept columns.

To the *Lutyens* fan Knebworth has more to give than the church: the GOLF CLUB HOUSE, 1908, indifferently Neo-Georgian, and HOMEWOOD, 1900, an eminently characteristic example of the architect's early style. Low ground floor with cottage windows and big weatherboarded gables, two to the garden, a group of three to the entrance. That in its feeling is not so different from, say, Voysey or Baillie Scott. But the entrance door has a rusticated surround carried up across the lintel, and above the lintel is a pediment with the tympanum between lintel and pediment simply left open, an extremely capricious effect.

KNEBWORTH HOUSE. The house, as it now appears, is essentially the work of the first half of the C19, partly *c.* 1815–20 and partly the work of Bulwer Lytton, the novelist, done *c.* 1840–45. The body of the house is one range of a two-storeyed courtyard house of *c.* 1500. The other three were pulled down in 1811. Fragments of original work have been re-erected in 1816 in the brick West Lodge, the composition of which is, however, also C19. The Great Hall is still in its original position, but what pre C19 work it contains is of the C17: the plastered ceiling with rectangular panels and the elaborate Screen with caryatid termini are Jacobean.* The magnificent panelling of the Hall culminating in the reredos behind the dais with its Corinthian columns and pediment across the whole width of the room is later still, about 1675 perhaps. The E front is of E-type with angle turrets to the projecting wings and a central porch. This is Tudor in outline and *c.* 1815–20 only in the details. The W front on the other hand is frankly a romantic paraphrase of the Gothic palace, unrestrained by archaeological considerations. In 1883 the E front was unfortunately enlarged by a third storey. In the same year a new office wing was erected. This has recently been removed and replaced by a new, very tactfully and soberly designed range (architect *Philip Tilden*).

KYTES *see* GARSTON

LANGLEYBURY

2¾ m. NNW of Watford, 1½ m. WSW of Abbots Langley

ST PAUL, 1865, by *H. Woodyer*. The exterior is unpromising, though ambitious for so small a parish. Flint. Nave, chancel, S chapel, and W tower with short spire. The detail rather coarse. Inside a most ornamental chancel arch, the very beau ideal for the pious and sentimental Victorian: musician angels on each of the two capitals and angels arranged radially on the arch. Otherwise also handsomely decorated. In the S chapel MONUMENTS of William Jones Loyd of Langleybury House † 1885 and of Caroline Gertrude Walker Loyd † 1893, the former with marble putti holding a portrait medallion, the latter with a seated, nearly life-size angel with raised arm in the cemeterial style.

LANGLEYBURY HOUSE (H.C.C. Secondary Modern School). Nucleus plain Early Georgian. Brick, two and a half storeys, with parapet, seven bays wide. The dates 1727 and 1729 on rainwater heads of the servants' block no doubt refer to the house as well. Good Later Georgian stable block with cupola and clock. Additions were made in the later C19 on all four sides.

* But the panels inserted in the side parts of the Screen with cartouches and arms must be a mid C17 addition.

LAWRENCE END
3½ m. N of Harpenden

Seven-bay, two-storeyed house of brick with purple brick chequer pattern, hipped roof, one-storeyed porch. Completed 1841 but still Late Georgian in character.

LAYSTON
1 m. NE of Buntingford

ST BARTHOLOMEW. Derelict at the time of writing. C15 W tower; big, with diagonal buttresses and a Herts spike, nave, and chancel. The nave details all C15, the chancel clearly C13 (big lancet windows on all three sides). The chancel arch, however (shafts and hollows in the diagonals), C15. The S porch also C15 (partly renewed). – Furnishings partly removed, partly neglected.

LEMSFORD

ST JOHN THE EVANGELIST, 1850, by *David Brandon* (GR). In the E.E. style (even the W tower, in spite of its Perp outline). Stone, not flint. Interior with naturalistic leaf capitals. Added in 1930 a S chapel for the Hall-Cain family. Perp with rich lierne-vault, by *F. E. Howard*.

LETCHWORTH

Letchworth, to nearly all those who know the name in Britain and abroad, means a garden city, in fact the first garden city ever built. The adventure began in 1903, several years before the Hampstead Garden Suburb and seventeen before Welwyn. The idea of the garden city came from Ebenezer Howard's book of 1898. To translate the idea into visual terms *Barry Parker* and *Raymond Unwin* had to make an organism out of a diagram. In this they succeeded. The Hampstead Garden Suburb makes that even clearer than Letchworth. For Letchworth, as the first exploratory pioneer job, suffered from some initial faults which it has never quite overcome. The principle of the garden city is one of controlled social and architectural structure and controlled growth. Number of inhabitants, type and location of houses, type and location of factories has to be kept in a certain relation to each other, with the result that the town should be an independent and self-sufficient unit. At Letchworth it took long to attract industry, and population consequently did not grow fast enough to justify an architectural display of public buildings as the plan had foreseen them along the large central square or green. In fact the visual failure of Letchworth is that very square, laid out in axis with the station and at right angles to another main axis. Coming from the station one has, as one should have, an initial feeling of urban bustle (a few shopping streets of tallish buildings). But then the square is reached, and the public buildings are mostly small, architecturally indifferent, and do not seem to be related to each other (Council Offices by *Bennett & Bidwell*, Grammar School by *Barry Parker*). The largest of them, St Francis' College (by *Morley Horder*; new extension by *L. H. Shattock*) stands in no comprehensible position and represents no scale echoed anywhere else. The domestic architecture of the early years, on the other hand, is eminently convincing. It is very similar to that of the Hampstead Garden Suburb, except that exposed brick is rarer. The style is mostly a free and comfortable Neo-Tudor with gables. The houses are detached or in groups of four. The streets curve, except for the main axes, existing trees are preserved, no garden walls since cut up for green – all principles adopted since for municipal estates. To the younger generation they have thus become a matter of course, but it should not be forgotten that they were for the very first time systematically followed at Letchworth. The old village of Letchworth lies outside the garden city, and it seems a pity that the *Parker-Unwin* plan did not choose to make use of the church and hall as a centre or sub-centre. It would have meant a welcome break in the architectural uniformity of the small-scale housing (cf., for example, Oxhey).

ST MARY. Flint; nave and lower chancel; no tower, only a timber bell turret. C13 windows in the chancel. – DOOR with C13 iron hinges. – PLATE. Late Elizabethan Chalice and Paten. – MONUMENTS. Stone effigy to a Knight, only 2 ft long, on a window sill. He holds his heart in his hands. – Brass to Thomas Wyrley † 1475 (chancel), to a husband and wife (later C15; nave).

LETCHWORTH HALL. Jacobean brick house with C19 and C20 additions. The tower especially, needless to say, is Victorian. The house should be approached not from the present front but from the NE. There lies the porch which gave access to the Hall. In the Hall the Screen is preserved, contemporary and not very elaborate. More elaborate the fireplace in the Parlour which lies in a wing projecting to the NW. The house has a variety of straight gables. The original plan was probably H-shaped.

WILBURY HILL, 1 m. W. Part of an Iron Age hill-fort, on the S side of the road, opposite the cemetery. The single rampart and ditch of the camp originally enclosed about 14 acres, with an entrance in the S bank. Stotfold Road runs along the bank on the W, and the line of the E rampart of this almost oval camp is probably followed by a hedge. The N part of the camp is skirted by the modern road (coinciding partly with Icknield Way). The fort was constructed *c*. 500–300 B.C.).

LEVERSTOCK GREEN
2 m. ESE of Hemel Hempstead

HOLY TRINITY. Designed 1846 by *Raphael Brandon*, consecrated 1849. A small flint church with double bellcote. The window tracery is Dec. – Original STAINED GLASS in the chancel windows. – ROOD SCREEN, STOLLS, and ALTAR by *Sir Walter Tapper*, 1932.

To the N WOODLANE FARM, C17 with C18 Gothick windows and other alterations. Original staircase.

LILLEY

ST PETER, 1870–1, by *Thomas Jekyll*, the Japan enthusiast who designed the woodwork for Whistler's Peacock Room. Of this un-Victorian sense of romance and delicacy the E.E. exterior of Lilley church betrays nothing (except perhaps for the brick and stone chequerwork parapet to the SW tower). On entering, however, one is puzzled by the fact that the porch under the tower is red-brick lined. The church itself is flint. Otherwise only a few indications of anything out of the ordinary run of churches. The chancel, for example, is not paved with red and yellow *Minton* or *Maw* encaustic tiles, as one might expect, but with tiles in two shades of soft green with an occasional *sang-de-boeuf*. The chancel ceiling is handsomely painted. Of the medieval church one feature remains: the plain Norman N arch in the chancel. It is of red stone, unmoulded, on the simplest imposts.

PUTTERIDGE BURY. Large Elizabethan-style mansion by *Sir Ernest George & Yates*, completed as late as 1911.

LITTLE AMWELL

HOLY TRINITY, 1863, by *Ewan Christian*.
HAILEYBURY COLLEGE, *see* p. 103.

LITTLE BERKHAMPSTEAD

ST ANDREW. Essentially 1857 and 1894. Of the church built in 1647 no telling features remain. – PLATE. Chalice and Paten, 1684; Paten, 1701; Paten, 1721; Almsdish, 1791; Flagon of Sheffield Plate, *c.* 1790.

Pleasant Georgian houses close to the church, especially LITTLE BERKHAMPSTEAD HOUSE, five bays, three storeys, with (later?) Greek Doric porch. Farther NE and belonging to The Gaze a high red brick Folly Tower, erected in 1789, perhaps with the bricks from an older house. It has tall blank arches, classical cornices, and battlements.

LITTLE GADDESDEN

SS PETER AND PAUL. Quite on its own outside the village. Architecturally less important than for its monuments. The W tower is not high. It is of flint and has diagonal buttresses. The rest of the church is cement-rendered, the treatment dating probably from the time when *James Wyatt* and *Sir Jeffry Wyatville*, busy with the rebuilding of Ashridge, rebuilt the s aisle and porch in 1812 and added the s chancel chapel in 1819. The s arcade is of 1876, the N arcade, with octagonal piers and hollow chamfered arches, as well as the tower, C15. – SCREEN. Much renewed. – BENCHES. Some with poppy-heads. – STAINED GLASS. Two *Kempe* windows of 1895 at the sw end. – PLATE. Mid C17 Chalice; Flagon, 1635; Paten, 1781. – MONUMENTS. An exceptionally full and varied series, especially important for the very progressive and Mediterranean style of those of the later C17 (*see* also Nettleden). Earlier only Elizabeth Dutton † 1611, the usual epitaph type with kneeling figure, removed to Gaddesden from St Martin-in-the-Fields, London, when that church was rebuilt in the C18. – Elizabeth Countess of Bridgewater † 1663, large classical monument without figures except for two small mournful putti. – Elizabeth Viscountess Brackley † 1669, epitaph with an inscription in a delightfully scrolly writing-master's script. – Henry Stanley † 1670 *aet.* 14, epitaph with two putti. – Dr H. Stanley † 1670, stately urn on pedestal.* – Third Earl of Bridgewater † 1701, good epitaph. – Jane Countess of Bridgewater † 1716, similar to the monument of 1663. Ann Norton † 1796, by *Ashton*, Grecian, with mourning female figure. – John William, seventh Earl of Bridge- 40b water, † 1823, a masterpiece of *Westmacott*, with a *tondo* with a labourer, his wife, and child, a dog and tools and wheat-ears, very Raphaelesque. – Francis Henry, eighth Earl of Bridgewater, † 1829, with seated female. An inscription notes specially that 'He bequeathed £8,000 as a

* In the floor of the Vestry memorial to the infant son of Dr Stanley with an inscription which runs as follows:

> TIBI GNATE USO
> LUCIS BREVI FUSO
> CITO QUE HIC CONCLUSO
> (MISERO ME DELUSO)
> HOC MEMORIALE
> BREVE ET CORDIALE
> CARMEN TRIPEDALE
> SAXULUMQUE QUALE
> CURTO NON STET MALE
> LONGUM NISI NIHIL VALE

reward for literary men for writing essays to prove the benevolence of God as displayed in the Works of the Creation.'

JOHN OF GADDESDEN'S HOUSE, opposite the NE entrance to Ashridge. Well restored and enlarged timber-framed C15 house with overhanging upper floor. The timber-roof of the Hall is original. If the date is indeed C15, as the Royal Commission assumes, then the house cannot be that built by John of Gaddesden who was Physician to the King from 1335 onwards and retired to his native village later in the C14.

MANOR HOUSE, 1576. Stone house with front of two turrets with stepped gables and a lower centre with a two-storeyed bay window. Mullioned and transomed windows. In the centre on the ground floor the Hall with a large fireplace and some C15 panelling brought from Ashridge.

54   ASHRIDGE (now Bonar Law College). Ashridge, in its vast
3a   park high on a ridge of the Chilterns, began its existence as the earliest English College of Bonshommes, founded by Edmund Earl of Cornwall, Henry III's nephew, in 1276. After the Dissolution it was in royal hands, and Princess Elizabeth lived here during Mary's reign. In 1604 it came to Sir Thomas Egerton, and that family remained in possession to the time when the present mansion was built. It is the largest of the romantic Gothic palaces near London and was designed by *James Wyatt* in 1808. His son *Sir Jeffry Wyatville* added in 1814–20 the N porch, the E wing with the staircase hall and the stables. The gardens and grounds were landscaped by *Capability Brown c.* 1760 and again by *Repton* in the early C19. To *Repton* the pretty, highly dressed features near the house are due, although they are not executed in conformity with the elaborate plans which he made and published. In the sun rose garden, for example, he intended to fill up a conduit; but the structure standing there now is by *Wyatville*. One of the few remaining fragments of monastic buildings faces the garden: the BARN, much altered by *Wyatville* who set the front back

to form a rustic verandah out of the original oak posts and added dormers and turret. Otherwise an UNDER-CROFT survives below parts of the Dining Room and Drawing Room (octagonal piers without ribs, and single-chamfered ribs).

The House is, no one can deny, a spectacular composition. The way in which *Wyatt, Jnr* has entered into the spirit of *Wyatt, Snr* is wholly admirable. The result is equally successful from the drive and from the garden. On both sides the chief accents are the twice stepped-back tower of the chapel with its two tiers of angle turrets and its tall slender spire, and the big heavy square tower above the staircase. The chapel projects towards the garden with tall Perp windows and an apse. It is connected with the main building on the r. by a Perp arcade now closed with brick and converted (by *Clough Williams Ellis* in 1929) into the Dining Room of the college. The main building is symmetrical with two bay windows and a narrow three-arched loggia in the middle with an oriel above. The E front is also symmetrical, with a central five-bay loggia. The entrance side is quieter. The main emphasis lies on *Wyatville's* porch, tall entrance hall windows, and stair-case tower behind. It has four plain bays of two and a half storeys to the l. and four to the r., and then on the r. follow nine further buttressed bays of only one and a half storeys. On the l. an Orangery wing branches off at a pic-turesque angle. The whole building is of Totternhoe stone.

Of the INTERIORS the most impressive are the Chapel and [55a] the Staircase. The CHAPEL consists of the apsed chapel proper with tall windows with two-centred heads and a fan-vaulted coving carrying a canted panelled ceiling, a pretty, typically C19 motif. The wooden fittings are by *Wyatville*. The ANTECHAPEL opens up into the tower, an effect as striking as any that *Wyatt's* more famous Font-hill may have afforded. In fact, in the absence of Fonthill, Ashridge is the best example of *Wyatt's* truly romantic handling of the Gothic style.

Wyatville's STAIRCASE HALL is perhaps a little drier, but certainly just as dramatic, very high, with a staircase starting in the middle with one short flight of stairs, turning at right angles against the back wall into two, and turning again and leading up in two long flights against the side walls to the first floor landing. The railing is of cast iron. On the first floor the hall is surrounded by arcades of four-centred arches with figure niches in the corners. There are more tall niches above, then a thickly corbelled-out gallery with a fine iron railing, and more arcading behind it carrying a fan-vaulted coving on which the lantern stands. This has a fan-vault with the fans surrounding a circle with a sun dial. The whole is designed with great elegance. The impression is one of dizzy height. The EN-TRANCE HALL N of the Staircase Hall is also excessively tall, or seems so because it is relatively narrow, and has a hammerbeam roof.

In 1860 *Sir Matthew Digby Wyatt* redecorated the DRAW-ING ROOM, gave it a copy of Guido Reni's Aurora ceiling and delicate Italian ornamental painting around, two colossal fireplaces with caryatids and door surrounds of colossal aedicules with free-standing columns and pediments. He also built a FERNERY in the garden.

Thirty years ago, it is said, the whole house had only two bathrooms.

LITTLE HADHAM

ST CECILIA. The church lies on its own to the N of the village Street and to the W of the outbuildings of Hadham Hall. It is a small church, of nave and chancel with W tower, N transeptal chapel, and S porch. The tower has diagonal buttresses and a spike. The tower arch dates it to *c*. 1400 or a little earlier. The nave has Perp windows. The chancel windows are renewed. The interest of the church lies in the S porch and the transept. The S porch is of the C15, lightly built of timber with wide open sides trefoil-cusped along the tops. The gable is bargeboarded, also with a simple trefoil cusping, ending on top in an ogee. The N transept is supposed to date from the late C16. It is of brick with elementary posthumously Perp three-light W and E windows and intersected tracery in the four-light N window. Inside, the transept opens in a wide four-centred arch. The PULPIT bears the date 1633. It has small-scale strapwork decoration, and a contemporary back and a big tester. Its decoration is the same as that of the PANELLING of the pew to its E and also some panelling in the N transept. The church has later box pews and the pulpit which is a three-decker (a rarity in Herts) is in its lower parts also later. – SCREEN. C15, of five one-light openings at each side of the entrance. – STAINED GLASS. A few C15 fragments in a S aisle window. – BRASSES to a Knight in armour (perhaps Thomas Baud) and his Lady, elegant, somewhat mannered figures, c. 1480; and to R. Warren, a priest, late C15, much rubbed off (chancel, S wall).

HADHAM HALL. Excavations have proved the existence of [61] a C15 house not on the exact spot or in axis with the present house. The brick outbuildings to the W are not in axis either and may partly be older than the house. They consist of the Gatehouse, added to an older building to its E, and originally no doubt higher than it is now, and a large brick barn (cf. Upp Hall). The mansion itself was built c. 1575 by the Capel family. It was much larger than it is now. All that survives is the W range with the main entrance and half the S range. Originally there were four ranges round an inner courtyard with the Hall probably in the E wing. E of this a later C17 Banqueting House was built, and yet further E the still existing terrace and a sunk formal garden with two pavilions at its NE and SE corners. Of all this traces and often foundations have been found. The house is of brick. The W range has the gateway between polygonal towers. The windows are all mullioned and the large ones transomed, and all have pediments, a feature which gives the building a somewhat classical air. Between the towers is a straight gable. The S wing has a low ground floor with brick arches, but the front and the upper floor inside have been entirely remodelled at about the time of Queen Anne. At the same time a wider staircase was built out close to the S end of the E side of the W range. To the N and NE is a late C19 addition in keeping with the rest. Not much of importance inside.

H—8

In and around the village many worthwhile timber-framed farmhouses and cottages. By the main crossroads a group with dates from 1672 to 1732. Good houses near Little Hadham also at FORD HILL and BURY GREEN.

LITTLE HORMEAD

ST MARY. The fame of this small and lonely church is its N DOOR, with the most lavish display of C12 ironwork, two large interlaced quatrefoil patterns in the centre, and borders of scrolls and trails. The door belongs to the N doorway which has one order of colonnettes with scalloped capitals and an arch with a thick roll moulding and a thin unusual triangular moulding. The same capitals and mouldings grouped inside in the awkwardly depressed chancel arch. The S doorway is also Norman and simpler. In fact the whole nave is Norman (*see* also one deeply splayed small roundheaded N window), the chancel E.E. (the S lancet windows are original). – The roofs are of the late Middle Ages, with rough tie-beams in the nave, with diagonal wind-braces in the chancel. – FONT. Early C14, octagonal, with very pretty blank tracery. – ROYAL ARMS. Dated 1660, small but nicely carved; above the chancel arch.

BALLON'S FARM, SE of the church. Timber-framed C17 house with two symmetrical gables to the street. Thatched roof.

LITTLE MUNDEN

ALL SAINTS. The exterior is not very promising. The usual unbuttressed W tower with spike, the usual flint nave and chancel, and a N aisle with N chancel chapel, all much restored. The interior much more interesting. The first bay of the N arcade has imposts with capitals of the C12, if not the C11, of three projecting rolls with herringbone hatching (cf. Walkern). In the chancel S wall is a C12 doorway, very plain and much renewed. That proves a nave and a chancel eight hundred years old. Next come the C14 contributions, the N arcade of two bays with octagonal piers and double-chamfered arches and the W arch into the chancel chapel. In the E respond of the arcade three pretty little ogee niches for statuettes. Half a statuette is still *in situ*. The W arch between chancel and chapel has a big crocketed ogee gable and serves as the canopy to a MONUMENT for an unknown Knight and Lady (tomb-chest with shields in quatrefoils and little mourners between). The costumes are clearly of the later C14. To the E of this arch, early in the C15, another was opened to house a second monument. The tomb-chest here is plainer, the costumes indicate the date suggested. The arch of ogee shape and panelled inside with a row of lozenges with quatrefoils. In the apex the figure of an angel. Also of the C15 the chancel arch and W tower. – SCREEN. From N aisle to N chapel. Plain C15 panel tracery.

LITTLE WYMONDLEY

ST MARY. Chancel, nave, and only slightly higher W tower of the C15. The rest 1875.

WYMONDLEY BURY, S of the church; surrounded by a moat. Brick, gabled, the N side symmetrically gabled.

WYMONDLEY HOUSE, near the W end of the village. Late Georgian five-bay, two-and-a-half-storey cemented front with a porch with unfluted Ionic columns.

WYMONDLEY HALL, to the r., on the way to the Priory. Early C17. Handsome timber-framed six-gabled front, the third to fifth symmetrical. Of these the third and fifth have bay windows below, while the fourth and sixth have only upper floor oriels. Good group of chimneys.

WYMONDLEY PRIORY, $\frac{1}{2}$ m. N. Of the Augustinian house founded in the C13 no more remains than a few odd C13 arches inside a farmhouse and one big aisled barn, supposed to be also of pre-Reformation date.

The village street is specially attractive.

LOCKLEYS *see* WELWYN

LONDON COLNEY

ST PETER. By *George Smith*. A lean, cemented façade in the *Rundbogenstil*, with vaguely transitional Norman detail.

The date is 1825, that is remarkably early for a Norman Revival. Aisleless interior. w gallery on thin cast-iron columns with Norman capitals. The STAINED GLASS of the E windows was designed by Ruskin's friend the *Dowager Marchioness of Waterford* and made by *Hughes* in 1865. It represents the Ascension in a broad pictorial, somewhat Raphaelesque, style.

62 ALL SAINTS CONVENT. Begun in 1899 by *Leonard Stokes*. A fine, very freely Neo-Tudor front, with much picturesque, original detail and yet strong and honest. Red brick, purple brick, and stone. The centre motif is a gatehouse with a figure frieze above the door. The l. and r. halves are only broadly symmetrical. They have several bay windows. To the r. the main front ends with a turret, and after that follows the lower Refectory with a large dais window. The style is similar to *Stokes's* later work for Emanuel College, Cambridge. – There is an equally fine cloistered garth inside. The CHAPEL was added in 1927 by *Comper*. It is yet unfinished. It consists so far of three bays of pale brick with tall pointed windows in which Perp and E.E. motifs are mixed. The interior is white, with the large baldacchino as the one all-dominating element (tall golden columns with curious little flowers painted on and a crocketed ogee top), a most surprising combination of the Italian and the English. The choir stalls also have slim Tuscan columns and yet little buttresses. Tree of Jesse glass in the E window. The extraordinary harmony of the interior is due to the fact that *Comper* directed everything from the baldacchino to the candle sconces on the walls, the candlesticks on the altar, and even the size and type of the candles.

LONG MARSTON

Of the medieval church only the w tower remains, hidden by trees. It is of flint and stone-chequer work and has no buttresses. The date is C15.

The new church of ALL SAINTS is by *Carpenter & Ingelow*, 1882, without a tower, quite modest, but well designed with Dec details. In it a large number of medieval fragments are re-used or displayed. The aisle piers are those which stood in the parish church at Tring until 1880 (a fine late C15 design). In the N wall is an early C14 window, then a Norman arch with shafts and dog-tooth ornament of the voussoirs, then a C13 window of two lancets, and then various small fragments. The PULPIT is ordinary early C17 work, the very renewed SCREEN at the E end of the S aisle dated originally from the C15.

MACKERY END see HARPENDEN

MARCHMONT HOUSE see HEMEL HEMPSTEAD

MARDEN HILL
¾ m. SW of Tewin

Built c. 1785–90 as a plain nicely proportioned block of 55b yellow brick with a bow window on the garden side. The Interiors were discreetly stuccoed. Had the house remained like that it would have been a pleasant but by no means a remarkable building. In 1819, however, *Sir John Soane* was called in. He added an Ionic four-column porch and made small alterations (his typical shallow incisive segmental arches) to the Entrance Hall and Dining Room. He altered the staircase and gave it a beautiful smooth and tense flow in a relatively narrow space. It starts with one middle arm and turns backwards in two to reach the upper floor. The handrails run on without any newel posts. The ironwork is classical and extremely simple. The skylight is an oval dome most sparingly decorated. The first floor room above the Entrance Hall, Soane's only other addition, is one of his masterpieces. Soane was specially ingenious in small spaces (*see* his own house, or the Dulwich Gallery, or Pitzhanger, Ealing). At Marden Hill he has divided the room into an oblong main part and a smaller part by the windows, also oblong but at right angles to the first. The two parts are separated only by a slight canting of the walls and by the design of the ceiling. The large oblong consists of a short segmentally vaulted bay, a square bay with a kind of cross-vault and a large rosette in the middle, a medieval boss, as it were, and another segmentally vaulted bay. The part by the window has the same rhythm but turned by 90 degrees and on a smaller scale. The centre here is a shallow saucer dome, and l. and r. of it are again shallow segmental vaults. The composition is so original as to be almost perverse, but the effect, although complex, is not at all confusing.

MARKYATE

ST JOHN THE BAPTIST. Below the A5 road in the SE corner of the grounds of Markyate Cell, reached from the E by an avenue of elm trees. Thin embattled W tower of red brick with blue brick chequer, and nave of 1734, enlarged by aisles with arched windows in 1811; chancel 1892. The arcades inside have roundheaded arches. The octagonal piers look decidedly later than 1811. Curved W gallery on thin iron columns.

MARKYATE CELL. Large Neo-Elizabethan brick mansion of 1825–6 by *Robert Lugar* (*see* his *Villa Architecture*), incorporating remains of the mansion built by Humphrey Bourchier in 1539–40. He had taken over the buildings of a nunnery founded early in the C12.

MEESDEN

ST MARY. Away from the village. The nave dates from the C12 (*see* the S doorway). The short transepts were added (or renewed) in the C13 (*see* the narrow two-bay arcades from the nave with octagonal piers and moulded capitals) but rebuilt in 1877. The chancel is of *c.* 1300 (*see* the renewed E window of three cusped lancets under one two-centred arch). The pretty timber bellcote with its shingled spire is C19. All this is in no way out of the ordinary. What, however, makes the church worth a special visit is the S porch, entirely built of brick, probably *c.* 1530 (cf. Wyddial). The two-light windows are of brick, the much-moulded doorway is of brick, and so are the diagonal buttresses and the crenellation with angle turrets and a niche under a stepped gable. Below the battlements trefoiled a

brick corbel-table (cf. Rickmansworth Rectory and Redbourn). – TILES. In the chancel a whole series of early
C14 tiles in dark green and yellow with circles, quatrefoils, etc. – PLATE. Chalice and Standing Paten, 1621. –
MONUMENT. Robert Yonge † 1626, with bust in circular
niche.

RECTORY (former Manor House). Five-bay, two-storey
brick house with hipped roof.

MINSDEN

CHAPEL. In ruins. The antiquarian will not find much to
instruct him, but the picturesque traveller much to delight him. Situated in a coppice, completely surrounded
by trees and undergrowth. The fragments of nave and
chancel stand irregularly to a height of 10 to 20 ft. They
are of flint and all details have decayed so much that outlines, door, and window holes now appear like designs in a
Henry Moore or Hepworth style. Inside the building and
closely around it is lawn. The ivy has been removed to
bare the wall surfaces.

MONKEN HADLEY*

The combination of Hadley Green and Hadley Common
results in one of the most felicitous pictures of Georgian
visual planning which the neighbourhood of London has to
offer. It is elusive to the descriptive word and eminently
English in character. The elements are the wide rather
shapeless Green to the N, by the Great North Road, and the
triangular Common farther S with the church between,
blocking the direct communication between the two. Both
Green and Common converge towards the church, the
Green funnel-wise, the Common less dramatically.

ST MARY. Built probably in 1494, the date appearing in an
inscription on the W tower. Flint and iron-stone with
white stone dressings. W tower with diagonal buttresses,
battlements and higher SW turret. C18 copper BEACON

---

* Parts of Hadley belong to the Urban Districts of Chipping Barnet
and East Barnet.

on top, a great rarity. Nave and aisles of two bays; the tower opens in a further bay into the aisles. In addition chancel aisles of one bay. Their arches have the simplest mouldings (concave double-chamfers). The nave piers have capitals only towards the arches, not towards the nave. The arches are four-centred. Squints from both chancel chapels to the chancel. – STAINED GLASS. E window by *Warrington*, 1846 (signed); s transept E window by *Wailes*; other contemporary glass. – PLATE. An unusually fine collection. Cup, 1562; Standing Cup and Cover, 1586; Flagon, 1609, of coffee-pot shape; Cup and Obelisk Cover, 1610; another, 1615, especially handsomely decorated; Paten, 1618. – MONUMENTS. Unusual number of small brasses: Lady, C15 (in front of the altar); two ladies (s transept E wall); man and woman, C16 (chancel s wall); woman in demi-profile, *c*. 1504 (s transept w wall); William Turnour † 1500 and wife and children (s aisle). – In addition the following later monuments: Sir Roger Wilbraham † 1616, by *Nicholas Stone*, epitaph with two busts of outstanding quality in oval niches, the attitudes of exquisite Mannerism. – Alice Stamford and her son, 1626, epitaph with painted portrait of the son, and painted decoration. – Elizabeth Davies † 1678, epitaph without figures, signed by *William Stanton*. – Richmond Moore † 1796, epitaph with female in mournful attitude by a broken column; unsigned.

Of the houses along the sides of Hadley Green and Hadley Common only a few are of high individual merit. It is their universally satisfying standard and their variety of scale, texture, and juxtaposition that makes them so enjoyable.

On the w side of HADLEY GREEN, OLD FOLD MANOR HOUSE, five-bay, two-storey Georgian, and OLD FOLD MANOR GOLF CLUB HOUSE, originally two cottages, now connected by an early C19 gateway with four columns and a broad parapet with Soanian incised line ornament. On the SE side of Hadley Green from s to N: OSSULSTON HOUSE, three-bay, red brick, with Gibbs surround to the arched door; then two Georgian cottages, then a wide gap; then HADLEY HOUSE, good mid Georgian five-bay red brick house with pediment and Roman Doric porch, with stables to the r., the most ambitious property along the Green; then FAIRHOLT, also mid Georgian, MONKENHOLT, Late Georgian, two cottages, two more houses, and the WILBRAHAM ALMS-HOUSES, 1612, six one-storey red brick cottages with two-light brick windows with arched tops to the two lights. The Almshouses mark the beginning of the funnel-like access from the Green towards the church and the Common.

From the N the beginning of the Green is the BATTLE OBELISK, erected in 1740 by Sir Jeremy Sambrooke (*see* Gobions); Portland stone. It records the Battle of Barnet of 1471. Then farther s DURY ROAD with on the r., on an odd island site, a Victorian brewery in the middle of all this Georgian domesticity (weatherboarded sheds at the back towards E), and on the l. Georgian houses: THORN-DON FRIARS, Early Georgian, and HADLEY BOURNE, with a seven-bay red brick façade.

To the N of the church THE PRIORY, with a few c16 remains but mainly early c19 Gothic Revival; a symmetrical front to the street. Then GROVE HOUSE, late c18, very thoroughly Neo-Georgianized by *H. A. Welch*, and BEACON HOUSE (with c17 remains). To the s of the church WHITE LODGE with a good though somewhat embellished Early Georgian doorcase. Two pretty Gothic cottages between White Lodge and the church.

The church closes the vista completely and only after one has passed it does the view open on to the Common with Hadley Wood as the background. The church is not much visible from the Common. The CHURCH HOUSE, c17 brick, stands as a partial screen in front of it; that is, E of the E end of the church. On the N side of the Common only MOUNT HOUSE, the individually best house of Hadley, mid c18, five-bay, red brick, with pediment and pedimented doorcase. On the s side quite a chain of nice houses: HADLEY LODGE, irregular with a handsome

four-column Ionic porch placed asymmetrically; GLADS-
MUIR HOUSE, five-bay, red brick, with Victorianized
front; HURST COTTAGE, five-bay, two-storeyed, early
C18 with an attached gabled Tudor cottage on the r.;
HADLEY HURST, good large house of c. 1710 with
stables. Curly broken pediment above the central door;
magnificent cedar tree in front.

MOOR PARK

51 The grandest C18 mansion in Herts. Built for Benjamin
Styles, a merchant who made a large fortune out of the
South Sea Bubble. It was said that he spent £130,000 on
the house. In fact it was not even a complete rebuilding;
Styles probably used the walls of the Duke of Mon-
mouth's house, which existed on the site. Nor was his
first building there. This was, it seems, George Neville's,
the Archbishop of York's, built late in the C15. Then
Cardinal Wolsey made Moor Park his chief country seat,
before he got involved in the development of Hampton
Court. Dorothy Osborne's Sir William Temple became
so enamoured of the gardens of the house as he knew
them that he called his own country house Moor Park.
Styles was principally advised by *Sir James Thornhill*. He,
or more probably *Giacomo Leoni*, designed the house in
1720. It is of five by nine bays, all cased with Portland
stone, with two and a half storeys and a top balustrade;
very classical. Its chief adornment is the four-column
portico on the entrance side. The giant columns are in the
Corinthian order with splendidly detailed capitals and
entablature; the coffering inside the portico is equally
splendid.
The garden side has an attached portico; the two side bays
at each side are emphasized by giant pilasters. The ground
floor has banded rustication and arched windows, motifs
more French than Italian.
Inside, all the display is concentrated on the ENTRANCE
HALL, of cubical shape, running up the whole height of
the house, with a gallery on first floor level, just as Inigo

Jones had done it at the Queen's House, Greenwich. But instead of Jones's chasteness there is here every device of magnificence. The ceiling has panels in feigned perspective, the centre one imitating the inside of a dome. The walls have large, brilliantly painted pictures by the Venetian *Jacopo Amigoni* who lived in England from 1729–36. They were much lighter originally than they are now. Their subject is the story of Io. The paintings are surrounded by putti and garlands. The front doorcases have the richest columns and pediments, putti by their sides, and allegorical females on the pediments, all this probably done by the two Italians *Artari* and *Bagutti*.

Through the Hall one goes straight on into the SALOON much less accomplished in its decoration of painted architecture and mythological stories. This work is attributed to *Thornhill*. The painting of the STAIRCASE is signed by '*F. Sleker Venetie*' and dated 1732. The oval dome, however, is no doubt of the time when the house belonged to Lord Anson (1755–62) or to Sir Laurence Dundas, for whom *Robert Adam* added side wings in 1763–4 (demolished in 1785). To Adam's style belongs the former BALL ROOM running the whole depth of the house. Its delightful ceiling decoration is by *Cipriani*.

The gardens were landscaped by *Capability Brown c.* 1755–60. The formal portion on the NE side dates from *c.* 1830–40.

The S Entrance Gates towards Batchworth Heath have a central Roman Doric archway.

In the grounds streets of private houses have been erected in the last thirty years or so. No. 6 TEMPLE GARDENS is by *Connell, Ward, & Lucas,* 1937, in the typical International Modern style of these architects. The curved outer staircases and the curved canopies should be noted. With the general rectangularity of blocks and windows they form the sort of contrast which abstract painters and sculptors of the twenties and thirties relished and which Le Corbusier introduced into architecture.

MERCHANT TAYLORS' SCHOOL (*see* Rickmansworth).

MUCH HADHAM

5 Of its own kind Much Hadham is visually probably the most successful village in the county. Its kind is that of the wealthy, in a way almost urban, village, with big Georgian houses in contrast with the more varied C16 and C17 cottages. The main street is long and of very high architectural quality. It has in its course two mansions big enough to possess proper ranges of stables and at its S end one in large grounds. The church stands away from the street, and close to it the Bishop of London's palace and the Rectory.

ST ANDREW. Quite a large church, all embattled, and one of complicated history. A C12 church can be surmised but has left no visible traces. About 1220 the chancel was rebuilt (blocked N lancet window). About the middle of the century a S aisle was added to an older nave, three bays long, with octagonal piers, plain moulded capitals, and double-chamfered arches. As building went on to the W taste changed and the last bays have slightly more complex capitals and arches. The N aisle is of two dates. Its E bay, wider than the others and probably originally opening into a Norman transept, is late C13; the other bays are early C14 (*see* the capitals of the octagonal piers, and the arch mouldings). The arches are sparsely studded with fleurons. Amongst the S aisle windows one original one is in the Dec style. The same style appears in the S aisle Piscina. The W tower followed under the aegis of Bishop Braybrooke of London (1382–1404). It is of three stages, embattled and has a tall spike. The buttresses are diagonal, the W window is tall. The tower arch has an interesting moulding. The C15 added the S porch, inserted the big five-light E window with panel tracery in two tiers and several other windows, and put in new roofs. They all survive and are worth study. The nave wall-posts rest on figures, the nave and chancel tie-beams are a little decorated on their undersides, the nave braces carry tracery, etc. – SCREEN. C15 with 'panel' tracery. – CHANCEL STALLS. With panelled back walls and poppyheads. – DOOR to N vestry. With big C13 ironwork. –

CHAIRS. Two big chairs of *c*. 1400; of uncommon interest. – PAINTING. On the N wall remains of ornamental Early Tudor wall painting. – TILES. A few C14 tiles inside the N chancel recess. – STAINED GLASS. In the head of the E window, unfortunately too high to be seen properly, two figures of male saints and a row of female saints, C15, apparently well preserved. – E window by *Burlison & Grylls, c.* 1875–80. – S aisle last window from W designed by *Selwyn Image* and executed 1891. – PLATE. Two Chalices and a small Paten of 1576; Paten of 1811. – MONUMENTS. Brass with demi-figure of a man, C15 (chancel floor). – Brasses to a man and woman, *c.* 1500; to Clement Newce † 1519, wife and children; and to William Newce † 1610, wife and children (nave E end). – Epitaph to Judith Aylmer † 1618, wife of the Bishop of London, with the usual kneeling figure. – Joane Goldsmith † 1569 (nave E end). – Dionis Burton † 1616 (next to the Goldsmith brass).

To the N of the churchyard stands THE PALACE, the Much Hadham residence of the Bishops of London, a long brick house with a many-gabled front. The brick casing of the later C17 covers a timber-framed structure of earlier date. The shape is that of an H. In the centre was the Hall, originally open to the roof. The old tie-beams can still be seen. Except for one C15 beam on the first floor, the old details, such as the staircase rail and newels, and some panelling, are of Jacobean type. To the S of the churchyard is the RECTORY of the early C17, but much altered.

The main street of Much Hadham is a delight from beginning to end, more sustainedly so perhaps than any other in Herts. The beginning in the N is THE LORDSHIP, an ambitious gentleman's house of *c.* 1740–5, with a stable block at r. angles to the l.; the house has nine bays and two storeys (originally three but converted into two about 1830), a three-bay pediment, a later Tuscan porch, and good iron railings and gates. At the back one wing survives of what was probably originally a much larger Tudor mansion. The wing opposite was re-cased in the C19. Outer S wing of 1912 by *Sir Reginald Blomfield*.

Inside a fine mid C17 staircase (not in its original position).

More or less opposite The Lordship are some gabled C17 houses, and then NORTH LEYS, of chequered brick, five bays wide, with straight door canopy on carved brackets, and also original ironwork to the street. From here the street is two solid rows of houses. The RED LION on one side, the NEW MANOR HOUSE on the other mark the beginning. The New Manor House is dated 1839, and may serve as a warning against that undiscriminating praise of the Early Victorian which one comes across sometimes to-day. The house is bargeboarded and gabled all right, but of stock bricks and symmetrical, no more than a drab suburban villa, picturesque merely in a routine way. After that, overhang cottages on both sides and such C17 mixtures as WOODHAM HOUSE with two symmetrical gables, but a doorcase of *c.* 1700 with carved brackets. The C16–C17 has also some pargetting to show, usually, of course, renewed, and occasionally fine exposed timbers, especially the OLD HOUSE on the E side, and of a slightly later date GREEN SHUTTERS on the same side. On the W side GAYTON'S is on a large scale, of brick, with three gables. Then, about halfway down, the most palatial mansion in the village is reached: MUCH HADHAM HALL, seen behind a large Wellingtonia, a five-bay house of 1735 with central Venetian window and hipped roof, and in line with it farther S the stable range with arched carriageway and four windows on each side of it. Opposite another early C18 house, the same usual type and of less unusual size; segmentheaded windows. On the same side, particularly pretty, CAMDEN COTTAGE, low with pargetting and an asymmetrical gable, followed by CASTLE HOUSE, a delightful, white, early C19 front of seven bays with a Gothick porch and arched windows with hood-moulds. Lower down on the same side MORRIS COTTAGE, with exposed timbers which may well be C16. Close to this is the entrance to MOOR PLACE, a house of 1775–9, not bigger originally than the best in the village, but placed in large grounds. The social scale operated effectively, without necessarily much architectural variety. Moor Place was designed by *Robert Mitchell*. It is of brick and has the usual five bays and two storeys. The distinguishing feature on the entrance side is the blank arches on the ground-floor. The interior has a fine central three-flight staircase with iron railings, much discreet stucco-work, and good fireplaces. A wing was added in the s by *Sir Ernest Newton* in 1907, lower, and in his best and most tactful Neo-Georgian.

s of Moor Place by the railway station an estate of nearly fifty houses by *P. Mauger & Partners*, begun in 1945.

Around Much Hadham many uncommonly well-kept former farmhouses and cottages, notably at HADHAM CROSS, YEW TREE HOUSE of the early C17 but with a date plate 1697, at GREEN TYE a cottage on the N side of the Green, and GRUDDS FARM with a moat, and at PERRY GREEN, e.g. BUCKLER'S FARM, well modernized in such features as the windows.

NAST HYDE
1¾ m. SW of Hatfield

GREAT NAST HYDE. Early C17 brick mansion of two storeys with gables; on the H plan, like North Mimms. The wings project farther to the N than to the S. In the middle of the S front a two-storeyed porch. The space between the wings on the N side is now taken by the C19 addition of a large hall. The original hall is, however, also preserved, as is the staircase with straight-sided balusters and the parlour. The windows are mullioned and transomed, of three to four lights.

E of Great Nast Hyde a house built in 1934 by *F. R. S. Yorke*.

NETTLEDEN

ST LAURENCE. A brick church of 1811 except for the low embattled W tower which is of flint and dates from the C15. Nave as well as chancel are embattled. The window tracery was originally no doubt simpler than it is now. – BRASS to John Cotton † 1545; the figure *c*. 4 ft long. – MONUMENT. Epitaph to Edmund Bressy † 1612 with wife and children, the usual kneeling figures.

NEW BARNET

ST MARK, Potter's Road, 1898, by *J. L. Pearson*, but not a spectacular example of that excellent architect's work. Nave only, the E end a temporary structure. Exterior flint with stone dressings, large Perp aisle windows with four-centred heads. The aisle arcades with tall piers; no clerestory.

THE ABBEY, 89 Park Road. The property was before the Second World War a Folk Museum. For the purpose a TITHE BARN from Birchington in Kent was re-erected here. At the time of writing it served as a Nestorian church. It has recently been converted into a museum and art centre.

This district, which is included in the East Barnet Urban District, is entirely part of outer suburban London.

NEWBERRIES PARK *see* RADLETT

NEWNHAM

ST VINCENT. A small church, but with W tower with stair-turret, S aisle and clerestory, and S porch. All this appears Perp, but the chancel has two small C13 lancet windows and the others of the early C14. And inside both the tower arch and the short arcade with low octagonal piers and double-chamfered arches are evidently C14. – FONT. Octagonal, Perp, with quatrefoil panels and shields on the bowl and blank arcading on the stem. – PLATE. Chalice and Paten, 1568. – TAPESTRY. 1949, by *Percy Sheldrick* in the style of 1500, in memory of Reginald Hine, the Hitchin historian. – BRASSES. Man, two wives and children, late C15 (chancel). – Joane Dowman † 1607 and children (chancel).

NEWSELLS PARK *see* BARKWAY

NORTHAW

ST THOMAS THE MARTYR, 1882, by *Kirk & Sons* of Sleaford (GR). In its rock-facing, its pinnacles on the W tower, and its flowing tracery quite alien in the county. The tracery of the w window is in fact very Sleafordish. – PLATE. Chalice and Paten, 1636; Paten, 1668; Flagon, 1749; Paten, 1785.

NE of the church the OLD VICARAGE (also known as Manorfields), a pleasing five-bay, two-storeyed, Georgian brick house. s of the church begin the grounds of NORTHAW HOUSE. The house is near their w end. It was built in 1698 and has the proportions of that date. It is seven bays wide with a three-bay pediment and three sets of quoins, at the angles, at the joints between first and second and sixth and seventh bays, and at the angles of the three-bay centre. A semicircular porch of late C18 style on the entrance side. The inside is not original.

SW of the grounds of Northaw House, in Coopers Lane, FAIRLAWN, another good Georgian five-bay house.

On the E–W lane s of the grounds of Northaw House, THE HOOK, an interesting house of its date, 1839. It was largely built from materials of Gobions (see p. 96), but has all the characteristics of the progressive villa as illustrated in Loudon's *Encyclopaedia*, the low-pitched, somewhat Italian roofs, the asymmetrical tower of moderate height, the occasional narrow roundheaded windows (a type of house which will no doubt one day be found as pleasing as a Tudor or Georgian house is found now). Inside, an excellent late C17 staircase brought here from Gobions or Gubbins (*q.v.*) when that house was pulled down. It has delicately turned and carved balusters of wide spiral, narrow spiral, and columnar shapes (cf., for example, Cheshunt Great House).

NW of The Hook and w of Northaw, NORTHAW PLACE, *c.* 1690 but much altered. Inside, a staircase with wall paintings in the *Thornhill* manner.

NORTHCHURCH

ST MARY. The w end faces the High Street across the turf of a treeless churchyard. The church has a Totternhoe-stone crossing tower; the rest is flint. The archaeo-logically, if not visually, most interesting fact about

Northchurch is that the s and part of the w wall are Saxon, and that the thickness of the wall at the w end proves the existence of a separate square w chamber w of the nave proper. The chancel is a C13 enlargement (*see* the large N lancet window now opening into a modern vestry). The masonry of the transepts is partly C13, partly C14. The crossing tower was rebuilt in the C15 and the arches on which it stands were then strengthened. It has a NW stair-turret. Porch and N aisle are C19. Of the nave windows the first has Dec, the second geometrical tracery. The chancel s windows are Early Perp. – CHEST. Flemish, *c.* 1500, richly decorated with tracery. – STAINED GLASS. E window of 1883, an early *Kempe*. Several other later windows by *Kempe* and his successor *W. E. Tower*. – BRASS TABLET to 'Peter the Wild Boy' who was found in the woods of Herrenhausen near Hanover; s wall, inside s door.

In the HIGH STREET by the churchyard two uncommonly fine C16 cottages of vertical timbers with brick filling. More half-timbered cottages on the opposite side of the road (Nos 13–25).

GRIMS DYKE (*see* Berkhamsted).

NORTH MIMMS

43ª ST MARY. In North Mimms Park, yet not near the house. The Vicarage of the late C17 close to the church, also in the park. The church has an interesting C14 building history. At the beginning of that century the chancel seems to have existed; in 1328–29 a N chapel was added with 2-light simple Dec tracery, and a N aisle with windows of three lights but the same reticulated tracery. The s aisle is nearly contemporary, as proved by the identical octagonal piers of the (3-bay) arcades with their moulded capitals and double-chamfered arches. A s chapel must also have been intended; for a blocked arch appears at the E of the aisle. But closer examination of the (triple-chamfered) chancel arch reveals on its E side the beginnings of a continuation which can only have been meant for a crossing tower. So the aisles were meant to open into transepts. This ambitious scheme is by no means frequent in C14 parish churches. The w tower (with diagonal buttresses, a C14 w door which has foliage capitals and fleurons in the voussoirs, 2-light bell-openings with transomes, and recessed spire) dates from c. 1440–50. – PULPIT. Elizabethan. One of the panels has a blank pointed arch instead of the usual squat round arches of so much Elizabethan furniture. – PLATE. Chalice c. 1570; covered Cup, c. 1610; German Tankard 1659 (on loan at the British Museum); Flagon, 1707; Paten, 1717. – MONUMENTS. Brass to a priest, c. 1360 with an excellent broad surround with figures in niches. God the Father with the soul of the deceased in a cloth and two angels by his side and in the canopy above the head of the priest. Obviously a Flemish piece. – Brasses to Elizabeth Knowles † 1458 and two children; a Knight late C15; a civilian and his wife (small figures), late C15; and to Thomas Hewes † 1587 and wife (all in the chancel). Tomb-chest of the C15 with shields in quatrefoils (Elizabeth Coningsby?). – Tomb-chest of the later C16 with the effigy incised on the lid; flowery pillow, flowery sleeves. – George Jarvis † 1716, epitaph with gesticulating demi-figure. – John Lord Somers † 1716, large standing wall monument in the chancel, with marble door at the foot, leading into the vestry. A life-size figure of Justice above against a black obelisk; two lions l. and r.

NORTH MIMMS HOUSE. More famous for its pictures than for its architecture. Yet the house is one of the best examples of the Late Elizabethan style in the county, inferior perhaps to none but Hatfield. It was originally a courtyard-house, but appears now on the H-plan. The N front of great perfection. Two storeys with large four-to five-light windows with two transomes, slightly projecting gabled wings, and a central porch without gable. Small cupola behind. The doorway, round-headed and flanked by remarkably pure Tuscan columns with triglyph frieze, originally led into the Screens Passage of the Hall. This room is now an Entrance Hall and contains an exquisite French chimneypiece of 1515. On the s side the arms of the H, in contrast to the N, project very far. They are in fact as long as the main range. Before 1846 a one-storeyed range closed the courtyard at their s ends. In 1846–7 corridors were added to the E and W wings; the courtyard was thus considerably narrowed. Finally, in 1893–4, *Sir Ernest George & Yates* built s of the original Great Hall a larger Hall with a central bay window. They also erected a long new SW wing of which only the ground floor loggia with mosaic vaults, lush white marble wall decoration, and an extremely juicy bronze gate remain. The gardens were designed by *Sir Ernest George*. The rose garden enjoys a special fame. This is the work of *William Robinson* himself, the reformer of the English garden towards the end of the C19.

NORTON

St Nicholas. A small church of no architectural interest, seemingly Perp but with a Norman chancel arch on the plainest imposts and an outer doorway of the s porch which looks like a Late Georgian doorcase. – FONT. Early C14, octagonal, with tracery and quatrefoil decoration. – PULPIT. C17, with canopy and elementary geometrical patterns on the panels. – BENCHES. Simple C15 shapes with little decorative buttresses. – PLATE. Early Elizabethan Chalice.

OFFLEY

St Mary Magdalene. Nave and aisles are medieval, built of flint and stone, and now cemented. The W tower is early C19 brick with typical Gothick windows of that date (e.g. quatrefoils); the chancel was remodelled *c.* 1750. It is the great surprise of the church, externally of Portland stone with square, pyramid-covered angle pinnacles, no s or N windows at all and only one lancet at the E end. Its interior will be viewed after that of the nave. This with its arcades of four bays must be – *c.* 1230; that is, the piers are octagonal, on shallow Attic bases, and

have capitals of individual upright stiff leaves as well as [21a]
the usual stiff-leaf formations. The arches are double-
chamfered. In the s porch a contemporary window or
small opening (Piscina?) is re-used. – FONT. A most interesting C14 piece, stone, polygonal, with tracery panels
of which some are still entirely flowing, but others equally
clearly Perp. So the date must be second half C14, and an
unexpectedly long survival of Dec forms is proved. –
BENCHES. C15, of simple, usual outlines, buttressed. –
TILES. Two in the s aisle wall with C14 or C15 patterns
and an inscription of 1777 that they were found in that
year 'which proves that King Offa was buried here'.
The name Offley was supposed to come from Offa, and
the tiles were regarded as Anglo-Saxon work. – PLATE.
A fine set presented in 1730. – MONUMENTS. Brasses to
John Sawmel † 1529 with two wives and son and to an
unknown man with three wives and nine sons, also early
C16 (both N aisle). – Spectacular monument in the s aisle
to Sir John Spencer † 1699, big standing wall monument
with reredos background. Semi-reclining figure in wig
and contemporary clothes and at his feet a Roman
matronly kneeling figure with one hand raised, talking to
Sir John. Two putti with crown and palm branch above.
A piece of the first order, variously attributed by Mrs
Esdaile to *E. Stanton* and *Nost.* – Epitaph to William
Chamber † 1728, by *William Palmer*; no figures but
good ornamentation.

The chancel of Offley church has to be treated
separately. It was rebuilt or remodelled by Sir Thomas
Salusbury *c.* 1750. It has a broad stuccoed chancel arch, a
roof altered and provided with a skylight later, and an
apse with a draped baldacchino and hanging-down drapes
round the E window. On the s wall Sir Thomas Salusbury
† 1773 and his wife, uncle and aunt of Mrs Thrale, have
their own monument, very pretentious and self-confident,
with the over-life-size standing figure of Sir Thomas and
Lady S. Tradition has it that theirs was a romantic story
of a troth long kept. They were parted but in the end
united. In the background in relief a rather vulgarly

detailed tree with big drapes hanging off it. Grey background and a grey sarcophagus. The monument was made by *Nollekens* in 1777, who also did the busts of Samuel Burroughs (father-in-law of a Salusbury) † 1761 and of Mrs Maude (friend of Dame Sarah Salusbury) † 1796 in the chancel arch, and another (unsigned) bust on the s wall (William Offley † 1789). – Other monu-

37b ments in the chancel chronologically: Sir Henry Penrice † 1752, and his son, excellent allegorical figure against a pink obelisk with a medallion with the profiles of father and son. Signed by *Sir Robert Taylor* ('invent et sculpr') on the drapery. – Sir T. R. Salusbury † 1835, bust by *T. Smith*. – Two memorials by *Sanders*, 1847 and 1855.

OFFLEY PLACE. *c.* 1825, said to be by *Robert Smirke*. Five-bay, two-and-a-half-storey mansion with cemented façade and Tudor porch. C17 work behind in one wing.

WESTBURY FARM. At the crossroads, half-timbered and plastered, of *c.* 1600 or earlier, with additions. In the farmyard a C17 brick and timber dovecote.

LITTLE OFFLEY, 1¼ m. NW. Late Tudor brick manor house on an H-shaped plan. Symmetrical front with two gables of different size on each end and a centre remodelled and provided with a pediment in 1695. Fine Elizabethan wooden fireplace with caryatids in one room.

OLD HALL GREEN

ST EDMUND'S COLLEGE. Better known as the Old Hall Green Academy. It was named officially St Edmund's College in 1793 and intended to be on the one hand the successor of the English College at Douai, founded in 1568, and the English school at St Omer (run by English Jesuits to the time of the dissolution of their order in France in 1762), and on the other of the small Roman Catholic school started about 1690 at Tayford and moved to The Lordship, Standon (*q.v.*) *c.* 1749 and to Hall Green in 1769. At Hall Green a brick house of 1630 was used which, with its two curved gables, still exists at the w end of the present College buildings. It stands together with divers cottages; and the Roman Catholic Parish Chapel, opened in 1818 (The Hermitage), blends in nicely with them, with its playful Gothick porch and its four arched windows. Its continuation by a light weatherboarded cottage front seems not at all incongruous.

The new college, reinforced by the immigrants from France, decided to build proper premises, an enterprise comparable in scale only with College work at Oxford and Cambridge, but far exceeding what English public schools did at that time. In 1795–9 a school was built, of fifteen bays width and three storeys height. The building which faces E is of stock brick with a three-bay pediment (also one on the W front, where a small cupola rises above it). The three main entrances and bays two and fourteen have surrounds of intermittent vermiculated *Coade* stone rustication. Inside on the ground floor a wide corridor or *ambulacrum* (painted in 1870 to designs said to be by *Führich* of Vienna). The Refectory (altered inside) was an addition of 1805. It is two-storeyed with arched ground floor windows and stands to the SE of the main block. The architect of these early buildings was *James Taylor* of Islington.

In 1845, that is after the Catholic Relief Acts, an important further addition was decided on, a chapel worthy of the traditions and ambitions of the College. *Pugin* was chosen to be the architect. He disliked the existing buildings violently. 'Priest factory' is the term he described them by. His addition in a spectacularly different style is the chapel N of the old building. It was completed in 1853, without the projected tower and spire. It consists of an ante-chapel like those of Oxford colleges and a long, tall, main chapel. The two parts are separated from one another by a big two-bay-deep rood screen, an object of Catholic tradition on whose re-introduction into C19 church architecture *Pugin* was specially keen. The style of the Screen as of the altar and reredos is E.E., but that of the window tracery is of *c.* 1300–30; that is, geometrical to flowing (E window). The furnishings are by *Pugin* too, the red, blue, and yellow floor tiles, and much of the stained glass. *Pugin*, moreover, built a house for the head-master (to the sw of the Refectory). It is in truth a small stock-brick villa, with a three-bay e front, decorated by two symmetrical bays and two symmetrical gables.

After *Pugin* the Scholfield Chantry was erected as a separate little rather heavy E.E. shrine, s of the Pugin Chapel. Its date is 1862, its architect unrecorded. The Galilee w of the Pugin Chapel came only in 1922 (architect: *F. A. Walters*).

Further large additions to the College in 1907–38 in a subdued Neo-Georgian style (by *F. A.* and later *E. J. Walters*; classrooms block *T. H. B. Scott*, 1922).

EARTHWORK. A rectangular enclosure with moat and mound 1,400 yds w of the Fox and Hounds Inn, above Collier's End on the main road N through Ware to Roys-ton. Between Collier's End and Old Hall Green is Roughground Wood, and the mound is in the NE corner of the wood. Around the mound is a moat 360 ft long and 86 ft wide. From one end of the moat a ditch runs sw into the wood and turns se parallel to the moat. The sides of the enclosure measure 300 ft and 176 ft. The mound marks the site of a C15 sunk-post windmill, nothing of which is to be seen above ground.

OLD RAMERICK *see* HOLWELL

OXHEY

The pre-C20 appearance of Oxhey is now completely lost. The village has grown into an appendix of Bushey, a suburb of Watford and even a suburb of London. The most interesting area is indeed the new L.C.C. housing estate in the centre of which wise planners have chosen to preserve a chapel and some old houses with their trees. The main house, OXHEY PLACE, it is true, is not older than the Victorian age. It is built in a Neo-Jacobean style. But close to it to the N a farmhouse with a good C16 oak ceiling. Also barns, and to the E a CHAPEL, the best individual building at Oxhey. It was built in 1612 as a plain rectangle of brick and flint with straightheaded Perp four-light windows. – Original w door. – Fine late C17 Font with Font Cover. – Reredos with twisted columns also late C17. – Altham epitaph of 1616 with kneeling figures, columns, and big semicircular pediment.

All around L.C.C. houses (many of the standard two-storeyed steel-frame type designed by *F. Gibberd*), and also several of the new H.C.C. SCHOOLS, both one-storeyed and two-storeyed especially the Hampden Secondary Modern School, Little Oxhey Lane, and the Clarendon Secondary Modern School, Chillwell Gardens, both two-storeyed (*see* Introduction, p. 28). Their variety of composition achieved with identical elements is worth special study.

PANSHANGER

For those who have an eye for the Romantic Gothick this house is of great interest. In 1808 the 5th Earl Cowper had an existing house drastically altered and enlarged by William Atkinson, a pupil of James Wyatt. It is a long low building with battlements and towers and is faced with Atkinson's patent cement. In 1800 G. A. Repton had submitted plans for a new Panshanger but they were not carried out, although the layout of the park is based on suggestions made by G. A. Repton's more famous father, the landscape gardener *Humphry Repton*. The view from the house past the groups of trees down to the lake created by a widening of the river Mimram is superb, It is one of Repton's most perfect schemes. The Red Book recording his plans is at Panshanger. The house itself is a demonstrative reaction against earlier Georgian ideals, not a square and solid symmetrically composed block, keeping proudly in opposition to the surrounding scenery, but a long and low, completely freely grouped front, 350 ft long, with battlements and turrets and occasional bay windows, and cemented to conceal its bricks. The original building is the r. half only, as one looks at the façade standing in the garden. The long and lower l. half was added by *W. Atkinson* in 1819–22 and largely rebuilt

after a fire in 1855. The interior was completely remodelled then. It is now in a grand rather pompous Neo-
Italian style with many columns and much thick, heavy,
and competent wood-carving. The architect responsible
for the conversion does not seem to be recorded.

PATCHETTS GREEN see ALDENHAM

PIRTON

A village with a remarkable number of good farm or manor
houses around.

St Mary. Broad crossing tower of stone with diagonal buttresses (rebuilt 1883). It is crowned by a Herts spike. It is
of the C12 as the arches inside prove. The nave has contemporary masonry but Dec and Perp windows. The
chancel windows are Perp, but the Piscina inside is C14.
The Perp s porch is the only flint-built part of the church.
The s transept is new. – GLASS. C14 and C15 bits in the N
and s walls.

In the village several worthwhile houses, notably three:
OLD HALL, sw of the church. Rectangular plastered flint
building with brick quoins and stone dressings. The entrance with three-light mullioned window above and a
gable is dated 1609.

RECTORY FARM. Stone building with a front of two lateral
gables and a central porch. The doorway is four-centred,
of brick. The windows, no doubt originally of three lights
mullioned, one renewed. Fine big barns by the side. Inside, a fireplace with caryatids and some oak panelling
from Hammond's Farm.

HAMMOND'S FARM. Gabled, of timber and brick, with a
four-centred brick doorway.

Away from the village chiefly two houses, one a manor house,
the other a moated farm.

HIGH DOWN. Beautifully placed on the edge of a wood.
Stone-built, with a porch with mullioned windows and a
gable; the arms allow the porch and probably most of the
house to be dated c. 1599 or a little later. The E front has
picturesquely varied projections and gables; the windows

are mullioned and transomed; the gables are barge-boarded. At the back a courtyard, now open to the E and formed of two lower and presumably older ranges. Four-centred brick gateway in the N range.

PIRTON GRANGE, 2 m. NW. A courtyard house inside a moat, of which three probably low ranges (except for the Bakehouse and Laundry) were pulled down in the C19. The remaining range has a centre remodelled *c.* 1700 (hooded doorway and sash windows), symmetrical gables of *c.* 1600 to the l. and r., and a lower gabled bay at the l. end of the front. E of it a gatehouse astride the moat.

PISHIOBURY
1 m. S of Sawbridgeworth

Remodelling or rebuilding of a Late Tudor mansion by *James Wyatt* in 1782. Red brick block of two and a half storeys with five-bay fronts. Castellated, and on the garden side with three-bay castellated pediment. Ground floor windows with four-centred arches, upper windows with hood-moulds. Inside, a fine square central staircase hall (open courtyard of the preceding house?). The staircase with delicate iron railings rises along three sides of the wall. Sparsely stuccoed vault and glazed centre dome. In the Dining Room Jacobean or slightly later panelling, stone fireplace with tapering pilasters and wooden richly carved overmantel. – Stables and Barn essentially still *c.* 1600. The lake and planting due to *Capability Brown.*

PORTERS PARK *see* SHENLEY

PUNCHARDON HALL *see* WILLIAN

PUTTENHAM

ST MARY. A small church with a low W tower with NW stair-turret higher than the tower. The masonry is flint and stone in a chequer pattern. The S aisle is stone with occasional flint, the clerestory has only two windows each side. The chancel is lower than the nave. The interior of the nave has three bays with slim octagonal piers. The S arcade has double-chamfered arches, the N arcade double-convex chamfering and fine capitals. Both are C14. The clerestory and roof are C15. – Below the beams are standing figures of saints. – PULPIT with very rustic C17 carving. – PLATE. Chalice, 1569.

PUTTERIDGE BURY *see* LILLEY

QUEEN HOO
1 m. NW of Bramfield

A delightfully well-preserved Early Elizabethan brick house, very small, and of an uncommon plan. The plan may be described as a half-E; that is, with two porch-like angle projections. They have corbelled-out gables on which even the honeycomb-decorated finials survive. The windows are mullioned and also of brick. The nearest parallel in style is The Lordship, Standon, but Queen Hoo was apparently never bigger than it is now (a hunting lodge, it has been suggested). Two fireplaces with depressed Tudor arches, and in an upper room remains of Elizabethan mural figure paintings.

RADLETT

CHRIST CHURCH, 1864, by *Smith & Son*; new nave and chancel added to the N in 1907 by *Oldrid Scott* (GR). The older part flint with red brick, yellow brick, and stone; Oldrid Scott's more restrained and more competent.

NEWBERRIES PARK, ½ m. E. This was once a fine mid Georgian mansion, with well-detailed, trim, Venetian windows, etc. At the time of writing rather neglected.

THE HOUSE BOAT, road house at the N end of the village, now British Physical Laboratories, 1935, by *W. R. Davidge*. Quite a suitable design for a road house, with a polygonal shingled centre, a brick part with port-holes, and roofs with ship's railings.

KENDAL'S HALL, 1½ m. S. Seven-bay, two-storeyed brick house. Central door with big segmental pediment on Ionic pilasters.

RADWELL

ALL SAINTS. Small church, mostly of the C19. No tower; but at the W end of the nave the last bay has an arch as if for a tower. − Carved ROYAL ARMS above C14 chancel arch. − COMMUNION RAILS. Early C17 square tapering balusters. − PLATE. Chalice, 1576 (1566?); Paten, 1793; two C18 plated Chalices and Patens. − MONUMENTS. Brass to William Wheteaker, wife, and son who † 1487; small figures (chancel). − Brass to John Bele † 1516 and two wives (nave). − Brass to Elizabeth Parker † 1602 (chancel). − Two small epitaphs with kneeling figures, 1595 and 1625. − Monument to Mary Plomer † 1605, the one object in the church describing a visit. Plinth with kneeling children, pilasters l. and r., achievement on top, and nearly life-size frontally seated effigy with baby by her side. Her foot rests on a skull, her hand holds an hour-glass. The carving is thoroughly rustic. The creases in the sleeve are still done with exactly the same carving convention as at Chartres about 1150.

RAMERICK *see* HOLWELL

RAVENSBURGH CASTLE *see* HEXTON

REDBOURN

ST MARY. A long, well-documented building history. W tower and nave Norman, N aisle arcade slightly later Norman, chancel early C14, S aisle mid C14; S chancel chapel and S porch 1444–55, clerestory c. 1478, N aisle c. 1497. Visually the best impression is obtained in approaching the church from the E. The E end is of stone and flint with the E chancel window displaying ogee-reticulated tracery and the big tiled roof coming far down. One small N window is also Dec. The S view of the church is distinguished against the N by brick battlements to the aisle, on a handsome arched and cusped brick corbel-table. The same design is used for the S chancel chapel which is a little higher than the aisle. The S porch has cusped niches l. and r. of the entrance. As for the tower it has the shallow buttresses (with bits of Roman brick re-used) and the roundheaded windows of its date. The stair-turret is also shallow. There is no crenellation but a tiny spike. Inside, traces of the Norman tower arch can be seen above the smaller later arch. The nave N arcade of three bays has Norman circular piers and scalloped capitals of the same shape as at Hemel Hempstead and, as there, with decoration to the scallops. The decoration seems simpler and a little earlier than that of the Hemel Hempstead nave. Arches of two steps with an outer billet label. Exposed remains of one Norman window in the N aisle. The S arcade is later: with octagonal piers, double-chamfered arches. The chancel arch with its moulded capitals and arch mouldings does not look later than c. 1300. The Piscina and Sedilia and a recess in the N chancel wall are ogee-headed. – FONT. Handsome, unpretentious early C18 design. – SCREENS. Good and well preserved C15 rood screen. Two broad and tall sections l. and two r. of the doorway. Each section of six lights with the centre mullion going up to the apex of the arch. The three l. and three r. lights taken each together under separate arches. Elementary Perp tracery. The coving of the former rood loft is happily preserved. It is now, with the parts above missing, all transparent like lacework: seven ribs fanning out from the main springers, and cusped tracery between. – PLATE. Chalice and Paten, 1577; Standing Paten and Flagon given in 1728. – MONUMENTS. Brass to Richard Pearson † 1512 and wife. Only the figure of the man and some children and that of a peacock are preserved (S chancel chapel). – Brass to Sir Richard Rede (?) † 1560, wife and children (chancel). – Epitaph to Eignon Benyon † 1717 and his wife † 1732, by *Thomas Bell* of London. The design copied from the Halsey monuments at Great Gaddesden, with the bust under a draped baldacchino. – Many minor epitaphs and tablets.

The church lies at the far W end of the triangular COMMON. There are several handsome houses and cottages (also thatched cottages) along it, especially on its E side, backing on to the houses in the High Street. GREYFRIARS, a gabled timber-framed cottage, and CUMBERLAND HOUSE, with a date 1745, seven-bay, two-storey brick house with Roman Doric doorcase and arched central window. In the HIGH STREET more such Georgian mansions, the biggest THE PRIORY, a completely urban early C18 house which might as well stand in Grosvenor Square: five bays, two and a half storeys, with segment-headed windows and the typical vertical strips and window surrounds of rubbed bricks. To its r. a long low nine-bay house of *c.* 1700, opposite RED HOUSE, late C18, and farther E REDBOURN HOUSE of seven bays and two storeys with three-bay pediment and added upper half-storey.

THE AUBREYS, 1 m. SW. Iron Age hill-fort, oval and comprising 22 acres of ground. The defences on the E and W sides have been damaged by ploughing, but on the NW, where there is a single bank and ditch instead of a double one, as on the other sides, and an entrance. Another possible entrance in the SE, covered by the house called The Aubreys.

REDHEATH
2½ m. W of Watford

The house, at the time of writing, was on the point of falling down. Only the W front stands as impressive as formerly: red brick, nine bays wide, three storeys high, with hipped roof and a broad central cupola. The clock on this is dated 1743. The central door sumptuously decorated with alternatingly rock-face-rusticated pilasters, a keystone head, and carved brackets supporting a shell-hood. The date 1712 is carved in. The house was built for Charles Finch.

REED

ST MARY. The sole importance of the church is the survival of Late Anglo-Saxon work in the nave. The angles of the nave have unmistakable long-and-short work, and in addition there is the N doorway, though the shafts with their volute or spiral capitals and the roll-moulding of the arch might well be later than the Conquest. Unbuttressed C14 W tower; chancel C14 (E end C19). – No aisles; the nave N windows late Perp. – PLATE. Chalice, and Paten, 1806.

REED HALL. A Tudor chimney remained when the house was rebuilt in the C18. Several more recent alterations.

RENSTREET FARM *see* BOVINGDON

RICKMANSWORTH

Rickmansworth was in the early Middle Ages Ryke-meres-wearth; that is, a rich moor-meadow; and indeed the characteristic features of the town are its rivers, lakes, and water-meadows, an area as broad as the whole town. It is only to be regretted that the bathing lake, one of the best near London, has been given the name Aquadrome.

ST MARY. Rebuilt in 1826 and again in 1890. The architect then was *Sir Arthur Blomfield*. To him belongs everything we see now except the yellow brick aisles with their typical Early Gothic Revival windows, and the W tower which was kept from an earlier building of 1630. It has thick clasping buttresses, battlements, and a spike in the Herts tradition. Blomfield's interior has the octagonal piers and two-centred arches of the county, and a clerestory. – STAINED GLASS, E window with Crucifixion by *Burne-Jones*, 1891. – PLATE. Chalice and Paten, 1509; Chalice and Paten, *c.* 1600; Chalice and Paten, 1628; Salver, 1692; Flagon, 1695. – MONUMENTS. Brass to Thomas Day and wives † 1613 (N aisle). – Plain tomb-chest of Henry Cary, Earl of Monmouth † 1661. – Epitaph to Sir Thomas Fatherley; later C17, with fine ornamentation.

Around the church lie the most interesting houses of Rickmansworth: THE BURY (Urban District Council), W of the church, and THE PRIORY. The latter is of brick and timber-framing and much renewed. The Bury is early C17 brick and timber-framing, roughcast, and has inside two original staircases and in one room panelling and two carved overmantels.

In CHURCH STREET not far from the church is the VICARAGE, the nucleus of which is late medieval half-timber work. The ground floor bay window has brick tracery at its foot. On the first floor an overhanging oriel. Picturesque gables. Many C18 and early C19 alterations.

The long HIGH STREET meets the short Church Street at right angles. It winds its way through the town from E to W. There are not many specially noteworthy houses in it. Most of them are by the E end: ST JOAN OF ARC'S CONVENT SCHOOL, the best Georgian house of Rickmansworth, the usual red brick, with the usual five-bay, two-and-a-half-storey elevation and a central pedimented door. Close to it (Messrs Adco) C18 STABLES (with cupola) of a former brewery. Farther W BASING HOUSE (No. 46), seven-bay, late C18, then Messrs Swanell & Sly, timber-framed cottages, and the SWAN HOTEL with Jacobean staircase, panelling, and fireplaces. The W half of the street was only built up in the C19, and close to its W end lies, completely rural, PARSONAGE FARM in Rectory Road.

Yet farther W in UXBRIDGE ROAD a POST OFFICE of 1950 (by *G. W. Pollard*) showing that the G.P.O. has now abandoned its Neo-Georgian tradition and is able to do neat and handsome modern work. Then YORK HOUSE SCHOOL, Georgian, five bays, two-storeyed red brick, and farther out LONGLANE FARM, timber-framing and yellow-washed brick with weatherboarded barns.

Special buildings: BAPTIST CHURCH, High Street, 1843. Of modest design, stock brick with lancet windows.

ROYAL MASONIC SCHOOL FOR GIRLS, 1928–33, by *Denman & Sons*. Large group with the classroom buildings all arranged in a semicircle. The rest is of brick and Neo-Georgian in style, the more representational buildings with somewhat magniloquent classical detail.

MERCHANT TAYLORS' SCHOOL, 2 m. E, nearer to Moor Park; 1931–3, by *W. G. Newton*. Not very large, friendly

H.—9

in the grouping. Brick, Neo-Georgian in style, with detail influenced by the Swedish Modern of *c.* 1925.

RIDGE

ST MARGARET. Nicely placed N of a village Green with some weatherboarded barns and a half-timbered cottage. The church belongs to the C15. It is of flint with stone dressings and has a low battlemented W tower with big diagonal buttresses, a tiled nave and lower chancel, and a very pretty C19 timber porch with bargeboarding and traceried openings on the sides (*A. Billing*, 1881). Aisle-less interior with two-light straightheaded windows and a good, lively king-post roof. – Large WALL PAINTING of St Christopher, mid C15, very raw. – PLATE. Chalice and Salver, 1740; plated Flagon, also C18.

ORCHARD MEAD. Almshouses, designed by *G. G. Swift* in 1844.

ROTHAMSTED
1 m. SW of Harpenden

MANOR HOUSE. Of the medieval house the masonry of the Hall, the central hall of the present house, facing S, remains, and that of the Offices and Kitchen to its E. In the Jacobean age the house was faced with brick and re-furnished, and about 1630–50 it was enlarged and externally altered. The show-side, the S front, is now of that period with mullioned and transomed wooden window casements, a three-storeyed central porch covered by a Gothick cupola and Dutch gables, two each side, to the l. and r., crowned by the typical alternately triangular and segmentheaded pediments (a first hint at the coming of the classical style). To the W there are three more such gables, and yet two more were added when in the 1860s the house was extended to the NW. That Neo C17 work was done very competently, but it seems unrecorded by whom. Many of the fittings were bought at that time by Sir C. B. Lawes-Wittewronge, and it is impossible now to recognize what belonged to the house originally. The Hall has linenfold panelling of *c.* 1550, the room to its r. a

big stone fireplace with caryatids and a lintel with four
birds carved in, the room to the r. of that a big Jacobean
wooden fireplace and a strapwork sopraporte. To the l.
of the Hall is a room with a late C16 wall painting of a
battle and opposite a stone fireplace. The Drawing Room
has an elaborate plaster ceiling and a sumptuous fireplace,
both c. 1900 by *Sir T. G. Jackson*. On the first floor is a
stone fireplace with a charming lintel with all sorts of
animals, including unicorn, camel, squirrel, and snake. –
The formal garden dates no doubt from the remodelling
of the 1860s. The fine avenue of elm trees was planted in
1721.

ROYSTON

Royston lies at the crossing of the Roman Ermine Street
with the pre-Roman Icknield Way, and it has been surmised that the strangest monument of Royston, ROY-
STON CAVE, close to the crossing, is in some way connected with this. It is a bottle-shaped cavern c. 28 ft deep
and at the foot c. 17 ft in diameter in which there are very
rudely carved reliefs of the Crucifixion, St Christopher,
etc. Their date is hard to guess. They have been called
Anglo-Saxon, but are more probably of various dates between the C14 and the C17 (the work of unskilled men).
At the important crossroads a monastery of Augustinian
Canons was founded in the C12. The parish church represents the survival of a part of their very large church.
ST JOHN AND ST THOMAS. The present church is large
and townish. It lies E of the old road and S of the new
main road of Royston. It looks all of a piece, but is in
fact a post-Reformation adaptation of the monastic
church. Of this the nave and aisles were pulled down. The
wall running W parallel with the N aisle wall of the church
is the N aisle wall of the monastic church. The W tower
stands where the nave must have ended. The rood-stair
has been traced one bay E of the tower. This first bay of
the present nave is different from the others. After that
the nave appears on the S side for two bays as a convincing
piece of mid C13 design, with piers consisting of four big
main shafts and four keeled diagonal shafts, and carrying

octagonal capitals and complexly moulded arches. The N
arcade and the rest of the S arcade have mostly octagonal
piers. But one on the N side has four main and four subsidiary shafts, presumably the result of the re-use of old
materials. This same very understandable device accounts
for the odd blocked archway in the N aisle and for details
of the W tower, and of the S aisle windows. The E part of
the nave is again a part of the monastic church which can
easily be reconstructed. It represents the originally aisleless E end of the chancel. On the N side one large lancet
remains complete and the springing of a second can be
recognized. On the S side the tops of all three (with dog-
tooth ornament) have been exposed in the masonry above
the arcades. – At what time these arcades were built so
entirely in the spirit of the old work cannot be said. The
Royal Commission is satisfied with 'in the C17 or C18'
and 'at some uncertain period'. Fresh detail research is
needed. The present chancel and most of the W tower including the W portal are C19. But the Piscina in the chancel is again a genuine C13 fragment. – PULPIT. Containing tracery from the former SCREEN of which other fragments have been used for a DESK. – SCULPTURE. Image
of the Virgin (headless) and of a bishop (also headless),
both of alabaster, C15. – STAINED GLASS. C15 angels in
a N window. – PLATE. Chalice, 1621; fine Paten, 1629;
Paten, 1718. – MONUMENTS. Alabaster effigy of a Knight,
two angels at the head, late C14. – Brass to William
Tabram, Rector of Therfield, † 1462, demi-figure under
cusped ogee canopy with thin pinnacles (nave). – Brass to
a man and woman, c. 1500 (nave). – Thin Brass Cross in
stone slab, C15 (chancel). – Against the outer N wall large
tablets referring to the BELDAM VAULTS close by, the
earlier with scrolly broken pediment records names from
1725 onwards, the later in a Gothic Revival style (very
Dec with crocketed ogee canopies) from c. 1830 onwards.

PERAMBULATION

The town consists chiefly of the four streets which represent
Ermine Street and Icknield Way: The HIGH STREET

leads down from the s to the main crossroads. It is narrow and straight. The chief houses are the BULL HOTEL, Early Victorian yellow brick; Nos 59–65 opposite, C15 plastered with overhang, supported on thin brackets; and Nos 43–47, a large early C18 house with a four-bay, three-storeyed centre with giant angle pilasters and four-bay lower wings. The windows are segmentheaded. More minor houses in the High Street recognizable by their classical cornices or by overhangs at the back. Parallel with the High Street KING STREET of the same character, but with only minor specimens. Off the High Street in JOHN STREET the stately former CONGREGATIONAL CHURCH of 1843 (giant Ionic columns *in antis* and big pediment) and the modest COURT HOUSE, debased Italianate of 1849. From here one arrives at THE PRIORY, apparently an enlarged Georgian house with quoins and pediment, probably built on part of the site of the domestic quarters of the monastery.

The High Street is continued past the crossroads in KNEES-WORTH STREET. Here are the remains of the Hunting Lodge which James I built for himself at Royston. What remains is a plastered cottage with overhang and then the so-called PALACE, a two-storey brick house with two big chimneys towards the street but the rest redone in the C18 with a shell-hooded door and a Venetian window above. N of this the street widens and some detached Georgian houses appear on the W: the ROOKERY (white brick) and YEW TREE HOUSE (red brick with segmentheaded windows).

The W–E axis has little to offer W of the crossroads (except the big WORKHOUSE of 1835). E of the crossroads it is called MELBOURNE STREET. On the s side of the street lies the church, on the N side chiefly the following houses: seven-bay early C18 (?) red and purple brick house with door on carved brackets and rubbed brick trim. Then BANYERS HOTEL, white brick, at an angle to the street. The three-bay centre with giant Ionic pilasters. Then a seven-bay stuccoed C18 front hiding a C17 back with four-light mullioned windows in two gables. Finally the

TOWN HALL of 1855, yellow brick, like a Non-conformist Chapel.

More Georgian houses to the E of the top of the High Street towards the Market.

In and near ORCHARD ROAD, just W of Huntingdon Road, an estate of *c.* 90 houses, also a two-storey terrace of houses for old people; 1945, etc., by *P. Mauger & Partners.*

THERFIELD HEATH, to the W. On the heath five round barrows and one long barrow, the only one of its kind in the county. Of the five Bronze Age barrows the diameters vary between 27 and 66 ft, and they stand 3–12 ft high. The long barrow stands 6–12 ft high and measures 125 by 65 ft.

SANDON MOUNT, Notley Green, in a field between Collins Lane and the road from Kelshall. The mound is covered by a clump of trees. Its diameter is *c.* 87 ft and it is surrounded by a ditch 14 ft across. A gap in the ditch in the NE corner marks a 16-foot-wide entrance. The mount itself was probably thrown up in the C13 as a look-out place or defensive earthwork, but in the late C14 or early C15 the site was used for the erection of a windmill, no trace of which is to be seen above the ground.

RUSHDEN

ST MARY. W tower (unbuttressed), nave, and chancel only. The chancel is of white brick and was built in 1849. The rest is essentially C15, including tower arch and chancel arch, but with the exception of the S doorway (capital with broad leaves) which proves that the nave walls must be C14. – FONT. Octagonal, Perp, decorated with small panels with quatrefoils or four-lobed leaves in three tiers.

Many very neatly kept cottages in the scattered village.

JULIANS. Essentially now a house of 1937–9, though much of the masonry is Early Georgian and some perhaps even Jacobean. The windows of the entrance side and more on the less formal N side are early C18. But doorway and window above, pediment, and lantern are all of the recent reconstruction. Inside, the extremely pretty staircase with slim twisted balusters is original, and most of the Dining Room represents a later C18 re-decoration.

RUSSELLS *see* WATFORD

RYE HOUSE *see* HODDESDON

SACOMBE

St Catherine. Nave and chancel, and sw tower, with low stair-turret. The latter was rebuilt in 1865. The whole church is very much renewed and architecturally of no interest. But it contains two monuments by two of the foremost sculptors of their periods : Thomas Rolt † 1758 by *Rysbrack*, an epitaph with flags and other trophies at the top and lovely cherubs' heads; and Elizabeth Caswall † 1815 by *Flaxman*, also an epitaph, rather frigid, with a standing allegorical figure with raised arm and a kneeling and weeping one opposite her.

Sacombe Park, built some time between 1802 and 1808. Yellow brick of two storeys and nine bays with a four-column, one-storey portico of Greek Doric columns on the entrance side. On the garden side two bow windows. In the centre inside, a staircase with restrained iron railing under an oval dome. The staircase starts as one arm, and turns at the first landing at right angles into two arms. They turn again at right angles and so reach an upper floor gallery (cf. Hyde Hall).

Old Rectory, Sacombe Green. An exceptionally picturesque timber-framed C15–C17 house. The history can be followed well. The oldest windows have wooden mullions set diagonally. Slightly later windows on the w side above the original ones. More alterations in the late C16 and C17 centuries. Carefully restored fairly recently.*

ST ALBANS

Introduction, p. 200. Verulamium, p. 201. The Cathedral, p. 202. Churches and Public Buildings, p. 219. Perambulation, p. 223.

* Cf. in detail *East Herts Arch. Soc. Trans.*, 1938.

INTRODUCTION

As one approaches St Albans, one's first sight from miles
away is a long ship-like nave and stumpy tower on a hill. It
is a typically English sight as one knows them from the approach to Lincoln and Ely, and the impression of the cathedral city is confirmed on entering the older streets with their
well-to-do Georgian houses. Yet St Albans became the see
of a bishop only in 1877. The glorious history of the church
is that of one of England's greatest abbeys. Its head was
made premier abbot of England in 1154. Its artists and its
chroniclers were famous all over England in the C13. Of the
domestic buildings of this powerful community hardly anything remains, and if it is always difficult to see with one's
mind's eyes what large Benedictine monasteries of the
Middle Ages have looked like, it is almost impossible at St
Albans. Much might still be recovered by excavation, but
the English have always been readier to raise funds for prehistoric or Roman research than for medieval. And so the St
Albans before St Alban, that is the Roman city of Verulamium is, thanks to the work of the last twenty or twenty-
five years, much better known than the Abbey. It was one of
the biggest and most important Roman towns on English
soil. Its site was in the valley of the river Ver, on the s side,
where now St Michael's Church stands. The Saxon abbey
chose a new place, on the highest eminence, and there the
cathedral still stands. To its s the monastic buildings extended down towards the river, the mill, and fishponds. To
the N grew the town. Of its beginnings we know little.
Privileges referring to the buying and selling of cloth were
confirmed by King John in 1202. The growth of the town
was marked (as in so many other places) by more and more
exasperated quarrels with the abbey. By the C15 the town
was however secure, and wealthy enough to raise a belfry.
The medieval town did not cover much ground. It was compact, except for the familiar ribbons of houses along the
main roads towards s, N, and w, that is towards the outlying
village churches of St Stephen, St Peter, and St Michael. A
nunnery had been founded near St Albans about 1140, but

its site was right outside the town, at Sopwell, by the river. After the Dissolution it was converted into a mansion of not inconsiderable size. The other important mansion of St Albans also lay by the river, at the foot of Holywell Hill: Holywell House, where Sarah Jennings, the future Duchess of Marlborough, was born. The Stuart and Georgian growth of St Albans took place along the three main roads too: Holywell Hill, St Peter's Street, and Fishpool Street; and this pattern was still virtually unchanged at the end of the C18. Only then new roads began to be built: the London Road in 1794, the Hatfield Road in 1824, and Verulam Road in 1833. The spaces between the old main roads were filled in only very gradually. There never was a building rush; for St Albans has not undergone any spectacular industrialization. The town had 6,000 inhabitants in 1801, 11,000 in 1851, 18,000 in 1911, 29,000 in 1931, and 44,100 in 1951.

VERULAMIUM

Verulamium was built near the site of a prehistoric city excavated some twenty years ago. This lay on the brow of the hill to the sw of the Roman town, was sacked by Boudicca in A.D. 61, and rebuilt on a larger scale shortly after. The early town is below the NW half of the later. The final Roman city was oval in shape like Wroxeter and Cirencester. Its walls were built c. A.D. 125–50. They were of flint with bonding courses of brick. In some places they still stand to the height of 12 ft. The outer ditch was 80 ft wide and 20 ft deep. There were four gates of which nothing remains visible, except for the plan of the London Gate at the end of Watling Street (c. 1¼ m. w of St Michael's). This is laid out in modern flint-work over the old foundations. The London Gate was 100 ft wide with semicircular towers. In impressiveness it must have far exceeded anything Roman surviving in Britain. The main street from the London Gate was 40 ft wide and 180 ft long. It led to a TRIUMPHAL ARCH of c. 300 of which the footings on one side are still visible. By the arch the street divided, and in the angle was a temple. One fork led to the FORUM. This was c. 200 by 300 ft in size and lay where the churchyard of St Michael's Church now is. The basilica was in the place of the church. Opposite were apparently administrative buildings and also (SW corner) a triumphal monument.

To the N of the Forum and a little away is the THEATRE, the one building excavated and restored. It is the only Roman theatre visible in Britain. The size is over 180 ft across, the shape is semicircular. There were about 1,600 seats. The stage part consists of the Postscaenium for stage properties, the Scaena or back colonnade, and the Pulpitum or stage proper. To the l. is a green-room.

S of the theatre was a TEMPLE of Romano-Celtic type, set in a vast court with internal and external colonnades. Houses have also been found, and one MOSAIC FLOOR with hypocaust heating underneath has been preserved *in situ*. Much more has been assembled in the Verulamium Museum and is there exemplarily displayed.

How much of Roman Verulamium still stood in the Middle Ages can hardly be estimated. Stukeley early in the C18 says that people for road-making were carting away 'hundreds of cartloads of Roman bricks'.

CATHEDRAL

9 INTRODUCTION. The first impression is one of unbalanced length : a nave nearly 300 ft long, and no attempt to match it by high towers. The crossing tower is sturdy and seems squatter than it is, because of its uncommon breadth. W towers are completely lacking. That is unfortunate; the medieval Norman building had planned two W towers, and in any case the crossing tower would have had a spire, as one was indeed built in the C13. A spike of Herts type existed as late as 1800 and was taken down only in 1832. In approaching the building and getting a closer view of its Norman parts, the most striking peculiarity is the russet and blackish-grey colouring of the Roman brick and flint, which was originally, of course, all plastered white. As it is the building has a sombre tone, decidedly joyless. And joyless also is the interior. We are never made to forget the overpowering weight of the walls. Piers and arches appear only

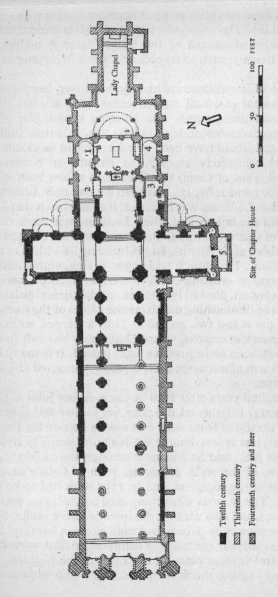

Lady Chapel

N

Site of Chapter House

0   50   100 FEET

■ Twelfth century

▨ Thirteenth century

▨ Fourteenth century and later

cut into them; no pier, no shaft becomes a being with an individual life. The grim austerity of all this is underlined by the shabby whitewash of the walls. There is nothing to attract, though much to respect and much to investigate.

Its peculiar architectural history, moreover, has deprived the cathedral of visual attractiveness. It is aesthetically a most unfortunate story. The Norman church (for of its Saxon predecessors nothing is left) was, it is true, built at one go and would have been as impressive in its gloom if it survived completely as, say, St Étienne at Nevers, or Tournus. Paul of Caen, the fourteenth abbot, built it between 1077 and 1088. He had been a monk of St Étienne at Caen when Lanfranc was its abbot. Rumour had it that Lanfranc was his father, and when Lanfranc was made Archbishop of Canterbury after the Conquest, Paul of Caen was made Abbot of St Albans. In his building he wished to outdo Lanfranc. His church was c. 360 ft long, with a nave of nine bays, a crossing with tower, a transept, and an apsidal chancel, flanked by shorter apsidal chancel aisles and by apses of diminishing depth on the E sides of the transept, two on the N and two on the S. Thus a stepped outline of seven apses was created, where Canterbury had only five. It must have been an impressive sight indeed. It is the richest development of a scheme first, it seems, conceived at Cluny in the C10.

A hundred years after Paul of Caen, Abbot John of Cella (1195–1214) lengthened the nave yet farther and began to erect a worthy w front with two towers outside the lines of the aisles, just as was done at Wells a little later. The style he used was E.E., and St Albans is amongst the earliest representatives of the style. However, John of Cella's finances were not of the soundest, and in 1197 work had to be suspended. The w parts were completed only c. 1230, without the towers, and also without the intended nave vaults. So in 1230 the nave at St Albans had nine Norman bays and four E.E., aesthetically not a happy combination. But worse happened. In 1323 five piers on the S side of the Norman nave collapsed causing much further damage, and so in a style blending with the E.E. w bays but conflicting with the Norman ones opposite, the s side of the Norman nave was rebuilt. There can be no peace for the eye in such conflicting surroundings.

The E parts of the abbey had in the meantime also been completely rebuilt. The need for room and also for altars was so great that even the seven apsed spaces were not sufficient. It is the development we find in most English cathedrals. The rebuilding began E of the crossing in 1257 and went on till the Lady Chapel was completed about 1320. This was slow work compared with that under Paul of Caen. His impetus was evidently lacking. Just as the builders of the w parts of the nave had given up the projected vaults, so the new chancel, retrochoir, and Lady Chapel had all been begun with the intention of stone vaulting and all ended with wooden vaults or ceilings. Had money or enthusiasm returned after that, the nave might have been entirely rebuilt as at Canterbury later in the C14 or at least entirely remodelled as at Winchester. The painful conflict between N and S would then have been avoided.

But the separateness of parts of St Albans goes still further. The monks' choir extends for three bays into the nave. A large C14 rood screen of solid stone ends it in the w and thus cuts off part of the nave and the view towards the crossing tower and the E. And another even bigger and heavier screen, the reredos, forms another division farther E.

Finally, to end this tale of unhappy circumstances, St Albans is the only one of the major churches of England which has a w front completely, or almost completely, Victorian. It is the work of *Lord Grimthorpe*, done at his own expense, in 1879. The cathedral was indeed in a sad state early in the C19. The Lady Chapel was walled off as a grammar school, a public way led through the chancel, and the w front was a ruin with the lateral porches walled up. Restoration began with a report of 1871 by *Sir G. G. Scott*. But work had to be stopped after Scott's death for lack of further funds. That was when Lord Grimthorpe, a lawyer, amateur theologian, and architect, aged 63, intervened, and as he is reputed to have spent £130,000 on the abbey it would be ungracious to speculate what Bodley or Pearson or Oldrid Scott would have made of so responsible a job.

THE NORMAN ABBEY. All that remains of the Norman style at St Albans (and it is much and of great power) belongs, with one exception, to the years immediately after the Conquest. Paul of Caen began it, probably in 1077, that is as soon as he had been made abbot to reform the lax Saxon monastery. His church was completed after only eleven years, a miraculous feat. Of its E parts, described above, little survives. We have to go to the transept and the crossing tower to receive the full impact of that mighty and graceless style. The building is of flint, with all strengthening at the angles, round doors and windows, and in similar places by means of Roman bricks taken freely from old Verulamium. Arches and windows are completely unadorned (no more than one step back instead of any mouldings). The walls are articulated by strip-like flat buttresses without set-offs (rather than lesenes). Paul of Caen might have seen these at St Étienne in Caen, begun in 1064 and consecrated about 1075–80. In the N and W walls of the N transepts the ground floor windows survive, and in both transepts the clerestory windows. Moreover, inside the transept the three equal openings to the chancel aisles and the apsidal transept chapels can still be seen. In the S transept two small windows remain above them. Of the S front of the S and the N front of the N transept we cannot say much, as Lord G. has given the one a spectacular group of E.E. lancets, the other a large rather thin rose-window. In their stead there had been big Perp windows. The interior system of the transept is of a tall ground floor, a triforium, and a clerestory with wall passage. The triforium has for each bay two pairs of openings. The colonnettes are circular or octagonal or of an odd, decidedly Saxon-looking baluster shape. This has been explained as a re-use of Saxon pieces; it may, however, easily be a survival of a tradition amongst craftsmen. The tympana of the arches are filled by a criss-cross of bricks, which was no doubt once white-

15b

washed, as all the rest. On the whitewash originally simple patterns were painted (an apparent alternation of red and white blocks of stone, for example, or a sham ashlaring by red lines to indicate joints or by zigzag lines.*

The crossing tower rests on immensely high arches. The supporting piers have a double-stepped section for each side. Above this is a triforium of three twin openings, and above this two large windows. The rest is hidden by a wooden ceiling painted early in the c 16 with pretty square panels. The exterior of the crossing tower is entirely of brick. The builders did not trust flint for construction so high up in the air. Above the first stage of windows is an outer gallery of four arches of twin openings on each side, and above this the bell-stage with two large twin openings and a curious piercing of the tympana by rows of little triangles. The angles of the tower are strengthened by buttress-strips which higher up develop into circular angle supports. The tower is embattled.

Of the E parts, as they were built by Paul of Caen, the beginning can be traced in the exterior on the N side and in the interior on both sides. The chancel aisles are groin-vaulted. On the S side a blocked arch in the first bay marks the former access from the chancel aisle to the inner transeptal chapel. In the second bay a pair of quite tall windows has been found and exposed.

The nave remains complete in the first three bays from 17 the crossing, at least at arcade and clerestory level. The flat ceiling is of the c 15 but of course replaces an equally flat Norman ceiling. w of the third bay only the N side is Norman. The nave has tall arcades with broad rectangular piers, in fact hardly piers at all, but chunks of solid wall masonry left standing. To appreciate the contrast between this raw treatment of the arcade and the articulate and elegant arcading of later styles one need only look at the c 13 work farther E. The Early Norman piers are, as it were, piers only potentially, not yet really. Their wall character is emphasized by the pilaster-strips or buttress-strips which rise on their surface and go right up

* Examples must also be looked for in the nave and the chancel aisles.

into the clerestory zone. Towards the arches the piers are double-stepped, a small progress against the single-stepping farther E. But there are not yet any further mouldings anywhere, nor any capitals, nor any ornaments.

Equally unadorned was no doubt the storey above the arcade. But here some alterations have been made which obscure the original state and have in fact until now prevented a full appreciation of the design of St Albans. As things are at present, one sees from inside a deep unmoulded arch above each arcade bay at the outer end of which is a three-light C15 looking window. These windows give no light. They lead into the roof of the aisle. An engraving by Kip and Hawksmoor of 1723 shows, however, that at that time the aisle roof did not reach up so high and that the windows were of quite a different shape. Evidence inside the present roof shows in fact that the window wall is a Norman outer wall. So St Albans had no gallery originally, as all the major Norman churches in England have, but only a triforium, that is a passage in the thickness of the wall of the passage itself; all traces have now gone, but to the l. and r. of the main upright pilaster-strips shallow piers can still be seen with their bases and unmoulded capitals on which formerly the arches towards the nave must have rested. According to Sir Alfred Clapham these were large, one arch for each arcade arch below, like at St Étienne in Caen, but a triforium as against a gallery can hardly be reconstructed with one arch of this kind and it seems much more probable that the triforium was indeed subdivided towards the nave, more or less as in the transepts. The large brick arches visible in the outer wall (i.e. the roof-space of the aisle) would then have been mere blank relieving arches. So the elevation of St Albans was not derived from St Étienne but from its sister foundation at Caen, Ste Trinité, which also possesses (an exception in Normandy as in England) a triforium instead of a gallery. The Trinité also was complete by the time Paul of Caen left Normandy. Details of the C11 triforium at St Albans have no doubt to be visualized as raw and bare as the arcade.

That St Albans, in the C12, did not shun ornament is proved by the SLYPE, that is the passage between S transept and Chapter House (*see* below) which is decorated with blank arcading with intersected arches. These arches have rings at close intervals so that they look like bent spinal cords. Some of the arcading is still *in situ*, but most of it has been re-erected against the S wall of the S transept. Below it is, also re-set, the highly ornate DOORWAY from the Cloister into the Slype. This has three orders, without any break between jambs and voussoirs, the outer of foliage scrolls, the middle one with two sets of roundheaded crenellations, one on the intrados, the other on the extrados. The inner order is C19 reconstruction. Amongst architectural fragments exhibited in the Slype there are many more pieces of C12 decoration.

THE THIRTEENTH AND FOURTEENTH CENTURIES. What reason can Abbot John de Cella (1195–1214) have had to lengthen yet farther the nave of the church, the nave being the least important part of an abbey church? Or was he only carrying out what had been planned from the beginning? He added three bays and started a proper W façade. The design is wholly in the Gothic style. No compromise with the existing nave is aimed at. Considering the fact that the Gothic chancel at Canterbury had been begun only twenty years before and Lincoln and Wells no more than five, John of Cella was certainly a modern-minded man. However, after only two years, work was stopped for lack of money, and much of what we see now goes back only to William of Trumpington (1214–35). The new bays of the nave have piers of an unusual section. They are basically square, with four attached shafts, but as the angles are broadly chamfered they appear as if they had semi-octagonal shafts in the diagonals. It is a somewhat heavy section, due perhaps to existing square Norman foundations for the lengthening of the nave? The arch mouldings are more complex than can here be described. The arches reach up higher than the Norman ones. Their apexes touch the sill-line of the triforium. For the E.E. extension also has no proper gallery.

The triforium is of two twin-openings per bay, with ample dog-tooth decoration along the sill and up the shafts, and with pierced quatrefoils in the spandrels. The most interesting thing about the triforium is, however, the fact that no differentiation is made between the curve of the inner arch of each light and that of the outer arch above both lights of one twin opening. Thus it looks as if the outer arch started with one broad complex set of mouldings from which some suddenly break off to form the smaller arch inside—a lack of articulation or logicality typically English. It exists at Worcester as well, probably a little earlier (Retrochoir consecrated 1218). Most of the work on this stage belongs to the second building phase. During the first, that is between 1195 and 1197, vaulting shafts of Purbeck marble had been attached to the spandrels of the arcade below. The triforium was prepared to receive their continuation up to the projected vault, but they were abandoned, as can clearly be seen, and with them the plan to vault the nave. The clerestory continues the wall passage of the Norman nave. On the outside it is handsomely shafted, with a larger arch for each lancet window and smaller, more pointed, blank arches between. The aisle windows were all altered by Lord G. Inside, the aisles have bare walls (none of the usual English blank arcading), but the S wall has tripartite vaulting shafts along the wall, as if for aisle vaults. The existing vaults, however, are C19. De Cella's W end was meant to be a grand show-piece, with two W towers standing outside the nave to widen the façade, and with three deep porches. The idea of towers was given up, the rest was built but fell into such dismal decay that it was almost entirely re-built by Lord G. Of the upper parts of the façade nothing is C13: a nine-light Perp window was demolished by Lord G. to replace it by his Late Geometrical one. The porches are original in their structure, but only in few details. The long Purbeck shafts carrying an outer skin of arcading in front of the blank arcading against the back walls of the porches, however, can be ascribed to the late C12. The inside of the front towards nave and aisles is richly adorned with blank lancet arcades. The capitals are of the crocketed as well as the stiff-leaf type.

The next addition to the church was the replacement of the Norman E end by one more spacious and more up to date. The work was started in 1257 close to the crossing. Here the Norman walls of the chancel and the first bays of the chancel aisles were left standing and tall blank arcades applied to the chancel walls. Two entrances into the chancel from the aisles with odd and very pretty little tripartite balconies above them (what was their use? they are inaccessible from outside) were provided. The balconies have three canopies each with three pointed and cusped arches and three crocketed gables. Farther E, that is in the Feretory or space for the Shrine, behind the altar and reredos, the chancel arcades are open, with piers of four major and four minor shafts. The aisles have quadripartite rib-vaults. Above the arcade is a small mostly blank triforium of even little cusped arches, and above that the clerestory with clusters of nook-shafts and wall passage. Here also a stone vault was planned, but only a wooden vault carried out. It is of C13 timber, but was repainted in the C15 and again recently by *J. C. Rogers* and *Professor Tristram*. The chancel ends to the E in an arcade of three bays* and a large and excellent group of a four-light Geometrical window and two flanking lancets. The large window has two trefoils in circles and above them a splendid large octofoil, similar to the contemporary chapter house at Salisbury. E of this the building is carried on one-storeyed, and on its general outline, especially from far away, this lowering of the roof line has an unfortunate effect. In plan the new E parts seem quite able to balance the long nave; in elevation they don't, except when the building is seen from the NE or SE. The E exterior consists of the Retrochoir and the Lady Chapel. Contrary to custom (cf., for example, 18a Exeter) the Lady Chapel was the last undertaking. The retrochoir carries on the line of the chancel aisles, but

---

* Into the springers of the arches odd little blank arcades have been carved, for no purpose which can now be understood.

uses an octagonal pier to separate the aisles from the roomy central span. This is not broader than the chancel but appears so because it is so much lower, and also because it has a flat ceiling. All this is not as it was originally intended. The foundations of columns have been found which would have divided the central span into three naves as is the case at Salisbury. Against the outer wall is renewed blank arcading, and above it open the windows. The window decoration, where it is preserved, is of the earliest bar-tracery type, two cusped lights with a foiled circle above. Others have the slightly later form of three unencircled quatrefoils above the two lights. Yet others (retrochoir aisle E, Lady Chapel vestibule N and S) go a decisive step farther away from the purity of the E.E. style.

The Lady Chapel itself must be called Dec, although it has none of the fantasies of East Anglia or Yorkshire. A special effort was made here (e.g., the outer walls of these E parts were intended to be, and were partly, stone-faced). A vault was also intended, but once more not carried out.* The outer walls have again blank arcading inside, all in its present form C19. The windows are sumptuously adorned. They have inside bell-flower decoration and in addition tier above tier of small figures on brackets. Their tracery is complex. It includes ogee reticulation and small ogee heads to the individual lights of the five-light E window. These are mostly oddly crowned by little crocketed gables, as if they were blank arches, although the glazing of the window goes on above them in the larger forms of the arch common to the whole five-light window. Otherwise there are intersections, unencircled trefoils, daggers arranged cross-wise so as to fill the oblong lozenge-shape at the top of a four-light window, a wheel of six cusped daggers in a circle, with mouchettes in the spandrels, etc. The Royal Commission dates all this as c. 1308. There is, however, no conclusive reason why it should not have been completed as late as c. 1320, which is a much more

* The present stone vault is C19. Before it there was a wooden vaulting.

likely date. If one looks at the Sedilia, for example, the charming blank arcading above has much crocketing but no ogees. Thus it appears earlier than, for example, the window above the Sedilia, which was (an extreme oddity) given the shape of a spheric triangle. If work was carried on at ground floor level, that is the level of the Sedilia, c. 1300–10, the more advanced tracery forms may well be a revision of the design made c. 1315–20.

In 1323 part of the s side of the Norman nave came down, and instead of a complete rebuilding of the nave, only this side (six bays long) was redone. The designer decided to keep to the general scheme of the C13 work farther W. He used piers of the same shape and only adjusted his capitals and arch mouldings according to a different taste. He abandoned the C13 vaulting shafts in the arcade spandrels, as he never intended vaults, and introduced pretty label stops instead in the form of heads : a King, a Queen, a mitred Abbot, and a layman, probably the master mason. His triforium also differs from that of the C13 in such details as the elongated cusping of the arches and the decoration of the spandrels. The earlier dog-tooth ornament was replaced by knobbly foliage. The clerestory fenestration is different too, as can be seen out-side from the s. In the aisles five-partite instead of tri-partite shafts are used and vaults actually carried out.

Some time later in the C14 vestries were built E of the s transept, where the Norman chapels had been. Their two doorways still exist, as does also the infinitely more elaborate late C14 doorway from the s aisle into the Cloister. This is set in a square frame, as pleased the taste of those who believed in the new Perp style. The door arch is very cusped. In the spandrels are those quatrefoils with shields which appear in the W doors of so many parish churches. To the l. and r. are slim niches with tiny lierne-vaults inside. For the Cloisters, see below (Monas-tic Buildings).

The C15, so prominent in most major churches, what-ever their original dates, is almost absent at St Albans (except for the nave windows above the Norman arcades).

Lord G. everywhere replaced it by his version of the E.E.

FURNISHINGS. ALTAR AND REREDOS. The reredos was erected by Abbot Wallingford (1476–92) and cost 1,100 marks. It looks repulsively un-genuine now with all its *Harry Hems* figures of 1884–90, but its structure is indeed essentially original, a solid stone wall with three tiers of thickly canopied niches. The schematism of the uprights and horizontals is far stronger than the fancy of the details (a typical Late Perp feature).* The relief now inserted in the reredos immediately above the altar is by *Sir Alfred Gilbert*. As the reredos cuts awkwardly into the chancel arcading short STONE SCREENS (with very plain Perp panelling) were erected in the chancel aisles. – ROOD SCREEN. The rood screen separating not the chancel (i.e. the area E of the crossing) but the monastic choir from the nave, stands three bays W of the crossing. It is also of stone and was probably built by Abbot de la Mare (1349–96). It has none of the grace and lightness of earlier C14 *pulpit* such as those of Exeter or Southwell. In its solid squareness with straight top and only a thin cresting it is wholly in the new Perp spirit. It has two doors, the lay-altar between them, and above this seven closely set niches for images with tall canopies above. More niches, strangely at a slightly lower sill level to the l. and r. of the doors. – CHOIR STALLS, 1905, by *Oldrid Scott*. – PULPIT. In the nave, big and circular, of stone, with C13 diaper patterning, designed and given by *Lord Grimthorpe*.

ORGAN CASE. By *Oldrid Scott*. – FONT and COVER, 1933, by *J. A. R. Blacking*. – SHRINE OF ST ALBAN. Erected *c.* 1320, destroyed in 1539, and found in 2,000 pieces in 1872. The base is like a tomb-chest with the usual quatrefoil decoration. In front of it detached buttresses, linked up, it seems, with the main structure only higher up. The base itself has four canted niches on each of the long sides, decorated inside with blank ogee-

---

* Fragments of original stonework from the Reredos removed at the time of the restoration are preserved in one of the E recesses of the S transept.

reticulated tracery. Crocketed gables above the niches, the spandrels with excellently carved but badly damaged figures, seated saints, the Martyrdom of St Alban, censing angels, etc. The top of this base formed the platform on which the shrine itself stood. This was always under the watchful eye of a *custos feretri* for whom a special raised box or bridge was constructed late in the C14. – This WATCHING LOFT has only one parallel, the one at Christ Church, Oxford. It is of timber, the ground floor made into cupboards and a narrow staircase, the upper floor coved out like a rood loft. The upper floor is one chamber, open towards the Shrine in eight twin-windows. The detail is all of the simplest Perp, again much like that of rood screens. The designing and carving was probably done by a workshop usually engaged on such jobs. – SHRINE OF ST AMPHIBALUS (N chancel aisle). Here also only the base remains, reconstructed in the C19. It is mid C14 work of clunch, whereas the major shrine of St Alban is partly of Purbeck marble. – DOORS. N wall, N transept, with big Norman iron hinges. – From S aisle to cloister, richly traceried, late C14. – The original W doors, also late C14, of similar design, now in the N transept. – BREAD CUPBOARDS. Late C16, small, in a W recess of the S transept, with balusters instead of doors. – TILES. A few C14–C15 tiles placed in front of an altar in the N transept.

PAINTINGS. St Albans possesses an amount of medieval wall painting unique amongst the major churches of England, even if far inferior to what, for example some French and German churches possess (St Savin, Reichenau). There are first of all traces in many places of the decorative motifs used to enliven the whitewashed wall surfaces, sham ashlaring, alternation of red and white courses, zigzag, foliage scrolls, etc. The whole church must be visualized painted in this fashion. Of the late Middle Ages are the pretty vine scrolls in a N transept N window and the dark green Tudor roses on a strong red background on the piers to the SE of the Shrine of St Alban. There are also traces left of the major figure motifs which must originally have been everywhere in the most important positions, e.g. a mid C13 Christ in Majesty with angels, on the E side of the arch between crossing and chancel. Similarly there is an earlier C13 figure of an angel on the E wall of the S transept and, on the E wall of the N transept, a C15 scene of Doubting Thomas against elaborate canopy work. Then two large C13 figures have been uncovered between the clerestory windows at the E end of the N aisle, and finally there is the decoration of the Norman nave piers themselves. Two of them have large C14 figures facing the nave, and five have the precious remains of C13 paintings originally no doubt above altars. It is a most interesting fact in itself that altars should have stood against all these piers in the nave of an abbey church. Each painting is of two tiers, and in each case the Crucifixion is on the upper tier. This repetition is again interesting, and equally interesting is the variety of treatment and sentiment, from the gentleness of the second of the painted piers (counting from W) to the majesty of the third, and the terrible distortion of the fifth. In date they range from c. 1215 (first) to c. 1275 (fifth).

LATER PAINTINGS. Last Supper; this cannot be the picture by *Fellows*, painted in 1701. It is obviously late C18. – The Passing of Queen Eleanor, by *Sir Frank Salisbury*, 1918, a piece of facile, colourful, historical fiction.

STAINED GLASS. Surprisingly little of interest. E window 1881, by *Burlison & Grylls*. Lady Chapel S and N windows by *Kempe*, 1896 and 1900. – PLATE. Chalice of 1560; two more C16 Chalices; Chalice, 1639; Paten, 1697; Spoon, 1709; Flagon, 1721. Spanish Crystal Cross, C16 (on the lay-altar).

MONUMENTS. The most important are the three CHANTRY CHAPELS to the N and S of the chancel. They are Humphrey, Duke of Gloucester's, 1447, Abbot Wheathampstead's † 1465, and Abbot Ramryge's † 1519. The most beautiful feature of the Gloucester Tomb does not belong to it, the late C13 iron grille of rectangular panels alternatingly built up of vertical and horizontal and of diagonal bars. The chantry itself has a large tripartite opening to the altar and above stonework of the design usual in screens, with piers between on which are three tiers of figures in niches. The vault inside is tra- [25] ceried. – The Wheathampstead Chantry has a wide four-centred arch closed by contemporary ironwork and a heavy straight-topped super-structure with the Abbot's emblem (wheat ears) and his device, Valles Habundabunt (of wheat). There is nothing fanciful about the architecture of this tomb. It is deliberately less sumptuous than that erected by Wheathampstead to his patron the Duke of Gloucester. The Ramryge Chantry of c. 1515–20 is the [26] most elaborate of the three, a tall ground floor with a close stone screen, again of the patterns used for stone rood screens, and above finer and thinner decoration with ogee arches and polygonal turrets. Amongst the carvings appear, apart from shields and Ramryge's emblem, the ram, the Instruments of the Passion and scenes from the Martyrdom of St Alban. The interior is daintily fan-vaulted. The door into the chapel is original. – The only other medieval stone memorial is a RECESS in the S aisle, arched and cusped, late C13. – On the other hand there is a large number of BRASSES preserved, and even more indents. Most of the figure brasses have been collected on a wooden board inside the Wheathampstead Chantry. They are all of the C15 and early C16 and of no special merit. Remaining on the floor Ralph Rowlatt † 1543, merchant of the Staple of Calais (s chancel aisle), and R. Beauner, c. 1455, and Sir A Grey † 1480 (chancel). In the chancel floor a fine tripartite brass canopy with concave sides belonging to the brass of Abbot Stone † 1451. But the finest brass at St Albans is the large plate of Flemish workmanship to Abbot de la Mare † 1396. It now lies on the tombchest of Abbot Wheathampstead in his chantry. It has broad buttresses on the sides of the figure with three tiers of pairs of small figures under canopies and two of single figures above. In the low top canopy the Lord holding the Abbot's soul in a cloth, and four angels, the whole done exceedingly delicately. – Post-medieval monuments are scanty and not of great interest. Painted epitaph to Ralph

Maynard † 1613 with kneeling figure (s chancel aisle), and below epitaph without effigy to Charles Maynard † 1665. – J. Thrale † 1704, epitaph with two frontal busts against an altar backplate with weeping putti l. and r. – W. King † 1766, epitaph of variously coloured marbles and with charming cherubs' heads at the foot (both s aisle). – Christopher Rawlinson † 1733, large epitaph with life-size figure of History seated on a sarcophagus against a black obelisk (N transept). – Mrs Mure † 1834, by *Chantrey*, pure white, with a kneeling female allegory and Grecian detail. – Bishop T. Legh Claughton, designed by *Oldrid Scott*, the figure by *Forsyth*, 1895; alabaster tomb-chest with recumbent marble effigy. – A. Blomfield † 1894, by *Sir A. Blomfield*, tomb-chest with tracery panels and poor figures between them (all these N transept).

MONASTIC BUILDINGS. Of these surprisingly little can now be seen. It amounts to this : the SLYPE along the s wall of the s transept.* Then the blank arcading and the springers of the vault of the CLOISTER. This went along the E half of the s side of the nave. The remains are clearly of the early C14. s of the Slype was the Chapter House whose site and size have been ascertained by excavations. s of this probably was the Dormitory, along the s range of the cloister the Refectory, and along the W range the cellars with probably the Abbot's Lodgings over, or extending separately farther W along the nave. The Guest House, Aula Regia, etc., were farther W still, not far from the GATEHOUSE which survives in all its bulk. It stands in a line with the s aisle of the church, *c.* 50 ft away from it, with the gateway leading from N to s into the abbey precincts. The building is due to Abbot de la Mare, that is belongs to the second half of the C14. It is of flint with stone dressings, a big, broad, fortress-like structure. The gateway is divided on the N side by a pier into a carriage-way and a pedestrian entrance, but on the s side there is only one very wide and high opening, flanked by rectangular turrets. The lierne-vault has a central octagon of ribs inscribed into a four-pointed star.

* On its Norman decoration, *see* above.

CHURCHES AND PUBLIC BUILDINGS

ST MICHAEL. One of the archaeologically most interesting 15a
churches in the county, which is not at once noticeable,
as the tower and the whole W end are *Lord Grimthorpe's*
work of 1898. On entering, however, an early history of
many stages becomes at once evident and is then borne
out by external features. The nave and chancel walls are
Saxon, probably of the C10. The nave windows with
arches of Roman brick are partly exposed. A similar arch
to a blocked doorway in the S chancel wall. The early C12
added aisles with very heavy low square piers (the Saxon
walls simply left standing). The S aisle was pulled down
later, but the blocked-up arcades remain. Early in the C13
the nave was heightened by a new clerestory. This with its
small lancet windows also remains. So docs the slightly
later Lady Chapel, that is the S chancel chapel, much
higher than the aisle so that the clerestory windows here
look into the chapel. The Lady Chapel has very tall roundheaded lancet windows. The E end has a group of two
with one circular window between, the whole framed to
the inside by shafts with moulded capitals and pointed
arches. The doorway from the nave into the chapel and
the S doorway to the church have plain double-chamfered
jambs and arches. Later alterations are the C14 ogee-
headed window and low outer recess in the S chancel wall
(the chancel E window is new), the Dec N aisle E window
of unusual tracery design, several Perp windows, and the
C15 nave roof on carved stone corbels.

FONT. Octagonal, Perp, with quatrefoil decoration. –
PULPIT. Hexagonal, early C17, with tester, decorated
panels, and daintily carved bookrests. – ORGAN, 1950, by
Welch & Lander. – PLATE. Large London-made Chalice,
Paten, Flagon, Almsdish, all of 1736; Almsdish, 1743. –
MONUMENTS. Brass to John Pecock † 1330 and wife (S
chapel). – Brass to a civilian (figure of the wife missing),
within the head of a beautifully ogee-foliated cross, also
c. 1330. – Brass to a Knight, *c.* 1400 (nave, E end). – The
international fame of the church is the monument to Sir

Francis Bacon, the philosopher and Lord Chancellor, † 1626, life-size marble figure seated comfortably and asleep, an exceptionally 'genre' conception for the date.

ST PETER. As far as the exterior is concerned *Lord Grimthorpe's* restoration of 1894–5 has made the church a wholly Victorian building. He added a w front (with a big, rather thin rose window and lancets facing the aisles, a w bay to the nave, rebuilt the N aisle, the crossing tower, and the chancel, and proudly placed above the rose an inscription: 'Templum hoc restituit Cathedrae renovator et auxit.' The transepts had already been pulled down in 1802. So now the only original feature outside is the s aisle windows, large, of three lights, with simple Perp tracery. On the N side Lord Grimthorpe corrected this mistake and made his Geometrical and Dec, as he had made his chancel E.E. So one can read a whole non-existing building history into the stones of the church. Inside, the nave arcades are old, of very tall piers of the usual C15 four-shaft-four-hollow section. The clerestory was rebuilt by Lord Grimthorpe. The angel corbels of the original roof were preserved. The outer wall of the s aisle has odd wall-shafts, also of C15 style, but possibly earlier than the nave arcade. They are shorter, too, so that they neither fit the nave piers nor the aisle windows. – PULPIT. With very rich Victorian carving, by *J. A. Goyers* of Louvain (1863). – SCREEN, 1905, by *Temple Moore*; correct without originality. – ORGAN and CASE. The organ was made by *Ralph Dallens* for St George's Chapel at Windsor, went from there to St Martin-in-the-Fields, and finally to St Peter's. Excellent scrolly carving. – STAINED GLASS. Plenty of fragments of C15 and later glass in the N windows, but much jumbled up. – The s window by *J. Caprounier* of Brussels, 1867. – The E window by Kempe's successor *Tower*, 1910, entirely in the Kempe style. – PLATE. Magnificent set of Chalice, Paten, Flagon, and covered Bowl, foreign, given *c.* 1667; Paten of approximately the same date; Spoon given *c.* 1720–30; Chalice and Paten given in 1785. – MONUMENTS. Brass to Roger Pemberton † 1627, wife and children. – Large finely classical Epitaph to Edward Strong † 1723, with bust at the top in a broken pediment. Strong was chief master mason to St Paul's Cathedral. The inscription says: 'In Erecting the Edifice of St PAUL, Several years of his Life were Spent, Even from the Foundation to HIS laying the Last Stone, And herein (Equally with its Ingenious Architect SR. CHRISTOPHER WREN and its truly Pious Diocesan Bishop COMPTON) He Shared the Felicity of Seeing both the Beginning and Finishing of that Stupendous Fabrick.'

ST STEPHEN. St Stephen, like St Michael, bears witness to those Early Norman decades when the cathedral was being rebuilt. The W front of the nave, of rough flint thickly embedded in mortar, has quoins of Roman brick and two small roundheaded windows. The front of the demolished N aisle which was left standing has one more such window. The N wall of the nave is a remarkable palimpsest. It contains one large Early Norman window (splay only inside; otherwise one might have been tempted to assign to it a pre-Conquest date). This was blocked and cut into by a wide Norman arch, probably to the aisle, which is in style similar to the arcade at St Michael's. It can hardly be later than *c.* 1120. This arch is also blocked. To the W of it an equally blocked pointed arch. Later, after the aisle had been pulled down, a pointed doorway was cut into the blocked roundheaded bay. The chancel masonry must also be Norman, as to it a S chapel was added early in the C13. The two S lancet windows are original. The S aisle arcade is again not of one date. The octagonal piers of the W bays have earlier moulded capitals than those farther E. The difference can easily be seen. The dates must be late C13 and early C14. The arches are of uneven width and height too, but all double-chamfered. In the C15 the W door was added and further odd additions were made in timber. Instead of a chancel arch there is a timber frame, and a similar timber frame at the W end carries a timber bell-turret, original even in the two-light timber bell-openings. – FONT. C15 with much figure carving of indifferent quality, small figures in cusped niches on the shapely demi-figures of angels with shields on the bowl. – LECTERN. Large Eagle Lectern of brass with an inscription : 'Georgian Creichtown Episcopus Dunkeldensis.' The inscription dates the lectern as between 1524 and 1543. – STAINED GLASS. Chancel N side by *Hughes*, c. 1866, rather pictorial and Raphaelesque; E window 1860, and S aisle window 1862, by *Clayton & Bell*. – PLATE. Chalice, Late Elizabethan; Salver, plated, 1718; Salver, 1789; Chalice, 1833. – MONUMENTS. Brass to William Robins † 1482, wife and children (chancel N wall).

CHRIST CHURCH, Verulam Road. Built in 1850 as a Roman Catholic church but soon taken over by the Church of England. The building is supposed to be a copy of the R.C. Church of the Archangel Raphael at Surbiton, Surrey. This was designed by *Parker* and illustrated in *The Builder* in 1847. Christ Church is of stone, in the Italian Renaissance style, and of ambitious proportions. The W tower is like a campanile, with arched openings and a far projecting roof. The windows are large twin-openings, the nave has arcades on columns. Only the chancel is straight-ended (an English custom which the architect evidently had no wish to abandon).

INDEPENDENT CHAPEL, Spicer Street, 1811. Three bays with three-bay pediment. Red brick with rubbed brick trim. The bays divided by 'lesenes'. Arched main windows with Gothic glazing bars.

TOWN HALL, 1829, by *George Smith*. The visual urban charter of St Albans. Until then the town had had the appearance of a mere country town; now it staked the claim to urban qualities. A giant portico of four fluted Ionic columns faces St Peter's Street and the N. It is placed on a plinth of full ground floor height with the main entrances between robust Tuscan pillars. The portico thus appears to stand too high as if it were on stilts. To the E and W large tripartite windows with straight lintels decorated by wreaths, all in the best Grecian taste. The idea of the whole composition seems to be taken over from Bishops Stortford (see p. 64).

GRAMMAR SCHOOL. The Grammar School was moved to the Abbey Gatehouse (*see* above) in 1871 and special buildings were erected. In 1907 new buildings including the Assembly Hall were started (by *P. C. Blow*). Further additions 1910 (School House), 1928, and 1936 (Science Block). Mostly flint with brick dressings, in a style mixing well with the surroundings.

ABOYNE LODGE INFANTS SCHOOL and GIRLS' GRAMMAR SCHOOL, Sandridgebury Lane (*see* Introduction, p. 28).

PERAMBULATION

The centre of medieval St Albans was the CLOCK TOWER, one of the rare survivals of an English belfry. It was built in 1403–12 and is of four stages, unbuttressed, with one-light pointed and cusped windows in straightheaded frames. Near the Clock Tower was the Eleanor Cross to commemorate the resting place of Queen Eleanor's dead body the night before it was conveyed to Waltham (*q.v.*). The Cross was pulled down in 1703 and a Market Cross built instead. This in its turn was replaced by the FOUNTAIN by *Worley* in 1874. From the W and E sides of the Clock Tower to the N two narrow streets run parallel: French Row and the Market Place. With their crazy overhangs at all heights and to all depths of projection they still convey a suggestion of the Middle Ages. Nos 1–5 FRENCH ROW are indeed pre-Reformation structures, even if the exteriors do not tell us much of that. But the beams inside the gateways of No. 1 and Nos 2–4 may well be as old as the C14. In the MARKET PLACE there is nothing visually so eloquent. The street has had too many recent alterations. Nos 29–30 indicate that in the C17 buildings were taller and more ambitious in the Market Place than in less important streets. No. 30 has two symmetrical bay windows, No. 29 three over-hanging gables. No. 29 is dated 1637. – Compare this with No. 17 in the HIGH STREET to the E of the Clock Tower. The High Street also has undergone too much modernization to be of value now. But No. 17 is dated 1665 and, although it is still gabled, it has now plaster decoration imitating rustication (the taste for quoins was coming) and plaster panels with wide foliage borders. – Chequer Street, running parallel with the Market Place farther E is again entirely changed. That completes the narrowest medieval nucleus of St Albans. The rest must now be treated by examining one after another the ribbons thrown out in the main directions.

From the crossing of Chequer Street and High Street, due s runs HOLYWELL HILL straight down to the river Ver. It is predominantly, but not entirely, a Georgian street. For the upper half the E side needs more attention, for the lower half the W side. Nos 1–5 are early C18, with unusually tall ground floors owing to the sloping away of the street. No. 1 has giant angle pilasters and an attic storey above the cornice which they carry. The symmetry of the façade is broken by the big segmentheaded carriageway. The feature repeats in No. 5. Nos 13–21 are more cottagey, but very attractive in the way in which their levels climb down. Nos 23–25 is the WHITE HART, a C15 timber-framed building, now much restored. Opposite it the first house of interest on the w side: No. 40, built in 1783 by *Sir Robert Taylor* for Sir William Domville, later Lord Mayor of London. It is a big four-square house of white, not red, brick. The façade is of the usual type: five bays, two and a half storeys, with three-bay pediment and a doorcase with attached unfluted Ionic columns and no pediment. Originality was not one of Taylor's virtues. Fine wrought-iron lampholders, fine mantelpieces, etc. Below No. 40 again no houses of individuality, but the same pretty stepping down of the skylines. Off Holywell Hill to the w SUMPTER YARD has only one house of note, the OLD RECTORY, five bays, two storeys, late C18, with Venetian windows flanking the doorcase.

To the E SOPWELL LANE runs parallel with the river, flanked by rows of minor two-storeyed houses,* until it turns towards the river. It was here, close to the river, that the SOPWELL NUNNERY stood. After the Dissolu-

---

* Including a former Primitive Methodist Chapel of three bays with pilasters, blank arches, and a one-bay pediment.

tion the buildings were converted into a private mansion,
and of this considerable ruins remain, all smothered in
ivy. They would look better if their shapes were bared
from the bulky foliage. Sopwell Lane was called the Old
Road when the London Road (*see* below) was the New
Road; that is, the former route to London went by the
Nunnery.

The direct continuation of Holywell Hill across the river is
St Stephen's Hill, leading up to St Stephen's. The
churchyard has on three sides good buildings: to the w
the KING HARRY, Georgian, of three bays and no par-
ticular merit except that it handsomely closes the vista
where the Watling Street enters the area of St Albans. Its
end is flanked on one side, E of the church, by the
VICARAGE, late C17, with quoins, five bays, two and a
half storeys, and a lower wing on the l. On the other side
of Watling Street, s of the church, Nos 2–8, a Late Georgian group, also of no special character in itself but good
as a foil to the church.

As the town of St Albans grew to the s down the hill and
then up again towards St Stephen's, so it grew to the N
until it reached St Peter's and to the w until it reached St
Michael's. The N growth has to be followed from the
point where French Row meets the Market Place. Here
the Market Place widens, after having received this
tributary. Then, as it reaches the Town Hall, it is joined
by Chequer Street and widens again. It is now ST
PETER'S STREET, a tree-planted street of the width and
character of such small-town high streets as one can see in
Herts at Berkhamsted or Stevenage. The visual peculiarity
at St Albans is that the lines of trees are not at equal dis-
tances from the l. and r. frontages. On the w side a good
start with No. 1, late C16 but refaced in the late C17 with
seven bays, two storeys, and three dormers. The centre on
the upper floor is emphasized by a door in a projecting
brick frame which leads to a balcony with iron railings.
After that nothing of importance on this side until St
Peter's Church is reached. But opposite, No. 14, THE
GRANGE, a country house rather than a town house, mid-

Georgian, of purple brick with red brick dressings, with a W front of the usual five bays, with the usual doorcase with attached unfluted Ionic columns, and a S front of two semi-octagonal bays with a Venetian window between. Nos 32–40 is one two-storey group, No. 32 early C18, No. 36 early C19 with Gothic glazing bars and former hood-moulds to the windows, No. 38 late C18. No. 40 is bigger and heavier than the others, mid C18, with a ponderous porch. Farther N Nos 58–60, the former St Peter's Workhouse, and then a row of small cottages, Nos 72–76, distinguished by the odd occasional use of oval windows. Then the church closes the N view of the street, which now continues narrower. Opposite the W front of the church an uncommonly good triplet of houses: No. 103, built c. 1829 by *George Smith* (of the Town Hall) in the Grecian taste, with a closed porch with Ionizing pillars. Next to this No. 105, slightly recessed, in the Tudor taste, an asymmetrical composition, stuccoed. Then IVY HOUSE, No. 107, built for himself by *Strong* (*see* St Peter's), four bays and three storeys, purple brick with red dressings, with giant angle pilasters and a doorcase with attached Tuscan columns, a frieze of metopes and triglyphs, and a pediment. Recent additions on both sides.

57b

The transition from town to country is (as so often) marked by Almshouses. N of St Peter's the PEMBERTON ALMS-HOUSES of 1627, a simple one-storeyed row of six, without gables or any other display features. SE of St Peter's in what is now HATFIELD ROAD the MARLBOROUGH ALMSHOUSES erected in 1736 by Sarah, Duchess of Marlborough. They are an uncommonly large composition, yet modest in height and lacking any representational effects. Open courtyard with a big cedar tree. Buildings on three sides. The wings of nine bays, the recessed centre of seventeen with a three-bay pediment with carved arms. In this centre the windows have stone surrounds. The others are of plain mullion and transome type, rather conservative.

60b

To the W of the Clock Tower a chain of streets, aesthetically as valuable as Holywell Hill and St Peter's Street but very different in character, because George Street – Romeland Hill – Fishpool Street neither go straight down the hill as Holywell Hill nor possess the spaciousness of St Peter's Street. They skirt the hill and very gradually reach the valley, and they meander in a felicitously accidental way. Starting from the Clock Tower Nos 18–28 GEORGE STREET are mostly medieval with overhanging upper storeys. On the other side only minor houses, except for No. 16 which is Late Georgian, distinguished by the excellent rounded corner (even the door, set in the curve, is rounded). The house leads on into ROMELAND which, with a few low cottages, connects the street with the green in front of the Cathedral. To the s of the Green ABBEY MILL LANE leads down to the river. At its end two remarkable buildings face each other: the FIGHTING COCKS INN, a small octagonal timber-framed house on a brick base, perhaps originally a monastic structure, and the former SILK MILL which dates from the later c18. The building is of brick, nine bays long and three storeys high, the gently arched windows broader than they are tall (as is typical of early factories), and with a small cupola.

Returning to Romeland the continuation of George Street is called ROMELAND HILL. On its s side is a piece of ground now a graveyard. Originally there had been a square called Roomland with the town pound. The churchyard which has replaced it is of 1812. To the N of the churchyard No. 1 Romeland Hill of only three bays, and then ROMELAND HOUSE, built c. 1710, purple and 58 red brick, seven bays, with three-bay pediment and broad pedimented doorcase on attached Tuscan columns. A Venetian window above it. Good plasterwork inside.

FISHPOOL STREET is a most pleasurable street to walk down, although there is no individual house of the quality of, say, Romeland House or No. 40 Holywell Hill or No. 107 St Peter's Street. Instead of describing consecutively it may therefore be better just to record that there is a variety of overhang houses (No. 13 of three storeys with plaster panels framed by foliage borders, Nos 38 and 42, and Nos 166–168 with a door with four-centred arch) and red brick houses of the usual square proportions (Nos 8, 56, 122), as well as of the long low type (Nos 59, 137). The only bigger house is ST MICHAEL'S MANOR HOUSE, late C17 of nine bays, with the entrance on the five-bay w side (a big porch on coupled Tuscan columns). At the foot of Fishpool Street the vista is closed by KINGSBURY MILL, a late C18 brick building with three white weather-boarded gables of different sizes against tall trees behind. Next to this KINGSBURY MANOR HOUSE, pleasant C18 house with a door taken from the Elizabethan Gorham-bury. Then the street turns, crosses the river, and carries on in a southerly direction towards St Michael's. Here, in ST MICHAEL'S STREET, Nos 14–18 show exposed timber-framing. At the far end on the r. is ST GER-MAINS, Late Georgian, stuccoed; on the l. DARROW-FIELD HOUSE or the Dower House (of Gorhambury), early C18, of chequered brick, five bays with a three-bay wing on the l. The doorcase is later, the Gates, sup-posedly Italian, date from the C17.

Houses such as this were on the outskirts of or outside the town when they were built. Right in the country was, for example, BLEAK HOUSE, in CATHERINE STREET and Normandy Road, which is now surrounded by other houses. It is also early C18, five bays and two storeys with lower three-bay wings. Above the Tuscan doorcase a win-dow with a projecting brick frame with ears. The other upper windows have slightly decorated brick lintels. In NORMANDY ROAD a cottage originally belonging to the same property. Door with straight hood on richly carved brackets.

Outside the town still to-day on the w THE PRAE, pretty, long, rambling early C19 house on the road to Dunstable; and on the E OAKLANDS, Hatfield Road, which is a romantic C19 conversion of a Georgian house. Tudor trim was applied and a castellated tower added which bears the date 1844. The additions were made for an F.S.A.

Between 1790 and 1830 three new main roads were created:
London Road in 1793, Hatfield Road in 1824, and
Verulam Road in 1830. In VERULAM ROAD first nothing
more remarkable than numbers of plain red brick cottages
which can thus be dated as *c.* 1830. Then DIOCESAN
HOUSE, a large detached red brick house, built as the
Verulam Arms and converted by *Caroë*. In LONDON
ROAD well-to-do stuccoed villas of about the same date,
planned together by *Smith*, e.g. Nos 25–27 with a verandah on pretty wooden skeleton columns, and Nos 174–
176, a Neo-Norman monstrosity, also by *Smith*. Flint with
red brick dressings, arched windows with Gothic glazing
bars, giant blank roundheaded arches and a zigzag of low-
pitched gables on top.

ST PAUL'S WALDEN

ALL SAINTS. A sizeable, low, all embattled flint church.
The W tower not high, with a higher SE stair-turret and
angle buttresses. The N wall of the nave is so thick as to
suggest an older age than the early C14 windows. The S
aisle arcade of five bays has octagonal piers also with early
C14 capitals and double-chamfered arches. Of the windows only one (with Kentish tracery) goes with that date.
The others are Perp, as are the upper portions of the
tower and the nave clerestory and also the S chancel
chapel (*see* its blocked arcade to the chancel, with stone
piers consisting of semi-octagonal shafts in the main
axes and hollows in the diagonals).

The chancel itself is the great surprise of the church. It[20b]
was remodelled in 1727 by Edward Gilbert of Bury
Street, London, and The Bury, St Paul's Walden. It is
separated from the nave by a gorgeous, if decidedly
worldly, screen with columns, carrying bits of entablature
and arches, and candelabra on top of the cornice. Inside,
the chancel is vaulted and stuccoed. On the S wall is a very
discreet memorial to the founder, a relief of an urn with
putti and E. G., Obiit 1762. – FONT. Octagonal, Perp,
with frieze of leaves and embattled top. – SCREEN. Two

sections of one light each, l. and r. of the entrance. Each light has a depressed ogee arch and some tiny Perp 'panelling' above. – STAINED GLASS. A beautiful Virgin of the early C14 in the tower W window. The figure of the Virgin is mostly brown and olive-green, the child is clothed in red. – E window (Strathmore Memorial Window) by *Hugh Easton*, 1946. – PLATE. Flagon and Standing Paten, 1680. – MONUMENT. H. Stapleford † 1631 and wife, small epitaph with the usual kneeling figures (s chapel, w wall).

THE BURY. Considerable *Robert Adam* and Neo-Elizabethan (1887) additions to Edward Gilbert's house of 1740. This is of red brick, two-storeyed, with polygonal bay windows and a central pediment. Robert Adam, *c.* 1767 added a Hall with segmental vault and apses at both ends, screened off by columns in Adam's favourite manner, and Drawing Room and Morning Room beyond the apses. The Drawing Room has bay windows on three sides. The main entrance to the house in the C18 was into the Hall. In the grounds GARDEN HOUSE, with Gothick pointed, ogee-arched, and quatrefoil windows.

STAGENHOE. Rebuilt after a fire of 1737. Stuccoed eleven-bay front. The outer two-bay wings two-storeyed, the rest three-storeyed. Three-bay sculptured pediment. Otherwise balustrades.

SALISBURY HALL *see* SHENLEY

SANDON

ALL SAINTS. Chiefly later C14. W tower originally unbuttressed but later propped up by big sloping brick buttresses without any off-sets. S porch tall with two-light windows. Nave with four-bay arcades to the aisles. Moulded capitals, double-chamfered arches. Chancel arch similar, but with double-hollow-chamfered arches. The chancel windows are Early Perp, that is also later C14: still steep, two-centred arches, but panel tracery. The tiny Easter Sepulchre inside the chancel (only 2 ft long) has a depressed arch and little crocketed ogee gables above it, and Sedilia and Piscina are also ogee-crocketed, which would indicate a slightly earlier date. – Indeed a contract exists between the Chapter of St Paul's in London and *Thomas Rykelyng*, stone mason, to pull down the old chancel at Sandon and rebuild it, and that contract is dated 1348. – PULPIT. Jacobean with much incised ornamentation. – SCREEN. C15, of simple design. – BENCHES. C15, complete with seats and backs, not only ends. – STAINED GLASS. Many higgledy-piggledy bits of pre-Reformation glass in the heads of aisle windows. – PLATE. Chalice and Paten, 1688. – MONUMENTS. Brasses to John Fitzjeffery † 1480 and wife; fine, slightly mannered figures; he in the spiky armour of the moment; *c.* 30 in. long. – Nicholas F. Miller † 1747, exceedingly good big epitaph with bust of the fashionable young man in elaborate surround of varied marbles. Who is the sculptor?

SANDON BURY. C17 brick house with slightly later s front of five bays and two and a half storeys. Large aisled barn with brick front, and derelict square dovecot. These two buildings seem of late C17 design with brick bands and horizontal and vertical oval windows.

SANDON MOUNT *see* ROYSTON

SANDRIDGE

ST LEONARD. An unpromising church when one approaches it from the w. The w tower and w end in general are all of 1886, and restoration has given the whole building too fresh an appearance. Yet the Roman bricks in the chancel masonry reveal a very great age, and inside a chancel arch of Roman bricks is preserved in the most curious of surroundings. These features may well belong to the church consecrated by Herbert Losinga, Bishop of Norwich (1094–1119). Of the later C12 the nave arcades of three bays with octagonal piers carrying square scalloped capitals with odd angle volutes. The arches have two roll mouldings. The C13 follows with the tower arch left standing when the new tower was built. It has two slight chamfers and rests on renewed shafts with original stiff-

23
30a
leaf capitals. Late in the C14 the renewal of the chancel and at the same time the erection of the stone rood-screen which (a most remarkable fact) respected the old Roman brick chancel arch. It was blocked, except for a doorway with fleurons in jambs and voussoirs and for charming little figures on sloping ledges to the E of it, and above is a two-light straightheaded window opening was made. To the l. and r. similar three-light openings. The whole would not look so improbable had not the restoration of 1886 replaced the upper E wall of the nave above the Screen and the Norman arch by wooden tracery. – FONT. Circular, Norman, with intersecting blank arches on colonnades. – PLATE. Chalice and Paten, 1776.

SARRATT

HOLY CROSS. Small church of flint, in its cross-plan and the masonry of short nave, transepts, and W parts of chancel C12 (see particularly the arches between these parts). The chancel was lengthened in the C13 (see the double Piscina) and again in the C14 (see the design of the renewed E window). The short W tower is of the C17 with an upper storey of the C16, which has pretty brick windows, brick quoins, and a brick top with saddleback roof. – PULPIT. C17, hexagonal with ornamented linenfold panelling and double balusters at the angles; square tester. – Plain old BENCHES in the N transept. – WALL PAINTINGS, very faded, on the E wall of the S transept. – PLATE. Paten, 1635; tall Chalice and Paten, 1764; Flagon, 1792. – MONUMENT. William Kingley † 1611 and wife, the usual epitaph with kneeling figures facing each other.
ALMSHOUSES. Opposite the church; plain red brick of 1821.

SAWBRIDGEWORTH

One of the best small towns of Herts, built not along a High Street like Berkhamsted or Stevenage, but within a square of main streets, all quite small.

ST MARY THE GREAT. A big church, unembattled except for the W tower. The tower seems to be C14 (see the tower arch) but was much repaired in brick in the C16. At that time a low stair-turret was added (cf. Hunsdon). The earliest remaining evidence of the history of the building is, according to the Royal Commission, a S arch in the chancel, now hidden. This is supposed to be *c*. 1300. The N aisle windows must be early C14 (E window replaced but probably correctly). The date goes well with the quatrefoil piers and chamfered arches of the N aisle arcade. The piers are the same in the S arcade but the arches seem a little later; and the doorway looks indeed later too. – FONT, *c*. 1400. Octagonal, with panelled stem and shields in quatrefoil panels on the bowl. – PULPIT, 1632, but still Jacobean in style. – SCREEN. C15. On each side of the entrance one very broad four-light division with panel tracery. – STAINED GLASS. E window, 1864, by *Hardman*, much less disciplined than at the time when Pugin designed for him. – MONUMENTS. The church is a veritable storehouse of monuments. The following fifteen deserve attention. In the CHANCEL: Reassembled (?) recess for a tomb-chest with three shields in richly cusped quatrefoils. Shafts to the l. and r. with diagonal honey-comb decoration. Ogee arches along the top and cresting above. Indents for brass at the back. Probably early C16. – Brass to Geoffrey Joslyn † 1470 with two wives, the figures 2 ft long. – Plain tomb-chest with almost completely defaced figures of John Joscelyn † 1525 and his wife. – Epitaph to Sir Walter Myldemaye † 1606, wife and son, with the usual kneeling figures. – Large standing wall monument to George, Viscount Hewyt, † 1689. Life-size standing figure *à la Louis le Grand*, one hand on hip, the other on a helmet. Red marble columns l. and r., and trophees outside them. Curly broken pediment on top. On the plinth two putti hold the inscription. – In the S CHAPEL. Magnificent large Brass to John Leventhorp † 1425 and wife, the frontal figures life-size. – Standing wall monument to Sir John Leventhorp † 1625 and wife. The two effigies, the lady in front, her husband behind and a little higher, lie under a deep coffered arch with Victories in the spandrels. Columns on the sides, fourteen kneeling children in relief on the plinth. – Jeremiah Milles † 1797 and his wife † 1835, by *Ternouth*, with a kneeling mourning woman. – In the NAVE: Late C15 fragmentary Brass; twelve sons and six daughters only. Brass to John Chauncy (?) † 1479 and his eight sons. – Sir Walter Hewyt † 1637 and wife † 1646, epitaph of black and white marble. Very unusual design. The two demifigures in one oval medallion hold hands. White columns with black capitals l. and r. White gable of two concave curves *à la chinoise*. – Viscount Jocelyn † 1756, excellent bust before grey obelisk. At foot tondo with mourning Justice. By *Bacon* (born in 1740; so the recoverment must be a good deal later than the Viscount's death). – In the S AISLE: Brass of Edward Leventhorp † 1551 and wife. He is in armour. – Brass of a woman, $2\frac{1}{2}$ ft long, *c*. 1600. – Inside the TOWER: C15 Brass to man and woman in shrouds. – Big Elizabethan Brass to Mrs Mary Leventhorp † 1566. – Standing wall monument to Sir Thomas Hewit † 1662, signed by *Abraham Story*. Black and white marble in a grand Baroque manner. Segmental pediment. Large inscription held by two putti.

In the nice collection of C18 gravestones.

PERAMBULATION

From the church Church Street leads to the crossing of the short main streets: to the S The Square, to the N Knight Street, to the W Bell Street. In all these there are worthwhile houses of the C16–C19, some timber-framed and plastered, some weatherboarded, and some of Georgian brick, e.g. No. 1 THE SQUARE, Late Georgian, FAIR GREEN LODGE, at the S end of the The Square, partly Early C18, and some houses and cottages to its S in VANTORTS ROAD. No. 1, The Square forms a pretty group with the end houses of Knight Street and No. 5C BELL STREET. In Bell Street also a weatherboarded house with far projecting hoist-loft, and farther W No. 11 (Red House) of *c*. 1720 five bays doorcase with fluted Ionic pilasters, No. 9 of the same type and No. 4 opposite (The Elms) also similar. Nos 36–46 (including the One

Bell Inn) are timber-framed and plastered and have such features as overhangs and (Bell Inn) small ground-floor bay-windows. In KNIGHT STREET Nos 14–42 a fine uninterrupted row of C17 to C18 houses. Nos 28 and 40 have giant angle pilasters, No. 28 also the rusticated door. pilasters and segmentheaded windows of the early C18. The same type exactly the WHITE LION INN in LONDON ROAD, the W boundary of the old town. The E boundary was the river Stort, and here by the river lies the exceedingly picturesque group of light weatherboarded MILL buildings, now of Messrs T. Burton.

HYDE HALL *see* p. 143.

PISHIOBURY *see* p. 187.

SHENLEY

ST BOTOLPH, 1 m. N of the village. The fragment of a larger building for which Maud, Countess of Salisbury, left money in 1424. Chancel and tower arch were pulled down in 1753. The wide nave was originally nave and s aisle. The outer walls are of squared flint with brick dressings. The windows have steep two-centred arches and elementary Perp tracery. – BENCHES. Some with poppyheads. – GALLERY. Remains of a Georgian gallery with Tuscan columns. – STAINED GLASS. Window in N wall, 1907, probably from *Morris & Co*. – PLATE. Chalice and Paten, 1798, Flagon, 1774. – MONUMENTS. Sir Jeremiah Snow † 1704, standing wall monument with two putti and an urn at the top. – In the churchyard plain tomb of Nicholas *Hawksmoor*, the great architect, who lived at Porters Park (*see* below) and died there in 1736.

In the village, LOCK-UP, C18, repaired 1810; brick, plastered, circular, with domed top like a beehive. Pointed door and small barred windows with the inscriptions : Be sober, Do well, Fear not, Be vigilant.

Several houses around the village. By far the most interesting of them :

SALISBURY HALL, 1 m. NE of the church. Brick house sur- 42a
rounded by moat. Built by Sir John Cuttes, Treasurer of Henry VIII, and modernized on the NW side by Sir

Jeremiah Snow late in the C17. The porch and pediment and the windows to the r. of it belong to his time; at the back all is Tudor work. Inside, the most important feature is six large plaster medallions (*c.* 3 ft diameter) and two half-medallions, all with profile heads of Roman Emperors. They are said to come from Sopwell Nunnery, St Albans (more probably from the house erected in its stead in the middle of the C16), and would deserve closer examination.

PORTERS PARK. One of the innumerable buildings of the Middlesex County Council SHENLEY MENTAL HOSPITAL. The house which belonged to *Nicholas Hawksmoor* (cf. above) is wholly altered. The stables keep more of their C18 appearance. The Hospital is a vast garden city, remarkably *riant* in its Neo-Georgian architecture and well-trimmed lawns.

HIGH CANONS, 1 m. SE of the village. Five-bay, two-storey house of 1773, in large grounds.

SHEPHALL

ST MARY. Small; nave and chancel with big tiled roof. N aisle of 1865; no W tower, only a bell-cote. The nave Roof has arched trusses with broad pointed trefoil tracery in the spandrels. – SCREEN. Simple, C15. – MONUMENTS. Several epitaphs to members of the Nodes family, 1695, 1697, 1713, 1731.

SHEPHALBURY. Gothic mansion of *c.* 1865 by *T. Roger Smith*. Red brick and yellow stone, E.E. detail, many gables, and a stair-turret.

SHEPHALBURY FARM. C17, with big chimney shafts and much pargetting (especially N gable).

SIX HILLS *see* STEVENAGE

SPELLBROOK
1 m. N of Sawbridgeworth

SPELLBROOK FARM. Early C18 with later C18 porch. Timber-framed and plastered, 5 bays wide.

THREE HORSESHOES INN. With exposed timber-framing; picturesque. (MHLG.)

STAGENHOE see ST PAUL'S WALDEN

STANDON

ST MARY. Unique in the county in two features: the large W porch and the detached tower to the S of the E end of the aisle. The church stands on rising ground, the E parts higher than the W end. Hence the chancel is raised by a number of steps, the most impressive effect inside. The chancel is early C13, as proved by two N lancet windows and the spectacular chancel arch with three orders of big polished shafts (renewed in G. Godwin's restoration of 1865 in pink marble) with shaft-rings and stiff-leaf capitals, and an arch with dog-tooth ornament (cf. East-wick). When, in the mid C19, the nave was rebuilt much wider than before, side openings were cut into the W wall of the chancel to allow a freer sight of the altar. Of mid C14 work the following survives: the W doorway, the four-light Dec W window with flowing tracery, the aisle windows, especially those to the W and E, and the ogee-headed recess in the S aisle. The arcade piers are assigned to the same date, but seem later. It is a big church. The arcades have five bays. They are tall and have piers with an un-common section (four attached semi-octagonal shafts and in the diagonals a keel between two hollows; cf. Tring) and two-centred arches. Above a (later) clerestory (with the windows above the spandrels, not the apexes of the arches). Of the C15 the tower in its present form and the big deep W porch with two windows on each side. – FONT. A very interesting early C13 design; octagonal, with two horizontal wavy bands of stylized leaves running around the bowl. – MONUMENTS. In the chancel Brass to a kneeling Knight, lower part only, 1412. – At the end of the nave Brasses to a civilian, mid C15; to a Knight of the Wade family † 1557. – In the N aisle plain tomb-chest, originally with brass-shields against the sides. On the lid the exquisite brasses said to be to John Field † 1474, a merchant of the 'Stapull of Caleys', and his son John Field, Squire, represented by the side of his father and in the same size (2 ft 9 in). The son is in armour. Both stand on hillocks with pretty flowers. Below the small figures of some children. The elder John Field had been rich enough to lend Henry VI £2,000 for the defence of Calais. – In the chancel standing wall monuments to Sir Ralph Sadleir † 1587 and Sir Thomas Sadleir † 1606. Both are monuments with recumbent effigies (Sir Ralph alone, Sir Thomas behind and a little above his wife) under arches (Sir Ralph's shallow and decorated with fleurons, Sir Thomas's deeper and coffered) and flanked by columns. In the spandrels of Sir Ralph's are Victories, in those of Sir Thomas's thin scrolls. The back walls have big bold cartouches, Sir Ralph's also excellent ribbon work. The tops are achievements; Sir Ralph's has also two obelisks at the angles. Both works come obviously from leading London workshops. By the side of Sir Ralph's monument his helmets (C16), sword (C14), spurs, and standard pole.

In the village S of the church the ENDOWED SCHOOL, a long, even, two-storey house with C16 timber-frame with brick-nogged infillings, considerably restored. To the N of the church a good early C18 brick house.

Half a mile SW across the river stands THE LORDSHIP. This includes the remains of an Early Tudor mansion, built in 1546 (see two date-stones). It had a central courtyard. All was pulled down except the W wing and half the S wing. In the W wing was the main entrance, in the S wing the Hall. The carriageway with its four-centred arch remains and the flanking turrets on the E. On the W only stumps. The NW angle turret of the range has been reconstructed on the old foundations. The S part of the W wing has several gables and an outer chimney. The interior is entirely remodelled, and a new wing to the E of the S end was erected about 1925 after a fire had burnt the Victorian living quarters.

STANSTEAD ABBOTS

St James. The interest of the church is its open timber S [22a]
porch, original C15 work, and its N chancel chapel added
in brick in 1577. The windows are still entirely Perp (E
window three four-centred lights under one four-centred
arch, N two-light straightheaded under hood-moulds).
The arcade inside also with its octagonal piers does not
betray any consciousness of the new Italian fashion. –
Inside there are few churches in the county which have so
well preserved an C18 village character. Whitewashed
walls, a C15 kingpost roof plastered, a three-decker PUL-
PIT and high BOX PEWS. – TOWER SCREEN. Tall and
solid; C17. – MONUMENTS. Brass to a Knight, late C15
(chancel). – Brass to W. Saxaye † 1551 (chancel). – Brass
to a man and woman, c. 1550, holding each other's hands
(nave). – Sir Edward Baeshe † 1587, wife and children;
the usual kneeling figures facing each other across a
prayer-desk. The children small below. Lavish strapwork
cartouche behind the main figures. – Robert Jocelyn
† 1806, by the younger *Bacon*, with two urns, anchor,
gun, and Sphinx (he commanded a ship at the taking of
Manila in 1762). – Four epitaphs in the nave; a study in
females mourning over urns: Philip Booth † 1818, by
Manning; H. T. Baucutt Mash † 1825, by *Kendrick* (two
females); Mrs Booth † 1848, no doubt by *Manning*;
Sir Felix Booth 'of 43 Portland Place', † 1850, by *Manning*.

St Andrew, 1880, by *Waterhouse*. An unimaginative
routine design, stone outside, nearly all happily covered
by climbers, red brick inside. – PLATE. Chalice and three
Patens, 1714.

Stanstead Bury, E of the church. An eminently picturesque front, the result of several centuries' alterations.
The shapes and textures and colours of the approach side
(W) must delight the eye of any painter. The house is the
outcome of the late C17 and early C19 remodelling of a
C15–C16 building of which the half-timbered stair-turret
and a brick wall and gable bear witness. A small addition

to the w front is of darker red brick and dates from *c.*
1700. The whole of the garden (E) front of seven bays
with three-bay pediment and dormer windows with alternately triangular and segmental pediments is late C17, as
is also the fine large staircase inside. To the s an early C19
façade of three bays and two storeys, as if the whole large
house were a villa in Hampstead. Originally the Tudor
mansion extended much farther to the s. Its building history is not sufficiently investigated.

BAESHE ALMSHOUSES, ¾ m. NW of the old church, built
early in the C17. Brick, two-storeyed, with three gables.
Altogether six dwellings.

BRIGGENS. The centre block was built *c.* 1725. Early C19
bow window added. Then in 1908 extensions to the NE
and NW.

The village street has one remarkable HOUSE. It is dated
1752 and appears from the front the usual five-bay, two-
and-a-half-storey red brick house of its date, with a handsome Ionic doorcase. But on its w side it has an apparently
contemporary circular stair-turret with embattled top, as
if it were a fortified manor house; an early example of
'Strawberry Hill' Gothic. At the E end of the High Street
in happy opposition to one another the RED LION INN,
early C17, with overhang and gables, the OLD CLOCK
SCHOOL, also of the C17, with its quoins and tiny cupola
with ogee top, and the Victorian MILL, now a factory, a
stock brick block of 1865, three by five bays with giant
blank arcades and a Greek temple roof.

STANSTEAD ST MARGARETS

ST MARGARET. Norman nave (*see* the small window in the
s wall). The chancel is Dec, obviously built for a church
more important than is the present one. Large E window
of four lights with early flowing tracery. Contemporary s
windows. On the N side the church had an aisle and a
chancel chapel which were later pulled down. Small
Georgian cupola. Inside low BOX PEWS.

STAPLEFORD

St Mary. The church stands outside the village. It has a Norman N doorway (one order of colonnettes, the left capital with upright oak leaves, the outer voussoirs zigzag, the inner zigzag on the intrados) and an altered C13 lancet window in the chancel. But its chief characteristic is its N tower which has the porch below, a weatherboarded upper stage, and then an octagonal timber stage and a spire. This changes a medieval church effectively into one mid Victorian. The tower was built in 1874. – PLATE. Chalice and Paten, 1712.

Waterford Hall, 1 m. S. Two-storey brick house of c. 1600. Traces of a mullioned brick window with hood-mould on the N side. Fine chimney stack.

STEVENAGE

St Nicholas. Away from the town to the NE, almost entirely on its own. A flint church with a low W tower with leaded spire. The upper parts and the diagonal brick buttresses are C15, but the tower itself (*see* its windows and W door) is Norman. The S view of the church is specially rewarding with the various steps in height and in depth. The church is entirely embattled. S porch at the W end of the S aisle, S transept added 1841. Most of the windows point to the C14 (chancel N and S; chancel chapels E straightheaded but with early C14 tracery; N chancel chapel N; odd windows in the aisles). The arcades between chancel and chapels are of the early C14 too. Those in the nave are C15 on C13 bases and shafts. The clerestory and the nave and chancel roofs are also C15. The niche for a statue in the NE corner of the N chapel may be C14 or C15. – FONT. Plain C13, with later ogee-shaped crocketed cover. – SCREENS. Complete set of screens between nave and chancel, aisles and chapels, and also chancel and chapels, the latter as usual more modest, but the principal ones also by no means as lavish as those of East Anglia. – CHOIR SEATS, C15, with MISERICORDS (mostly leaves; also an angel with spreadout wings, and a face with leaves growing out of the mouth). – STAINED GLASS. E window, 1842, S chancel window, 1848, both supposed to be by *Wailes* (TK); but can they be by the same artist? The E window has four saints, with canopies, in traditional colours. The S window is a three-light Noli me tangere in gaudy colours (still the painterly approach of the C18 and by no means yet medievalizing). – PLATE. Chalice and Paten, 1634; Flagon and Paten, 1683. – MONUMENTS. Brass to Stephen Hillard, *c.* 1500, largish figure of a priest in vestments. – Mutilated effigy of a lady wearing a wimple; an angel and a priest by her pillow; *c.* 1300.

The RECTORY W of the church is by *Sir E. Newton*, 1919.

HOLY TRINITY, 1861, by *Blomfield*. An early church of his, before his style became smooth and competent and stale. Nave and chancel only, with a bellcote. Flint with stone, red brick, and white brick adornments. Tiled roof with bands of fancy tiles. Plate tracery. A new larger nave and chancel were added by *Tate & Popplewell* in 1881–5, 'and a very good match they made' (GR).

SIX HILLS, ¾ m. S. Barrows. Probably of Roman date and constructed for burial purposes.

PERAMBULATION

Stevenage is for the time being still chiefly the High Street with three short branchings-off on the E. But the New Town, one of the planned satellite towns of after the Second World War, is growing. It will have its centre S of the present town, industry chiefly W of the railway, and residential areas mainly to the E on the hills extending up to 2 m. in that direction, and as far S as Shephall.

The attraction of Stevenage HIGH STREET is the haphazard tree-planting and the fact that at the N end it widens into a triangular Green and halfway down to the S it narrows for a while by the placing of an island in it. The narrow street thereby formed on the E is Middle Row. Starting from the N the BOWLING GREEN has on its own N side unfortunately nothing to act as a sufficient back-drop to the approaching High Street. At the E corner is the GRAMMAR SCHOOL, quite extensive now, and incorporating a small one-room building of (redone) brick with open timber roof which is the school, originally founded as Alleyn's Grammar School c. 1562. On the w end Nos 1–7 JULIAN'S ROAD, a group of early C17 cottages. In the HIGH STREET on the E side, still facing the Bowling Green, No. 3, a four-bay C18 front, stuccoed, and No. 5, THE GRANGE, a broad twelve-bay red front with central canted bay window and large carriageway on the l. The house was a coaching inn and dates from the Early Georgian time. A little farther s THE YORKSHIRE GREY, also an inn, lower, with five widely spread windows and door with pediment on Tuscan pilasters. The C18 carries on on the E side, while on the w less happens; it is a pity, however that the architecture of the Woolworth store does not take any notice of the character of the rest of the street. Nos 29–35 on the E again a pleasant Georgian brick group. No. 37, a cross-gabled C16 house, starts the narrower part of the High Street. MIDDLE ROW which splits off here, to join the High Street again lower down, is all red brick cottages, so consistently so that one may well feel reminded of Holland. Opposite on the w side at the junction of the High Street and Middle Row is No. 66, dignified early C19 white brick; No. 68, *temp.* William and Mary with an eight-bay front and narrow angle pilasters; and Nos 70–72, also c. 1700. The E side is here less interesting and does not produce anything special to its s end. On the w side there are still Nos 94–98, timber-framed with symmetrical gables, and No 106, Late Georgian brick of five bays and three storeys with a doorway with pediment on carved brackets and a charming iron lantern-holder over. Off the s end of the High Street at the beginning of LETCHMORE ROAD immediately behind Holy Trinity the former WORKHOUSE, the best timber-framed building of Stevenage; C16 with symmetrical gables to the l. and r. on an overhanging upper floor.

From here, turning E the NEW TOWN is reached, or from the High Street by Sish Lane. Most of the area so far built is called Stony Hall. Its visual focus is a long seven-storeyed block of flats by *Yorke, Rosenberg, & Mardall*, just off Sish Lane. It faces the future centre of the town. Immediately in front of the flats lies an area for the planting of trees, and then the group is closed a little lower down by a number of four-storeyed flats. The high block is built with a reinforced-concrete frame, long open-access balconies at the back and divers kinds of small motifs as light relief. In the front view this hankering after variety has led to a curious, not easily comprehended, rhythm. The concrete framing shows round one group of window-balcony-window on the left and round five such groups on the right. Two similar groups between, however, have the framework hidden, and on top of that they possess a different, alternating rhythm of windows and balconies. The functional justification is a different size of flats behind, but the aesthetic effect remains somewhat restless for the monumental centre of a neighbourhood. Most of the smaller housing is two-storeyed in terraces.

The following details may be mentioned. SE of Stony Hall lies Bedwell North and East, S of Bedwell North Whomerley Wood, and SW of this Monks Wood. The architect to the Corporation is *C. Holliday*. The projects called Stony Hall South and the Stony Hall shops, Whomerley Wood, and the Monks Wood shops were under the charge of *Stirling Craig*; Sish Lane North and Monks Wood Hostel of *Cynthia Wood*; Stony Hall East, Bedwell North and East, and the Monks Wood Public House of *Oliver Carey*; Monks Wood and the Sish Lane Hostel of *L. W. Aked*.

In the New Town one uncommonly good public house the TWIN FOXES by *C. Holliday*, *O. Carey* and *L. G. Vincent*, outstanding in its combination of actively modern forms with the traditional English pub. Also two notable schools.

BARCLAY SCHOOL, Walkern Road. Co-educational Secondary Modern School by *Yorke, Rosenberg, & Mardall*. The size is remarkable and explained by the planned development of Stevenage New Town. The composition of the school is free and felicitous as well as functionally sound. The building has no façade, indeed no face. Yet it is not at all utilitarian in any derogatory sense. A nice variety of blocks and of materials (light brick, breeze blocks, random rubble, light weatherboarding). Excellent details, fixtures, and fabrics inside, e.g. a William Morris wallpaper on the focal wall of the Dining Hall. A specially interesting detail is the main staircase carried up on a concrete spine without jointing into the wall or resting on a wall. In front of the entrance against a curved screen *Henry Moore's* 'Family', man, woman, and child.

WALKERN ROAD SENIOR MIXED SCHOOL (*see* Introduction, p. 28).

STOCKING PELHAM

ST MARY. Small church, of chancel and wide nave (the Royal Commission suggests it might originally have had a wooden S arcade because the S wall is not in line with the chancel). Mid C14 according to the remaining chancel N window and the remarkably original nave window. – No furnishings of interest.

STORTFORD HALL *see* BISHOPS STORTFORD

TEMPLE DINSLEY

An Early Georgian house* of moderate size (seven bays, two storeys, segmentheaded windows with stone keystones, and rubbed brick surrounds, central three-bay pediment) so much enlarged by *Lutyens* in 1908 that the whole appears entirely a Lutyens house. He added to the main front on each side three-bay extensions with semicircular windows in the top floor, and three further two-bay ranges with roofs so steeply pitched that these wings become the composition's main feature. Also extensive office ranges.

TEWIN

ST PETER. A small church on the edge of a scattered village but with the RECTORY close by, a five-bay, two-storeyed

* A cottage outside the grounds is dated 1717.

Georgian house with a timber-framed weatherboarded barn, and a stable also timber-framed but with brick in-fillings. – The church is partly still of the C11 (*see* a tiny window on the N side of the nave and the uncovered re-mains of inner surrounds of windows on the s side). The chancel was rebuilt or remodelled in the C13, as is proved by s lancet windows. Also of the C13 the s aisle with lancet windows and an arcade of octagonal piers with simply moulded capitals. Of the C15 some inserted Perp win-dows, the whole very low w tower with diagonal buttresses and a spike, and the nave roof. A little later still the timber s porch, badly converted, when the chief monument of Tewin was removed from its original place outdoors and squeezed into the porch. As this has a high obelisk as its main motif, the effect is painful. The MONUMENT is to General Joseph Sabine, Governor of Gibraltar, † 1739. Below the obelisk on the pedestal in the front an ex-quisitely carved relief of a Roman general (portrait?); on the sides and back trophies and arms. There is a number of good epitaphs in the church (1709, 1727, 1733, 1789) and also a BRASS: Thomas Pygott † 1610 (s aisle). – FONT. Fluted C18 bowl.

MARDEN HILL: *see* p. 165.

TEWIN WATER, 1 m. WNW. Called 'a new and handsome house' in 1819. Handsome the house certainly is, in the Neo-Greek way, with a w front of seven bays, the centre recessed and adorned by a pair of coupled Ionic giant columns, the wings by Ionic angle pilasters. The s front has two shallow bow windows, attached coupled Ionic giant columns between, and a little curved forward bal-cony between them. No pediment, just a plain attic.

THEOBALDS

Theobalds was built by William Cecil, Lord Burghley, Queen Elizabeth's leading statesman, about 1564. When James I visited the palace he was so pleased with it that he induced Lord Burghley's son, Robert Cecil, his own prime minister, to exchange it against the old and gloomy

brick palace of Hatfield. During the Commonwealth
Theobalds was dismantled and all but pulled down. About
1765–70 on a site close to it four small country houses
were built instead, known, it seems, as Theobalds Square
Of these one remains, OLD PALACE HOUSE, a modest
five-bay, two-storey house, apparently with one-bay side
wings. It has now an early C19 iron verandah. The second,
THE CEDARS, was severely damaged by fire during the
C20 and not reconstructed. The other two, Cecil House
and Jackson's School, have gone. Of Burghley's palace
only one strip of brickwork exists now *c.* 15 ft high. It
forms part of the gardener's cottage of Old Palace House.
It seems to have been the S W corner of the Burghley mansion. In addition stretches of the old wall have been identified.

About ½ m. W is the entrance to what is now known as
THEOBALDS PARK. The monumental entrance is nothing
less than *Sir Christopher Wren's* TEMPLE BAR, erected in 56
Fleet Street, London, in 1672, and transferred to its
present site in 1878. It is a very big gate, much bigger
than photographs make one expect. It has two orders of
pilasters, the lower rusticated Tuscan, the upper Ionic.
The upper storey rises only above the centre part of the
lower (on the scheme of the Italian church façade of the
Baroque). The main gateway has a wide depressed segmental arch; the entrances for pedestrians are curiously
narrow in comparison. The upper storey is flanked by big
volutes, again as in Italian church façades. They are
decorated with gristly, typical mid C17 forms. In the top
pediment a tablet flanked by cornucopias. The quantity
and character of the details seems rather French than
Italian. The ephemeral architecture of triumphal arches,
as publicized in engravings may have influenced Wren.

THEOBALDS PARK is a mansion of five bays and two and a
half storeys with forward-curving one-storey colonnades
and small outer wings. The centre of the garden side is
simply a bay window. But to make up for that plainness
there are to the l. and r. of the bay window Venetian windows on two floors. The house was built in 1768. Some

time later, probably about the middle of the C19, the space behind the colonnades was filled in and structures put up with large Venetian windows towards the garden. Yet later, an Edwardian addition was made of somewhat pretentious character, a broad big tower on the garden side on the l. Its details are reactionary for its day. The clients were not well advised in the choice of their architect. The original part has an Etruscan Entrance Hall and to its l. a staircase with iron railings curving up to the upper floor under a ceiling also decorated in the Etruscan taste. Below the house to the s is an ornamental lake formed out of the New River.

THERFIELD

ST MARY, 1878, by *G. E. Pritchett*. He used the chancel N and s windows of the old church. Small fragments from other parts of it are kept in the vestry. Also in the vestry COFFIN LID with foliated cross and C14 MONUMENT with tiny recumbent effigy and two female figures. Under the tower wooden epitaph to Ann Turner † 1677, with ornament, figure of Father Time, and a Skeleton.

Many good old houses in the scattered village (Elm House, Tuthill, The Limes, etc.). The best is the RECTORY, no doubt the former manor house. It has a C15 and an early C18 half. The earlier half is a rarity in the county. It has a N front of two parts, to the l. a two-light window converted into a door, and above the long windows of the former Chapel. The pointed E window of this can also still be traced. The r. part of the old half on the N side is gabled and has a stair-turret. On the ground floor is a four-light window, on the first floor one of two lights. All these windows, also those on the less well preserved s side of the house, are straightheaded, but the individual lights are pointed and cusped. – The r. half of the house to the N and s is clearly early C18: four bays, two storeys, with mansard roof.

THERFIELD HEATH (Barrows): *see* Royston.

THORLEY

ST JAMES. Norman s doorway. Colonnettes with spiral-fluted shafts and capitals with elementary upright leaves at the angles. Arches with two orders of zigzag. Nave and chancel have C13 lancet windows preserved. No aisles. w tower C15, unbuttressed, with low stair-turret and spike. Tall C15 tower arch; the chancel arch of double-chamfered orders could be C13 still. The chancel Sedilia, however (ogee-headed), must be of the C14. The E and w windows C19 (1846, by *Pritchett*). – FONT. Square, C12, of Purbeck marble, with five shallow blank arches on each side. – REREDOS with side-panels of naturalistically carved flowers and leaves; High Victorian in style (by *J. Day*). The church was restored in 1854 by *Vulliamy*. The PULPIT and COMMUNION RAILS were designed by *Sir G. G. Scott*. – STAINED GLASS. w window, *c.* 1853, still in the painting style of the C18, that is pre-Puginesque. – PLATE. Chalice and Paten, 1562; Patens, 1809 and 1818; Flagon, 1839. – Many minor epitaphs.

THORLEY HALL, close to the church. Good C15 farmhouse with C18 modernizations (s front). Elements of the C15 can still be traced inside.

THROCKING

HOLY TRINITY. The most interesting part is the w tower; of the C13, flint-built and unbuttressed below (*see* the two deeply splayed lancet windows), but completed in brick with roundheaded windows, a corbelled-out stair-turret, and a parapet (originally with pinnacles) in 1660. An ornate brick plate outside records the date. The rest of the church is Perp. – FONT. Octagonal, Perp, with various tracery patterns on the panels of the bowl; the stem is also panelled. – BENCHES. Four in chancel with poppy-heads. – MONUMENTS. Two black floor slabs with unusually fine coats of arms, one to Thomas Soane † 1670, the other to Robert Elwes † 1752. In 1753 *Rysbrack*, one of the two most distinguished sculptors of the period in England, made the noble epitaph for Elwes: a large, very classical pedimented inscription tablet and a Rococo cartouche with coat of arms beneath; no figures. – Hester Elwes † 1770, by *Nollekens*, also an epitaph; with a seated female figure by an urn; the decorative detail remarkably Neo-Grecian for its date.

THUNDRIDGE

Of the old PARISH CHURCH, ½ m. to the E of the new, only the W tower survives, hidden by trees and covered by creepers. In it is a Norman doorway, not in its original position, with zigzag and dog-tooth decoration. To the N of the church even more immersed in the trees is one tall brick chimneystack of THUNDRIDGE BURY, the former manor house.

The new church ST MARY dates from 1853. It is by *Benjamin Ferrey*, rockfaced and with a tower alien to Herts in that it has no battlements but a stair-turret with a spirelet. – PLATE. Flagon, 1775; Chalice and Paten, 1837. – MONUMENTS. Caroline Hanbury † 1863, by *Theed*. Relief of a meticulously carved monument under a weeping willow. – R. C. Hanbury † 1867, also by *Theed*, with a dull figure of Faith.

YOUNGSBURY, the new manor house, ¾ m. NE. The front part is dated 1745, the back early C19. Later alterations. (POLES. By *Sir Ernest George*, late C19. Red brick, in the Jacobean style, with curved gables. Large curved scholastic looking additions.)

Small OBELISK erected in 1879 to the memory of Thomas Clarkson, who resolved on this spot in 1785 to devote his life to the abolition of the slave trade. The monument stands by the side of the main Cambridge road (Ermine Street).

TOTTERIDGE

Totteridge is characteristic of the outermost perimeter of London: a village church still preserved and otherwise small Georgian and big wealthy Late Victorian and Edwardian houses.

ST ANDREW, 1790. Aisleless nave of brick with arched window in Gibbs surrounds and heavy W pediment. Pretty weatherboarded bell-turret of 1706. W porch 1845. Chancel and window tracery 1869. – PAINTINGS. Virgin and Saints, demi-figures, by *Lorenzo Lotto*; an early work, presented by Lord Rothermere. St John on Patmos and the Woman of the Apocalypse, both sketches, by *Benjamin West*, uncommonly dramatic, almost in a Tintoretto way. – PULPIT. Jacobean, from Hatfield church. – STAINED GLASS. Chancel by *Clayton & Bell*, nave S and N, one window each, by *Kempe*, 1896 and 1903. – PLATE. Cup, inscribed 1614. – PROCESSIONAL CROSS. Italian, late C13. – MONUMENTS. John Puget † 1805, by *John Bacon, Jnr*, epitaph with urn. – Second World War Memorial, by *T. J. Rushton*.

Several noteworthy houses close to the church. VICARAGE, *Sir Charles Nicholson's* first building, 1892, very simple; BARN, weatherboarded, just NW of the church; GARDEN HILL and SOUTHERNHAY, W of the church, the former Early, the latter Late Georgian.

From the church TOTTERIDGE LANE runs E towards Barnet and W towards Edgware and Elstree. The following houses in the E half (from E to W) deserve mention: disused CONGREGATIONAL CHAPEL, 1827; OLD HOUSE at the NE corner of TOTTERIDGE GREEN, plain Georgian; THE CROFT at the SW end of the Green, very picturesque Late Victorian with three ranges and a court, roughcast, with Tudor windows, somewhat *à la* Voysey, by *Collcutt*, 1895. – W of the church: THE PRIORY, three-gabled Jacobean but considerably altered and restored. Then a group of pretty Georgian cottages, then GRANGE MANSIONS, a late building by *Nicholson* in the Neo-Georgian style, with Garage originally the stables of The Grange; then the MANOR HOUSE, a good five-bay mid Georgian house; Gothick GATE LODGE to Loxwood; TOTTERIDGE PARK, early C18 and early C19 but enlarged and altered out of recognition; DENHAM FARM HOUSE, with Late Georgian façade to an earlier timber-framed house, and opposite DENHAM, 1877, by *Norman*

Shaw, a picturesque, asymmetrical half-timbered house with Stables. On the same side farther W FAIRLAWN, 1710, but much altered. THE WARREN up a lane to the s is also by *Nicholson*, and also of no special character.

TRING

There is not much of architectural importance at Tring except for the church. It lies back from the HIGH STREET which here widens into a kind of square with the architecturally deplorable Rose and Crown Hotel on the other side. The High Street has nice houses; one of them (No. 23) of three storeys and four bays, late C18. – In AKEMAN STREET an odd former Nonconformist chapel with two short projecting wings, and Nos 91–92 of good C16 half-timber work. In WESTERN ROAD some pretty Early Victorian houses ending in the BRITANNIA INN facing W with its porch, that is away from the town, to welcome visitors. On the other side behind the High Street a fine C16 barn in PARSONAGE PLACE.

SS PETER AND PAUL. The s side appears from the High Street across the churchyard; flint with random stone, an oddly mottled effect. It is not specially long and the tower is not specially high. It is embattled throughout, with chequerboard patterning in the s porch and nave battlements. The earliest part of the church is the chancel with a tall C13 lancet window in the N wall. Otherwise most of what is visible is C15 to C16, except for the tower whose arch to the nave is clearly of early C14 date. The tower has angle buttresses and a SE stair-turret higher than the tower battlements. The broad spacious nave has N and S aisles of six bays with unusual piers which have four attached shafts and in the diagonals thin fillets between hollows. They were renewed in the restoration of 1880–2 (by *Bodley*), the originals going to Long Marston. The capitals and arches remained. The shafts are continued in the clerestory zone by stone shafts on figures of animals, and these shafts support the old roof. The clerestory windows are of three lights, simple Perp, as are the aisle

windows, except the larger ones at the E ends of the aisles.
– STAINED GLASS by *Kempe*, S chancel windows 1886
and 1890, several others of the 90s. – PLATE. Chalice,
1565; two large Flagons and Breadholder, 1713; Breadholder, 1723. – MONUMENTS. The monument to Sir
William Gore † 1707 and his wife is very sumptuous. It
proudly faces the porch and is the first thing that strikes
the visitor to the church. The sculptor may be *Nost*. Sir
William, in the robes of a Lord Mayor of London, and
Lady Gore lie comfortably on the concave sides of the
plinth of a big urn against an elaborate pedimented back
architecture. – John Gore † 1763, a dainty epitaph of
varied pale marbles with a small medallion against an
obelisk; two putti outside the flanking pilasters. – W.
Kay † 1838, by *J. Browne*, with a big seated female figure.
TRING PARK, a former Rothschild mansion, brick with
French pavilion roofs; nothing outside specially splendid
or showy.

TYTTENHANGER

Large brick house with the ends projecting slightly on the N 48b
or entrance side and a little more on the S or garden side.
The brick quoins, the brick window frames, the wooden
mullions and transomes of the windows, the heavy window pediments on the S side, alternatingly triangular and
segmental, the hipped roof and the rather squat cupola,
all is characteristic of a date *c.* 1660. Cussans indeed,
without quoting any authority, says that Tyttenhanger
was built by Sir Henry Blunt shortly after he had come
into possession in 1654. The magnificent staircase inside 49
with a balustrade of sumptuous openwork foliage scrolls
also goes well with that date (cf. Ham House, Surrey;
Forde Abbey, Dorset). The most characteristic features
of the 1650s, however, are the extremely odd surrounds
of windows on the S and W sides, the undisguised
asymmetry of the W side, the quite crazy doorcases in the
staircase hall, with frames growing angular excrescences
halfway up the sides, and at the top retracted friezes
carrying pediments and similar mannerisms. They are of

wood but remarkably similar in design to the stone doorway at Balls Park, Herts. Only the outer s doorway at
Tyttenhanger with a scrolly open segmental pediment on
delicately carved brackets looks embarrassingly accomplished for a pre-Wren date. Tyttenhanger, together
with Balls Park, belongs to a group of mid C17 houses for
which Mr Colvin has recently suggested *Peter Mills* as
the architect. The attribution is based on the fact found
by Mr Colvin that Mills designed Thorpe Hall in
Norfolk.

On the second floor CHAPEL with two-decker pulpit set
awkwardly in a window corner, and Ten Commandments
above the fire-place. Hour-glass attached to the pulpit.
In the attic behind the dormer windows a Long Gallery
runs along the whole length of the house. – Much linenfold and Elizabethan panelling re-used.

UPP HALL
1¼ m. SE of Braughing

Fine early C17 manor house of brick with straight gables.
The main front to the W, originally with a porch. The
window openings are very wide and had no doubt brick
mullions and transomes (cf. Hadham Hall). Only in the W
gables, below small circular openings, do brick mullions
and hood-moulds survive. Projecting wings on the E side.
More spectacular than the house itself its brick BARN,
140 ft long with diapers of vitrified headers. A number of
the original pointed-arched openings remain.

VERULAMIUM *see* ST ALBANS

WALKERN

ST MARY. The exterior does not tell of anything earlier
than the C14, until the s doorway is reached which is
clearly Norman (one order of colonnettes). It leads into
the s aisle where there is also one fairly large blocked Norman window. The arcade of two bays between aisle and
nave must be Early Norman. The arches are unmoulded

and rest on imposts of the simplest shape. One consists of four little rolls projecting in steps and decorated herring-bone-wise (cf. Little Munden). As, moreover, there is no central pier but simply a piece of thin wall left standing, one can assume that that wall is pre-Norman. The N arcade of three bays has octagonal piers with simple moulded capitals and double-chamfered arches; clearly C13, though the windows, as those of the S aisle, are Perp. The chancel was, in an extremely ham-fisted way, made E.E. by *Gough* in 1878 and 1882 (arcade to the added N chapel with two Gargantuan arcades each of two lights with elementary plate tracery). But the Sedilia and Piscina are original C13 work. The W tower is quite tall and has no buttresses. The W window shows that it was built early in the C14 (ogee-reticulated tracery). The tower arch is double-chamfered. – FONT. Octagonal with coarse cor-belled-out shafts in front of the diagonal panels (C14?). – SCREEN. C15. – MONUMENTS. Extremely good effigy of Purbeck marble representing a Knight with flat-topped helm, mid C13 (S aisle). – Brasses to a man and woman, formerly with scrolls; good quality (N aisle). – Brass to Edward Humbarstone † 1583 and wife (nave W end), with palimpsest of Flemish brass. – Epitaph with two of the usual kneeling figures, 1627 (nave). – Epitaph of David Gorsuch † 1638 and wife, also the composition of the two kneelers facing each other, but, in accordance with the later date, rather livelier figures, a more classical sur-round, and some thick fruit hangings. – In the Church-yard a scrolly obelisk (like a candelabrum) on four scrolly feet (Susannah Elwes); Early Georgian no doubt.

CONGREGATIONAL CHAPEL, 1810. Just a gabled, lightly bargeboarded front with doorway and one arched window above.

Opposite MANOR FARM, one of the usual five-bay, two-storey Georgian façades but perhaps structurally earlier; for the octagonal brick DOVECOTE with blank horizontal oval windows is no doubt late C17 (cf. Sandon). – More interesting houses along the village street to the S: the WHITE LION with a chequered brick five-bay centre and earlier end-gables, one with an early C19 Gothic doorway; ROOKS NEST FARM with one wing of timber-framing and brick, the other of brick with projecting porch. The latter wing has large mullioned brick windows.

WALKERN HALL. Early C19 house of five bays and two and a half storeys with two-storey lower wings. Greek Doric four-column porch, balustraded top.

WALKERN MILL, 1831, of brick, with small roundheaded windows.

WALL HALL see ALDENHAM

WALLINGTON

ST MARY. Perp throughout. Fine S porch with tall entrance and three-light windows. Airy nave with a large S window and large N aisle windows. Arcade to the N aisle with piers with four shafts and four hollows in the diagonals. The N aisle roof is original. The chancel opens in a four-centred arch to a N chapel. The rest of the chancel was rebuilt in 1864. – FONT. Octagonal bowl of Purbeck marble with two shallow pointed arches in each panel. – SCREEN. C15, with very simple tracery. – BENCHES. Completely preserved C15 benches with thin backs. – STAINED GLASS. C15 bits in the N chapel. – PLATE. Cup, 1754; Paten, 1840. – MONUMENTS. Tomb-chest without effigy; on the sides alternatingly broad panels with shields and narrow niches with small C15 figures under crocketed ogee canopies.

WALTHAM CROSS

There is now no break along the Roman Ermine Street between London and Middlesex and between Middlesex and Herts. Some fifty years ago there still was. One can notice between Enfield and Waltham Cross where the pre-Victorian ribbon of houses comes to an end, where the Victorian additions come to an end, and where first the former and then the latter begin again on the Herts side. Only a quarter mile from the border stands

32a WALTHAM CROSS, one of the Eleanor Crosses, that is the crosses erected by Edward I to commemorate the resting-places of his dead queen, Eleanor of Castile, on the way from Harby in Leicestershire where she had died to Westminster Abbey. There were twelve in all. Most of them have disappeared; only those at Northampton, Geddington, and Waltham remain. Charing Cross was the last of them. The Waltham Cross was begun in 1291. The masons were *Nicholas Dyminge de Reyne* and *Roger Crundale*, and the sculptor or *imaginator* was *Alexander of Abingdon*. The Cross was heavily restored. In fact the second and third stages were rebuilt in 1833 and again in 1883. In 1950 yet another restoration was begun. In the history of Gothic architecture in England, the Eleanor Crosses are of considerable importance. They (and St Stephen's Chapel, Westminster) mark the earliest departure from the purity of the E.E., that is the classic Gothic style, and the dawn of the Dec style with its complexities and sophistication. The Waltham Cross is hexagonal first of all, which is an odd shape, without the axial clarity of the square, circle, or octagon. A glance at the main stage with the figures will explain what is meant by this. There are three figures standing in niches under canopies, the niches framed by the buttress-like supports of the canopies. But on the remaining three sides the rhythm changes and although there are also niches they are not framed by buttresses but have one buttress each right in the middle, in front of the niches, a typical Dec complication. The statues also have no longer the crispness and sharpness of E.E. sculpture (e.g. at Westminster Abbey *c.* 1260–70) but a tendency in the draperies to congeal, as it were, and in the whole figures to become part of a general flowing undulation. Decoration is profuse. The lowest stage has blank two-light arches crowned by crocketed gables and with quatrefoils in the spandrels, still a pure Geometrical kind of tracery. The foliage of the capitals is naturalistic, as far as that can still be seen, and no longer stiff-leaf. The spaces to the l. and r. of the gables are decorated with diapering. All this does hardly go beyond Westminster Abbey. But the upper parts of the second stage have become a jungle of crockets and finials. The self-discipline of the E.E. style is evidently disappearing.

What there is of interest in Waltham houses is in the HIGH STREET, especially S of the Cross on the W side HAROLD HOUSE, No. 73, of yellow brick, with an Ionic doorcase and a pediment decorated by a cartouche with the date 1757; and N of the Cross on the E side GREENFIELD HOUSE with a late C18 porch.

HOLY TRINITY, towards the N end of the High Street, was built in 1832. It is of yellow brick and has the tall, rather gaunt character of churches of that time. The one-light and two-light Perp lancets (an odd combination) are characteristic. No aisles, no galleries. The E parts were remodelled very well in 1914 by *Ayres*. Tall double transeptal openings with piers without any capitals. No E window at all, but N and S windows concealed by an arch across the chancel at the entry to the altar-space.

THEOBALDS: *see* p. 246.

WARE

11bST MARY. The parish church lies in the centre of the town at the very crossing of High Street and Baldock Street. It is a typical Herts town church, of flint, all embattled, and all too thoroughly restored. Nearly all the windows are renewed, and it is often not possible to say how accurately. Those of the show sides of the transepts are an invention of *G. Godwin*, who restored the church in 1848. (Further restorations 1885 and 1905.) The existence of transepts is the only unusual feature of the church. The W tower is tall, in fact of five stages, has thin angle buttresses and the characteristic Herts spike. Of the windows the most interesting (probably old, because hardly the sort of thing the Victorians would have invented) are those with flowing, that is *c.* 1330, tracery in the S aisle. The only detail in the church which goes farther back is one fragment of a S chancel window found and left uncovered. It proves the chancel to be C13 work. The rest of the window was destroyed when *c.* 1400 a S chancel chapel was built and connected with the chancel by an ambitious double bay

one wide arch subdivided into two by a Purbeck marble
shaft (with the well-known four-shafts-and-four-hollows
profile) and by a spandrel pierced by Perp tracery. The
nave arcades of four bays plus one taller and wider arch
corresponding to the transepts is later still. It has tall slim
piers of a typical complex C15 profile. Only inside the
arches are small capitals employed between shaft and
arch, the main mouldings towards nave and aisle run
through uninterrupted. – Pretty C15 recess in the N transept. – FONT, c. 1400; the most richly decorated medieval 30b
font in the county; octagonal, of stone, with quatrefoil
panels on the short stem and on the big bowl figures of the
Virgin and the Archangel Gabriel, St Margaret, St Christopher, St George, St Katharine, St James, and St John
the Baptist. Between them demi-figures of angels alternately carrying musical instruments and Instruments of
the Passion. The carving is rather coarse and stocky. –
PULPIT. Mid C17 with raised panels but still tapering
pilasters at the angles. – COMMUNION RAILS. S chapel
mid C17, from Benington, unusual shape, as if panelling
were made transparent by leaving only the broad frames
and taking away all the infillings. – PANELLING. S chapel.
Handsome late C17 work with a top band of openwork
foliage scrolls. – DOOR from chancel to N vestry. C14 or
C15, with three locks. – STAINED GLASS. E and W windows by *Wailes*, 1849–50, strident colours, and the types
of the figures not inspired by the style of c. 1300 but
rather by the Nazarenes or Raphael. – Chapman Allen
window, S aisle, c. 1885; a characteristic example of the
gradual influence of the Pre-Raphaelites on the typical
Victorian glass style. By *Shrigley & Hunt*. N transept N
window, c. 1910, by *Whall*, inspired by the Pre-Raphaelites but refreshingly different from the ordinary run of
early C20 windows. By the same one N aisle window,
1905. – PLATE. Chalice, 1618; Paten, 1806; small Chalice,
1806. – MONUMENTS. Brasses to Elene Warbulton † 1454
(N transept); to a lady, c. 1425 (N transept); to W. Pyrry
† 1470, with wife and children. – Pretty Epitaph to R.
Atkinson † 1756, by *H. Cox*. The usual obelisk but at its

foot to the l. a row of books, to the r. a Rococo cartouche with arms. – W. Murvell † 1826, by *Rouw*, heavy and severely Greek epitaph, white marble. – The churchyard has nice cast-iron gates and railings.

THE PRIORY (Urban District Council). The remains not of a priory but of the house of the Franciscans at Ware. The present large house grew out of it after the Dissolution and exhibits easily recognizable C17 and C18 work. What is earlier and goes back to the Franciscans and the C15 is the S side and part of the W side of the Cloisters with openings consisting of three lancet lights under a four-centred arch, and a range projecting to the W from the W wing. This has straightheaded two-light windows on two floors with pointed and cusped heads to the individual lights, and an open kingpost roof now no longer accessible. What was the use of the range at the time of the friars is not known (guest house?).

INFANTS SCHOOL, Park Road (*see* Introduction, p. 28).

PERAMBULATION

From the centre Baldock Street leads N, the High Street E to the bridges across the river Lea and the New River. Both streets have much to recommend them, mostly in their combination of C16–C17 timber-framed and gabled with C18 red brick houses. In BALDOCK STREET the best building of the earlier type is the BULL INN with overhang, two gables, and two first floor oriel windows. Opposite Nos 43–49 are the usual plastered C17 cottages. The best brick houses are Nos 27 (five bays, three storeys, Ionic doorcase) and No. 35, both first half C18. The same story *en miniature* Nos 10–12 and No. 8, the former timber-framed, the latter brick. At the N end of Baldock Street lies on the r. THUNDER HALL, a tall Jacobean brick house with central (former) porch and gable. It was remodelled and cemented over early in the C19,* when also a gatehouse and cloisters were added so that now the whole building seems of that period. Opposite is CANONS

* It is said by *Wyatt*. Does that mean the elder or the younger?

HOTEL, yellow brick with a Greek Doric porch. Then
one of the most interesting buildings of Ware; CANONS
MALTINGS which incorporates a range of two-storeyed
red brick malthouses of *c.* 1600. The W side has a row of
buttresses, the E side one three-light brick window with
hood-mould, still with four-centred heads to the individual lights.
The HIGH STREET runs parallel with the river Lea. The
houses had originally gardens stretching down to the
river, and perhaps their most unusual feature is that a
number of them has gazebos of brick or weatherboarded 7a
by or overhanging the river. Otherwise the street has also
the alternating rhythm of the gabled and picturesque with
the straight and regular. Nos 84–88 with three gables and
some good ceilings inside is the best C16 example. In
complete contrast to it Nos 74–76, a two-storeyed, urban,
eight-bay, stock brick façade with the shop windows set in
blank arcades. Opposite Nos 61–65 are plastered, two-
storeyed, and gabled houses of the C17; No. 65 has some
C15 details remaining inside; No. 67 is mid C18 of purple
brick with rubbed red brick dressings. The same difference is repeated between Nos 51–53 or 35–37 and the
good Georgian fronts of Nos 43–47 between them. An
effect worth noting is how WEST STREET runs parallel
with, and close to, the High Street but opens out into it
in one place about the middle of its course. Here, nobly
recessed from the High Street, stands the OLD TOWN
HALL, a plain Regency house of seven bays with a heavy
unfluted Ionic. EAST STREET also runs parallel to the
High Street. It must be visited because it has in No. 2A
a dated example of the usual purple brick front with
rubbed brick dressings (1709; with curly lintels to the
second, fourth, and sixth upper windows). Next to it an
archway below a niche opens in a house of about the
same date. It leads into BLUECOAT YARD. Here on the
r. is Bluecoat House, the former manor house of Ware,
a C15 timber-framed house (*see* the front door and some
beams inside) altered in the C16 and C17. It was the
Bluecoat School from 1674 to 1761. Opposite it a long

terrace of almshouse-like cottages was erected in 1698 for nurses and children. They are still entirely pre-classical in their character, timber-framed with horizontal windows and dormers. Back to the High Street where, towards the E end, there is one more good early C18 house: No. 21 with a carriageway and next to it a door-case with Gibbs surround.

From the E end of the High Street straight on into STAR STREET with perhaps the most interesting building of Ware, Messrs Albany's CORN STORES. They incorporate a large C17 quadrangle of storehouses originally with an open courtyard. The upper floor is reached by outer ladders under lean-to roofs and has open timber roofs all the way round. Such large commercial premises of so early a date are rare indeed.

Across the river and the New River to LONDON ROAD. Facing the bridges the former AMWELL HOUSE, John Scott's the Quaker poet's house (Ware Grammar School for Girls), a stately red brick mansion of c. 1730 with three-storey centre of five bays and far-projecting two-storey wings with Venetian front windows. MILBROOK HOUSE, to the E, now also belongs to the Grammar School. It is of c. 1820, yellow brick, and has at the back an odd battlemented bow window with Gothick windows. John Scott's gardens were extensive, and their pride, his GROTTO, fortunately still exists (Scott's Road). It was built in the 1770s and is, though on a small scale, far more complex than Alexander Pope's at Twickenham. Com-pared with the grotto at Stourhead, on the other hand, it is minute. But that only enhances the enchantment. It con-sists of quite a number of passages and chambers laid out as intricately as the catacombs of Rome. They are to a varying degree lined with flints, shell, quartz, bits of glass, etc. The daylight is not entirely excluded; in two places a sudden glimpse of the greenery of the garden is caught by a small two-light Gothick and a still smaller circular win-dow. Moreover, the largest room has an indirect skylight. But the second largest room is all in darkness, a room with a central pillar and originally a number of ribs towards the walls in the fashion of Gothic chapter houses. The patterns of the shell decoration vary from chamber to chamber, sometimes a complete lining, once cemented walls with a 'polka-dot' pattern of shells, and once a trellis pattern. The largest rooms are only 12⅓ ft and 6½ ft in diameter.

FANHAMS HALL, 1¼ m. NE. A Queen Anne house of moderate size with a delightful staircase, converted by *W. Wood Bethell* in 1900–1 into a vast Neo-Tudor affair (e.g. with a gallery 107 ft long). The plasterwork by *Lawrence L. Turner*.

EASNEYE, 1½ m. SE, *c.* 1868, by *Waterhouse*. Red brick, with much diapering, masses of stepped gables, details of tracery, etc., in the E.E. style and much use of red terra-cotta. Rather harsh and unsympathetic in the general effect.

WARESIDE

HOLY TRINITY, 1841, by *Thomas Smith*. Of stock brick in the Norman style. Nave, wide transepts with galleries in them, and apse (polygonal outside). In front of the altar rails the Puginesque brass to a vicar who died in 1845.

A quarter of a mile S of the church a half-timbered house proudly dated 1843 and indeed happily incorrect in its arrangement of the timbers.

WATER END FARM *see* WHEATHAMPSTEAD

WATERFORD HALL *see* STAPLEFORD

WAYTEMORE CASTLE *see* BISHOPS STORTFORD

WATFORD

Watford with *c.* 73,000 inhabitants is by far the largest town of Herts. It is clearly a town of its own, yet with its red London buses, its terminus of a London tube line, and its many names and fascia-boards of shops familiar to the Londoner, it never allows one to forget that in many ways one is still in London when one walks through Watford. The urban area of Watford is wider than its population figure would make one expect. It extends to the sw through Bushey and Oxhey and in the se towards Rickmansworth. New estates of council houses, both H.C.C. and L.C.C., are growing up rapidly, and Watford's own development is steady too, since the town's industries, chiefly brewing (Benskin's) and printing and its allied trades, are not suffering much under trade crises.

The old Watford of pre-Victorian days is still easily discernible. It consists of the church and its closest surroundings and the long High Street leading down towards the river Colne and on to Bushey and London. The river skirts on two sides the hill on which the town stands. The railway crosses the river valley by a fine long and high brick VIADUCT once apparently one of the main sights of Watford.

St MARY. Hidden from the High Street by a screen of low houses and placed in a large churchyard with an abundance of old trees.* The church itself is of flint, long, broad, and low, with a big, solid w tower. The tower has diagonal buttresses, battlements, a NE stair-turret, and a spike. The chancel dates from the early C13, as can be seen inside from the double Piscina and the chancel arch. Its capitals and double-chamfered arches repeat in the low long s arcade of the nave. The N arcade is C15, yet at first sight very similar. Both arcades have octagonal piers and two-centred arches. The differences lie in the taller piers, the more finely moulded capitals, and the slightly taller hollow-chamfered arches. The outer walls of the aisles, the clerestory, the nave roof with beams resting on carved angels, the s chancel chapel with tall slim octagonal pier and four-centred arches, and the tower are also C15. The N chancel chapel (Morrison Chapel) was added in 1595 (see the Tuscan columns of the arcade to the nave – cf. Hatfield church – and the mullioned and transomed E window). – PULPIT, 1714, by *Richard Bull*, with daintily carved borders to the panels, etc. – VESTMENT CUPBOARD, c. 1730, Flemish or French, with the four evan-

* The churchyard was altered in 1952.

gelists in medallions. – PLATE. Chalice, 1561 ; Chalice and Cover, 1610; two Flagons, 1628; two Breadholders, 1637; Almsdish, 1642. – MONUMENTS. Brasses to Hugh de Holes † 1415 and his wife † 1416 (?), largish figures, of good quality; the man, in judge's robes, bigger than the woman. – Brass to three retainers of the Morrison family; two of them died in 1610 and 1613. – In the Morrison Chapel wall monument perhaps to Bridget, widow of Richard Morrison of Cassiobury and later wife of the second Earl of Bedford, who built the chapel in 1595 (no inscription): the usual kneeling figure between two columns. The monuments to her son and grandson are the chief glory of Watford church and among the best sculptural works of their date in the county. Both are by *Nicholas Stone* and both of alabaster and touch. Both also are of the most ambitious type : standing wall monuments with life-size figures. Sir Charles Morrison † 1590 (made 34 in 1619). He rests semi-reclining between columns supporting two segmental arches and a larger segmental arch above. To the l. and r. outside the columns two kneeling figures against baldacchinos of richly crumpled fabric. No Jacobean mannerisms are left, and the skill of portraiture is admirable. Opposite the monument to Sir Charles Morrison † 1628 ('splendidissimo et clarissimo viro'). He lies semi-reclining behind and slightly above his wife's recumbent figure. The monument this time is a tall four-poster and above the two segmental arches are two gables. Two kneeling figures outside the columns as in the earlier monument. – Many minor later monuments, e.g. Anne Derne † 1790, graceful epitaph of varied marbles, by *J. Golde* of High Holborn.

ST ANDREW, Church Road, 1857, by *Teulon*. Rather restrained for that architect. s aisle added 1865.

HOLY ROOD (R.C.), Market Street, 1883–90, by *Bentley*, then about 45 years old. One of the noblest examples of the refined, knowledgeable, and sensitive Gothic Revival of that time. The flint exterior combines vestries and other outer rooms into a square plan. The main accent is the square NW tower. In addition two turrets with copper spires. Flint with stone bands in the Herts tradition; the tracery C14, but other detail clearly influenced by Arts and Crafts innovations. Plain nave, transept of two bays width with two-storeyed opening to the nave. This and the elevation of the chancel with square ambulatory and well-passage above it, in front of the large upper windows, are remarkable yet not obtrusively original.

BAPTIST CHURCH, Clarendon Road, 1876–8, by *J. Wallis Chapman*. In a semi-Italian Romanesque style with apse towards the street and attached campanile with pyramid roof. Purple brick with red brick dressings.

TOWN HALL, Hemel Hempstead Road and Rickmansworth Road, 1940, by *C. Cowles-Voysey*. At the main traffic junction of Watford and repeating in its plan the lines of the two streets and the roundabout between them. Above the concave centre a Swedish-modern lantern. The building is otherwise in chaste Neo-Georgian forms. With the Hospital next to it, the Library, and the Swimming Baths, it forms the nucleus of a civic centre for Watford.

MINISTRY OF LABOUR HEADQUARTERS, built close to Watford Junction railway station as the London Orphan Asylum by *H. Dawson* in 1869–71. Large group of brick buildings in an undistinguished Gothic style.

MRS ELIZABETH FULLER FREE SCHOOL (*see* below).

(*see* below)

PERAMBULATION

The visual centre of Watford is now by the Town Hall. It was once by the church. Around the churchyard there still are on the N a row of nice low cottages, on the S the MRS ELIZABETH FULLER FREE SCHOOL, a delightful three-bay brick building of 1704 with arched windows, stone quoins, door with segmental pediment and central cupola, and on the W the BEDFORD ALMSHOUSES, founded in 1580. They have a five-gabled plastered front with the two outer gables a little smaller than the others. Round the corner in KING STREET: WATFORD PLACE, a white villa of *c.* 1825 with four-column Ionic portico, and in VICARAGE ROAD the Morrison Almshouses, re-built in an uninteresting Neo-Gothic style in 1824.

From the churchyard to the N and E the HIGH STREET can be reached. In NEW STREET a four-bay, three-storeyed brick house of early C18 type. At the corner of Church Street and High Street a C16 half-timbered house with overhang. To the N the prevalent character of the High Street is C20 urban. To the S there are still stretches of small old houses of quite a county town character, especially Nos 129, etc., and on the other side Nos 154, etc. A little lower down BENSKIN'S BREWERY, the stately C18 dwelling-house towards the street (five bays, two and a half storeys, with three-bay pediment and lower outer wings) and behind it the tall Victorian brewing premises of yellow brick. On the other side of the road some maltings of 1836 still exist. Yet lower down the High Street on the E side No. 223 with good doorcase (fluted Ionic pilasters and Venetian window above), on the W side Nos 244–248, an eight-bay, cemented late C17 house. The end is Frogmore House on the E side, immediately by the gasometer, a four-bay, three-storeyed house of c. 1700 with rusticated doorcase with Roman Doric pilasters, carved metopes, and a hood on carved brackets.

The High Street N of the church is not entirely without older houses but they rather tend to be overlooked. Note HALSEY HOUSE (Conservative Club) on the W side, long Early Victorian stuccoed façade, and on the E side MON-MOUTH HOUSE, a completely reconstructed early C17 brick house. The exterior has now four gables; some interior features are preserved in their original state. Past the Town Hall in the HEMEL HEMPSTEAD ROAD, No. 3 (Education Offices), the best classical house at Watford: late C17 front of nine bays but not as wide as that number of windows would make one expect. The bays are very narrow projections with squeezed-in windows. The central three bays also project, a lively rhythm of forward and backward movement. – A little to the N in CHURCH ROAD the SALTER'S COMPANY ALMSHOUSES, 1863, by *John Collier*, an almost ideal example of charitable mid

Victorian architecture. One long central range and two short projecting wings. Red brick, Tudor style. The centre motif completely asymmetrical with a tower and a stepped gable. Fine cedar trees between the buildings. Ornate iron gates to the street.

Farther out to the NW (1½ m. from the centre) GROVE MILL HOUSE and HEATH FARM HOUSE, good farmhouses, and THE GROVE. The Lodges towards Hemel Hempstead Road of late C18 stuccoed architecture. The house was built by *Sir Robert Taylor* in 1756, enlarged *c.* 1780 and again *c.* 1850. It is a block of red brick with stone quoins. The centres on the two principal fronts are emphasized by angle pilasters. The E part is older than the larger W part. On the other side of Hemel Hempstead Road is RUSSELL'S, now a H.C.C. Home, a good red brick house with pediments on two sides. It has the date 1718 on a weathervane. The S entrance is oddly placed in the central bow window. Much new H.C.C. housing of good design to the NE of Russell's and beyond the North-Western Avenue. Between Kingsway and Leavesden High Road one of the new H.C.C. SCHOOLS (*see* Introduction, p. 28).

Back to Watford by the North-Western Avenue. Just beyond its E end in COLNE WAY (and off St Albans Road) ODHAMS PRESS, big brick factory with long low bands of windows, a symmetrical façade by *Sir Owen Williams*, 1937.

LANGLEYBURY *see* p. 152.
REDHEATH *see* p. 191.

WATTON-AT-STONE

ST ANDREW AND ST MARY. An all-embattled flint church of the C15 with two porches, a rood stair-turret on the S side, and a tower stair-turret rising higher than the tower battlements. The N porch is two-storeyed with a broad stair-turret on the E side. The view from the NE towards all these various castellated parts is especially enjoyable. Most of the windows are renewed but represent the Perp 'panel' tracery of the originals accurately. The E window is original. The interior has a four-bay arcade with particularly characteristic Late Perp piers. They are of a complicated section (the same as at Ware) with a double curve and several hollows and have capitals only to the innermost shafts under the arches. The main mouldings carry on into the voussoirs without any break. A Perp N chapel was added in 1851 and provided with a Neo-Jacobean tunnel-vault. – MONUMENTS. Brass to a Knight in armour under ogee canopy with thin buttresses and pinnacles. The figure is said to represent Sir Philip Pele-tot † 1361. It is 4 ft 9 in. long and restored (N chapel). Brass to a civilian, C15 (N chapel). – Brass to a Knight in armour, early C16 (N chapel). – Brass to a civilian, head-less, C15 (N aisle). – Brass to a lady, Early Elizabethan, lower part missing (nave, E end). – Brass to a priest, mid C15, very good large figure (4 ft 9 in.; chancel). – Large incised alabaster slab to John Boteler of Woodhall and his two wives. One of them died in 1471. The inscription runs at the head end, the wrong way up. John Boteler's date of death remained blank (N chapel). – Standing wall monument to Philip Boteler † 1712 and wife. Frontally kneeling figures in a shallow Gothic recess, he in contemporary costume, she as a Roman matron. They suffer from lack of leg space. – Sir Thomas Rumbold † 1791, by *Bacon*, with a delicate relief of a mourning female in a tondo. Two urns in the shallowest relief to the l. and r. – W. R. Rumbold † 1786, with a big urn wreathed with an oak garland. Probably also by *Bacon* but unsigned.

The best thing in the village is a baluster-shaped early C19 cast-iron PUMP. It stands close to WATTON HALL, a timber-framed plastered house with three parallel overhang gables to the street. N of them three trefoil brick arches, no doubt Early Tudor, have recently been discovered underneath the plaster.

BROOM HALL, ¾ m. W. Late C16 brick house with central porch, central chimney, and on the upper floor partly original windows with brick mullions and four-centred heads to the individual lights.

WATTON WOODHALL *see* WOODHALL PARK

WELWYN

Nowadays people often forget that Welwyn is not a garden city but an old little town of much charm and far enough away from the garden city not to be entirely swamped by suburban developments however tasteful.

ST MARY. The exterior is too drastically restored to have preserved any of its original character. The SW tower, nave, clerestory, N aisle (with its odd N gable), S aisle wall, and S chancel chapel were newly built in the 1910. Inside, the chancel has a long lancet window in the S wall and two blocked ones in the N wall. The E end has a group of three stepped-up lancets, with Purbeck marble shafts inside. The Double Piscina has pointed trefoil heads. The chancel arch is double-chamfered on broadly moulded capitals. The forms of these and the arches are repeated in the S arcade of four bays. – SCREEN and COMMUNION RAIL destroyed by fire in 1952. – PLATE. Chalice, 1666; Paten, 1678; Flagon, 1750. – MONUMENT. Edward Young, author of *Night Thoughts* and *On Original Composition*, who was Vicar of Welwyn from 1730 to 1765.

Plenty of enjoyable houses near the church. Immediately to the SE one of brick and timber; opposite this, across CHURCH STREET, a Georgian five-bay house. At the end of Church Street Wendover Lodge, white Late Georgian three-bay house with additions. In MILL LANE the former ASSEMBLY ROOMS, just S of the White Horse Inn, red brick, low, of five bays, now divided into cottages. At the S end of Mill Lane more minor Georgian architecture.

Facing the entrance of the road from St Albans the WHITE HART and its neighbour, both red brick Georgian. The White Hart was largely built *c.* 1760–5. A little to the W School Lane leads to NEW PLACE, built in 1880 by *Philip Webb* for his brother. It is of brick, L-shaped, with Webb's typical sash-windows with relieving arches, but buttresses and a steep-pitched roof. To the N of the White Hart High Street runs towards the church. By the crossing of the river Mimvam BRIDGE on the way towards the church by the bridge BRIDGE COTTAGE with iron verandah and monkey puzzle, and BRIDGE HOUSE, and opposite this a house with pretty semicircular porch. w of the church the WELLINGTON HOTEL with some old half-timbering but usually c. 1725, and then at the exit to the N more detached Georgian houses. Not one of all these houses is of the first order; but their grouping around the church and the streets fanning out from it is attractive.

LOCKLEYS. Nine-bay brick house of 1717 now a school. Two-storeyed with angle pilasters and attic above the cornice. Doorway with segmental pediment on Roman Doric columns. Segmentheaded windows. The dressings of fine rubbed bricks. – In the grounds an important ROMAN VILLA has been excavated. This was originally built of timber and mud in the C1 A.D. It was then a rectangular house of five rooms with an open colonnade in front. In the C2 wings were added and the colonnade was rebuilt. The plan of the villa marked in turf and brick.

WELWYN GARDEN CITY

Welwyn Garden City was planned and built entirely after the First World War. It is thus a later creation than Letchworth and the Hampstead Garden Suburb and differs in characteristic ways from both. It is not pioneer work like *Parker & Unwin's*, but the architects of Welwyn, *Louis de Soissons* and *A. W. Kenyon*, have evidently learnt from the mistakes of the pioneers.

Welwyn Garden City extends on both sides of the railway 63b which runs here in a straight line roughly from S to N. To the E of, and close to the railway is the industrial area; for a garden city as against a garden suburb must possess enough industry to ensure it an independent life. Architecturally best amongst the factories are the SHREDDED WHEAT COMPANY, 1925, by *L. de Soissons* and ROCHE PRODUCTS, by *Otto Salvisberg* of Zurich,

1938–40 (addition 1952). Towards w from the railway station runs a short boulevard with planted centre. This meets at right angles the main N–S artery, also a parkway. At its N end a semicircular exedra is intended to have important public buildings. At present the main public buildings and also the five-storeyed Stores, and the shopping area are all by the station and the parkway. This urban-looking area is something that the Hampstead Garden Suburb lacks and that Letchworth received only slowly and never adequately, owing to its arrested growth.

The residential layout is clearly derived from the *Unwin* ideas and patterns. Old trees are meticulously kept, straight roads are rare, and closes everywhere determine the pattern. The predominant style of the houses, however, has characteristically changed since Letchworth. It is now a quiet comfortable Neo-Georgian, no longer olde-worldy. The brickwork is mostly exposed.

LUDWICK CORNER, Cole Green Lane. By *Sir Ernest Newton*, 1907.

PENTLEY PARK JUNIOR MIXED AND INFANTS SCHOOL and HOLLYBUSH LANE SECONDARY MODERN SCHOOL (*see* Introduction, p. 28).

The original Welwyn plan provided for a growth to *c.* 50,000 inhabitants. In 1948 the Welwyn area was thrown together for planning purposes with Hatfield New Town, and a revised plan worked out (consulted architect and planner *Louis de Soissons*). The future populations for the two are now 36,500 for Welwyn and 25,000 for Hatfield. Building schemes of the last few years are SOUTH PARKWAY, LEMSFORD LANE S of this, and, at the other side of the railway, about 1½ m. to the E HOMESTEAD COURT (with several blocks of flats of no special architectural interest) and, again to the E, COLE GREEN LANE. Here houses are by *Hening & Chitty*, and *P. Mauger & Partners*.

WEST HYDE

ST THOMAS, 1844, by *Thomas Smith* (GR). Flint with cemented brick dressings. In the Norman style. Nave,

transepts, and narrower chancel. A porch and a corresponding excrescence in the angles between transepts and
chancel. A roof ridge runs through the transepts and the
crossing at right angles to the nave; an odd effect.

WESTBROOK MAY *see* BOXMOOR

WESTMILL

ST MARY. It is only by looking at the SE angle of the nave
that one can recognize the Anglo-Saxon origin of the
church. No other feature as early as that exists. The next
in order of time is the N arcade (two bays). Two pointed
arches, unmoulded, are cut through the Saxon N wall.
They look later C12. Then comes the chancel, with one
straightheaded C13 window. The others are C19.
Altogether the church is too much restored to be very
rewarding. The chancel arch is C15, the very tall tower
arch and the whole W tower with diagonal buttresses and
Herts spike essentially *c.* 1500. – FONT. Octagonal, Perp,
with fleurons in quatrefoils, circles, etc.; also blank tracery.
– CHANCEL SEATS. Some with poppy-heads and very
gaunt long human heads. – BENCHES. Simple C15, buttressed. – COMMUNION RAILS, with twisted balusters,
late C17. – PLATE. Chalice, 1563; Paten, 1630; large
Paten, 1713.
A pretty group of cottages along the S side of the churchyard, started at the E end by the early C18 brick mansion
WESTMILL BURY (five bays, two storeys) and its fine
brick-fronted barn.

WESTON

HOLY TRINITY. The uncommon importance of the church
is its Norman crossing with the four crossing arches and 16a
the lower part of the tower complete. In addition the N
transept with two Norman windows is preserved and the
blocked arch which opened no doubt into an apsidal
chapel. The S transept also survives though entirely

altered. Presumably the church had two apsidal transept chapels and an apsidal E end. Of the Norman nave one can say nothing. The Norman parts are of flint with stone dressings. The upper part of the tower was built in 1867. The crossing piers have capitals a little more complex than most such Norman arches in Herts, and abaci with a little billet or crescent decoration. The present nave and S aisle (octagonal piers, double-hollow-chamfered arches) with clerestory are Perp. The clerestory windows now look into the heightened aisle. The nave ceiling is divided into square panels; the beams rest on grotesque head corbels. The chancel was rebuilt in 1840 by *Thomas Smith* in the Norman style. It seems odd to us now to see how a hundred years ago such a brick chancel with such ornate Norman trim was considered a match for the austerity of the original work. – FONT. Octagonal, Perp, with quatrefoil panels. – STAINED GLASS. Chancel N and S window still with what may well be glass of *c*. 1840. – PLATE. Chalice, 1638; Paten, 1661.

A good village with many pretty houses on the W side away from the church.

WHEATHAMPSTEAD

St HELEN. A big flint church with a chancel as long as the nave and a dominating crossing tower with a broached lead spire starting like a pyramidal roof (an odd outline due to the C19 restoration). Of a Norman church the foundations of an apse have been discovered. The nave no doubt corresponded to the present nave. The chancel was added *c*. 1230 (*see* the fine group of three lancet windows in the E wall, with nook shafts inside, and the N doorway with dog-tooth decoration). The crossing tower with its heavy treble-stepped piers belongs probably to the later C13. The early C14 is responsible for the W door (with its ball flower ornament) and the S aisle and S porch. The two-light windows at the aisle W end and the octagonal piers with their moulded capitals and double-hollow-chamfered arches are typical of that date. Of the same date are the transepts, and here much money must have been available and an architect with a good sense of display. The N transept N window is of five lights, the S transept S window of four. Both have ogee-reticulated tracery. Moreover, the S transept E window has some very original finely ogee-cusped tracery and big fleurons inside along jambs and voussoirs. In the N transept the windows have even two orders of (smaller) fleurons. The E window has fleurons outside as well, and inside below the sill a delightful blank frieze of crocketed ogee arches with brackets for statuettes. Nothing else of the Dec style in the county, with the exception of the E end at St Albans, is quite so rich. The same designer inserted equally original windows in the chancel N and S walls. The N arcade of the nave is later than that of the S, although the N aisle has windows of early C14 date. The clerestory windows were given their present shape in 1863–6. The only notable contribution of the later Middle Ages is the charming canopied Piscina in the chancel tucked in diagonally by the Sedilia. – FONT. Early C14, octagonal with quatrefoil circles on finely carved but somewhat decayed leaves. – PULPIT. Jacobean, from the former chapel at Lamer House. – BENCHES. In the N transept. From the same chapel; two benches dated 1631. – SCREEN. Fragments in the N transept and at the W end, Jacobean, and probably made up of fragments from a former W gallery. – PAINTING. Mount of Olives by *King*, 1821, large figure. The frame is in a thin Gothic taste. – STAINED GLASS. *Kempe*, 1893, N aisle, first window from E. – MONUMENTS. A large number. Brass to Hugh Bostok and wife, *c.* 1436 (N transept); good large frontal figures; the parents of Abbot Wheathampstead of St Albans. – Brass to John Heyworth † 1520 and wife (N transept), small figures slightly in profile. – Man and wife with children, *c.* 1520 (N transept). – Headless Lady, leg of a Knight and dog at his foot, C15 (S transept). – Brass Indents chancel N with stone surround. – John Heyworth † 1558 and wife (N transept), the figures small, incised in a marble slab, with a modest architectural surround; at the foot simplest strapwork (cf.

Harpenden, Cressye). – Sir John Brocket † 1558 and wife (s transept) : alabaster tomb-chest with recumbent effigies. The decoration with figures and heraldry is just on the point of leaving the Gothic style and going classical. No refinements. – Garrard Monument N transept, the largest in the church, undated and not fully identified. The date must be in the 1630s, and the design is conservative for that date. Alabaster semi-reclining figures, the husband behind and slightly above the wife, big architectural surround and columns, coffered arch, and allegorical figures in the spandrels of the arch top achievement. – Many Garrard tablets in the N transept, one of them, hung up much too high to be seen, is by *Thorwaldsen* (Charles Drake G. † 1817 : two Grecian figures holding each other by the hand; in the style of Athenian stelae).

WATER END FARM, 1¾ m. E, originally a manor house of the Jennings family. The house lies picturesquely by a ford. It is of brick, has quite an ambitious symmetrical W front with three straight gables, three shallow two-storeyed bay windows, and two small straight-headed doorways. Fine large decorated chimney-stacks. The house is said to have been built about 1610.

ROMAN REMAINS, on the N side of the road from St Albans to Welwyn. The remains probably represent the capital of Cassivelaunus, the British chieftain who opposed Julius Caesar in 54 B.C. On the slopes above the river Lea are two stretches of earthworks, the W known as the Devil's Dyke on account of its size. This is 1,400 ft long, 130 ft wide, and originally 40 ft deep. On the E side of this 100-acre enclosure is another ditch, known as the Slad, 1,200 ft long, 80 ft wide, and 15 ft deep.

WHITWELL

A pretty village with, along the High Street, the Youth Hostel, red brick, of three bays, c. 1700, and three other houses of brick and of half-timber work (Bull Inn).

WICKHAM HALL see BISHOPS STORTFORD

WIDFORD

St John the Baptist. Unbuttressed Perp w tower with low rectangular stair-turret, characteristic tower arch, and recessed spire. Nave and chancel under one roof. s porch C19. In the nave above the s doorway a reset C12 zigzag arch. One s window with Dec tracery, the rest Perp and much of the tracery new. – PILLAR PISCINA. A Norman block capital with the front semicircle decorated; early C12, it seems. – DOOR, C14 with C13 ironwork (says the R. Commission). – WALL PAINTINGS. E. and N walls of chancel. On the N wall Christ of the Apocalypse with sword; c. 1500. – PLATE. Specially good Chalice of 1562 with Paten.

WIDFORDBURY. C17 farmhouse, but to its E, now used as churchyard wall, the brick wall of a much larger former house with C16 bricks, a four-centred arched doorway, and a larger doorway of the Elizabethan period with pilasters and round arch. Also near the farmhouse an octagonal C16 DOVECOTE.

BLAKESWARE, 1 m. w. Rebuilt in 1878 by *George Devey*. The material is red brick, the style Neo-Tudor. The composition and details both as good as the time could make them. The house clearly shows what difference the employment of a sensitive architect makes, even when he works in terms of period imitation.

WIGGINTON

St Bartholomew. Small late medieval church, completely renewed in 1881 by *Will. White*. The w end had a separate w chamber. The little C19 turret sits on the joint between it and the nave. – STAINED GLASS. *Kempe* window of 1892 (SS Stephen and Laurence). – PLATE. Chalice and Paten, 1569; the rest 1877.

GRIMS DYKE (*see* Berkhamsted).

WILBURY HILL *see* LETCHWORTH

WILLIAN

ALL SAINTS. In the chancel is a C12 blocked doorway. The rest appears C14 and chiefly C15. The chancel E window is specially attractive with two orders of shafts inside. Early in the C19 the E end received some blank Dec arcading and a reredos to match. – SCREEN. Little of the C15 left. – CHANCEL SEATS. With poppy-heads; also one with an elephant and castle and one with St John's head on the charger. – PLATE. Chalice and Paten, 1718. – MONUMENTS. Brass to Richard Golden † 1446, frontal, in priest's vestments. – Epitaph with the two usual kneelers to E. Lacon † 1625 and an even humbler one with kneelers to John Chapman † 1624. – Sir Thomas Wilson † 1656 and wife, with two frontal busts in oval niches above long inscription.

Near the church the VICARAGE, a small timber-framed cottage, and PUNCHARDON HALL with a C18 seven-bay brick front.

WOODHALL PARK
1¼ m. SE of Watton-at-Stone

53 The house was built in 1777 by *Thomas Leverton*, the architect who probably designed Bedford Square in London. It was an oblong white brick block of seven bays and two and a half storeys connected by one-storeyed links with higher pedimented one-storeyed wings with large Venetian windows. The house itself towards the garden has rustication to the ground-floor three-bay centre and on it a one-and-a-half-storey attached order of Ionic columns. The outer ground-floor windows have pediments on brackets, all very nicely detailed. About 1795 the wings were extended on the entrance side and a one-storeyed porch of four pairs of unfluted Ionic columns was added. *Leverton's* interiors have a style decidedly their own, different from Adam's or Chamber's or Holland's. This comes out most clearly in the central staircase hall, profusely but very delicately decorated with plaster *a*

l'antique. Oval panels are specially favoured, but the dome lighting the room is circular. The staircase ascends in an elegant sweep without inner supports. It is in one flight without intermediate landings along three walls and leads to a first floor gallery. The Entrance Hall between portico and staircase (originally the Saloon) is decorated in the Etruscan taste. The central room towards the garden has arched windows and blank arches along the other walls. It was originally the entrance. Above it the best room of the upper floor, with a specially pretty ceiling.

WOOLMER GREEN

St Michael, 1899–1900, by *R. Weir Schultz*. The exterior in no way remarkable (tower projected but not built). But inside the low panelled room with a big panelled pointed wagon-roof and tie-beams has much character. Rood screen with naturalistic leaf and fruit tracery. The apse arch is lower than the small apse itself.

WOOLMERS or WOOLMER PARK
2 m. SW of Hertingfordbury

The garden front has two canted bay windows at the ends and a long one-storeyed colonnade of severe Tuscan columns between. This seems to date the house as *c.* 1810–20, and the entrance porch, staircase, and passage to the staircase correspond to that date. Yet it seems likely from documents that the brick structure itself was built before 1800.

WORMLEY

St Laurence. To the N of the house and away from the village. A small church consisting of nave and chancel only, to which in the C19 a S aisle, S porch, and stone bell-cote were added. One N window of the nave and the N doorway prove the Norman date of the nave. The chancel has been too much restored to preserve any original features. – FONT. Norman, circular, of very uncommon design. An upper frieze of broad upright leaves, and below this panels separated from each other by thick cable mouldings. In the panels rosettes and groups of upright leaves. – PULPIT. Jacobean, with termini-caryatids at the angles. – PAINTING. Last Supper, presented by Sir Abraham Hume of Wormleybury in 1797. Ascribed to *Palma Vecchio* and purchased from a monastery of Rocchelin Canons near Verona. – PLATE. Flagon, 1625; Pewter Almsdish, 1699. – MONUMENTS. Two white memorial epitaphs, both with sculpture by *Westmacott*; one to Lord and Lady Farnborough, 1838 and 1837 (with a large kneeling female figure), the other to Sir Abraham Hume † 1838 (with portrait bust).

WORMLEYBURY. The house is a square block of yellow brick consisting of basement and two and a half storeys. To the S is a central canted bay window. There was at first no other outer decoration. In this form the house was (according to Mr Christopher Gotch's unpublished thesis) built by *Robert Mylne* in 1767–69. Rainwater heads bear the date 1767, and also one referring to the preceding house: 1734. Mylne was architect to the New River Company (*see* Great Amwell). For the embellishment of this plain house *Robert Adam* was called in. He adorned only three rooms, but made an exquisite job of them. The Entrance Hall has attached columns, an aedicule on Roman Doric columns on each side (a typical early Adam motif), and most delicate stucco work. Even more profuse is the stucco decoration of the Drawing Room, and here *Angelica Kauffmann* provided her much favoured little painted roundels, etc. – The staircase has an oval dome and classical iron railings. It leads up to a gallery on the first floor. The stucco panels of the staircase walls vary surprisingly by size and shapes. The motif in one set of them is a large pitcher. All much in the Wedgwood taste. Adam worked at Wormleybury in 1777–9. Shortly after, in 1781–2, Mylne was again paid for work at Wormleybury, and as the sums are considerable, the best work is no doubt the giant portico of stone, added on the entrance side. The garden front was left un-

touched. In front of this lies a made lake, really a widening of the river, and the principal view from the house is
focused towards a big urn on the other side of the lake. –
The stables with a clock turret are close to the house on
the w.

The village stretches along the high road from London, the
same pattern as at Enfield or Broxbourne. It has the usual
remains of gabled and plastered houses (THE LIMES
GARAGE), red brick Georgian houses (WORMLEY
HOUSE), and early C19 yellow brick houses (ARCH
PRODUCTS to the s of Wormley House; with unfluted
Ionic porch and the ground floor windows in blank
arcades).

WYDDIAL

ST GILES. A Perp church, over-restored in the C19. Un- 20a
buttressed w tower, C19 s porch. The special and great
interest of the church is its N aisle and N chancel chapel,
both built of brick and dated by a brass inscription 1532.
The windows are of the usual three-light type under one
arch, all of brick.* The arcade of three bays has brick
piers of the usual type with semi-octagonal shafts and
hollows in the diagonals. The arches are treble-chamfered,
the middle chamfer being hollow. The arch to the N
chapel is also of brick. This triumphant entry of brick
into church building is a significant sign of the Tudor age.
The N chapel has SCREENS to W and S of elaborate early 27
C17 design and BOX PEWS to match in the aisle. –
STAINED GLASS. In two N windows eight smallish panels
with Scenes from the Passion; Flemish mid C16. –
PLATE. Paten, 1734. – MONUMENTS. Brass to John Gille
† 1546, with wife and children (chancel). – Brass to Dame
Margaret Plumbe † 1575, large demi-figure praying
(chancel wall). – Epitaph to Sir William Goulston † 1687,
with twisted columns carrying a scrolly broken pediment
and marble busts in grey niches above the inscription.

WYDIAL HALL. Built after a fire of 1733. Large white
balustraded house of five by seven bays with canted bay

* A late C16 N doorway is of stone.

windows on the E. But the big outer chimney on the S side, the square two-storeyed porch in the middle of the E side, and other details indicate that enough of the Elizabethan or Jacobean period remained to be made use of. The appearance of the older house is known from Chauncy (1700).

YOUNGSBURY *see* THUNDRIDGE

GLOSSARY

ABACUS: flat slab on the top of a capital (q.v.).

ABUTMENT: solid masonry placed to resist the lateral pressure of a vault.

ACANTHUS: plant with thick fleshy and scalloped leaves used as part of the decoration of a Corinthian capital (q.v.) and in some types of leaf carving.

ACHIEVEMENT OF ARMS: in heraldry, a complete display of armorial bearings.

ACROTERION: foliage-carved block on the end or top of a classical pediment.

ADDOSSED: two human figures, animals, or birds, etc., placed symmetrically so that they turn their backs to each other.

AEDICULE, AEDICULA: framing of a window or door by columns and a pediment (q.v.).

AFFRONTED: two human figures, animals, or birds, etc., placed symmetrically so that they face each other.

AMBULATORY: semicircular or polygonal aisle enclosing an apse (q.v.).

ANNULET: see Shaft-ring.

ANTIS, IN: see Portico.

APSE: vaulted semicircular or polygonal end of a chancel or a chapel.

ARABESQUE: light and fanciful surface decoration using combinations of flowing lines, tendrils, etc., interspersed with vases, animals, etc.

ARCADE: range of arches supported on piers or columns, free-standing; or, BLIND ARCADE, the same attached to a wall.

ARCH: round-headed; i.e. semicircular pointed, i.e. consisting of two curves, each drawn from one centre, and meeting in a point at the top; Segmental, i.e. in the form of a segment; pointed; four-centred, see Fig. 1(a); Tudor, see Fig. 1(b); Ogee, see Fig. 1(c); Stilted, see Fig. 1(d).

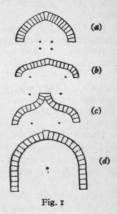

Fig. 1

ARCHITRAVE: lowest of the three main parts of the entablature (q.v.) of an order (q.v.) (see Fig. 11).

ARCHIVOLT: undersurface of an arch (also called Soffit).

ARRIS: sharp edge at the meeting of two surfaces.

ASHLAR: masonry of large blocks wrought to even faces and square edges.

ATRIUM: inner court of a Roman house, also open court in front of a church.

ATTACHED: *see* engaged.

ATTIC: topmost storey of a house, if lower than the others.

AUMBREY: recess or cupboard to hold sacred vessels for Mass and Communion.

BAILEY: open space or court of a fortified castle.

BALDACCHINO: canopy supported on columns.

BALLFLOWER: globular flower of three petals enclosing a small ball. A decoration used in the first quarter of the C14.

BALUSTER: small pillar or column of fanciful outline.

BALUSTRADE: series of balusters supporting a handrail or coping (q.v.).

BARBICAN: outwork, constructed like a gateway, defending the entrance to a castle.

BARGEBOARDS: projecting decorated boards placed against the incline of the gable of a building and hiding the horizontal roof timbers.

BASILICA: in medieval architecture an aisled church with a clerestory.

BASTION: projection at the angle of a fortification.

BATTER: wall with an inclined face.

BATTLEMENT: parapet with a series of indentations or embrasures with raised portions or merlons between (also called Crenellation).

BAYS: internal compartments of a building; each divided from the other not by solid walls but by divisions only marked in the side walls (columns, pilasters, etc.) or the ceiling (beams, etc.). Also external divisions of a building by fenestration.

BAY-WINDOW: angular or curved projection of a house front with ample fenestration. If curved also called bow-window; if on an upper floor only also called oriel or oriel window.

BEAKHEAD: Norman ornamental motif consisting of a row of bird or beast heads with beaks pointing downwards and biting usually into a roll moulding.

BELL-COTE: turret usually on the W end of a church to carry the bells.

BILLET: Norman ornamental motif made up of short raised rectangles placed at regular intervals.

BLOCK CAPITAL: Romanesque capital cut from a cube by having the lower angles rounded off to the circular shaft below (also called Cushion Capital) (Fig. 2).

Fig. 2

BOND, ENGLISH or FLEMISH: *see* Brickwork.

BOSS: knob or projection usually placed to cover the intersection of ribs in a vault.

BOW-WINDOW: *see* Bay-Window.

BOX PEW: pew with a high wooden enclosure.

BRACES: *see* Roof.

BRACKET: small supporting piece of stone, etc., to carry a projecting horizontal.

(a)

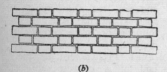

(b)

Fig. 3

BRICKWORK: *Header:* brick laid so that the end only appears on the face of the wall. *Stretcher:* brick laid so that the side only appears on the face of the wall. *English Bond:* method of laying bricks so that alternate courses or layers on the face of the wall are composed of headers or stretchers only (Fig. 3a). *Flemish Bond:* method of laying bricks so that alternate headers and stretchers appear in each course on the face of the wall (Fig. 3b).

BROACH: *see* Spire.

BROKEN PEDIMENT: *see* Pediment.

BUTTRESS: mass of brickwork or masonry projecting from or built against a wall to give additional strength. *Angle Buttresses:* two meeting at an angle of 90° at the angle of a building (Fig. 4a). *Clasping Buttress:* one which encases the angle

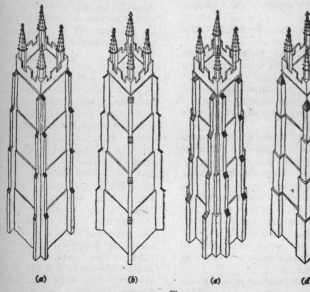

(a)   (b)   (c)   (d)

Fig. 4

(Fig. 4*d*). *Diagonal Buttress:* one placed against the right angle formed by two walls, and more or less equiangular with both (Fig. 4*b*). *Flying Buttress:* arch or half arch transmitting the thrust of a vault or roof from the upper part of a wall to an outer support or buttress. *Setback Buttress:* angle buttress set slightly back from the angle (Fig. 4*c*).

CABLE MOULDING: moulding imitating a twisted cord.

CAMBER: slight rise or upward curve of an otherwise horizontal structure.

CAMPANILE: isolated bell tower.

CANOPY: ornamental covering above an altar, pulpit, niche, etc.

CAP: in a windmill the crowning feature.

CAPITAL: head or top part of a column (q.v.).

CARTOUCHE: tablet with an ornate frame, usually enclosing an inscription.

CARYATID: human figure used instead of a column.

CASTELLATED: decorated with battlements.

CEILURE: panelled and adorned part of a wagon-roof above the rood or the altar.

CENSER: vessel for the burning of incense.

CENTERING: wooden framework used in arch and vault construction and removed when the mortar has set.

CHALICE: small cup used in the Communion service or at Mass.

CHAMFER: surface made by cutting across the square angle of

a stone block, piece of wood, etc., at an angle of 45° to the two other surfaces.

CHANCEL: that part of the E end of a church in which the altar is placed, usually applied to the whole continuation of the nave E of the crossing.

CHANCEL ARCH: arch at the W end of the chancel.

CHANTRY CHAPEL: chapel attached to, or inside, a church endowed for the saying of Masses for the soul of the founder or some other individual.

CHEVET: French term for the E end of a church (chancel, ambulatory, and radiating chapels).

CHEVRON: sculptured moulding forming a zigzag.

CHOIR: that part of the church where divine service is sung.

CIBORIUM: box or container for the consecrated bread. Also used to mean a baldacchino (q.v.).

CINQUEFOIL: *see* Foil.

CLAPPER BRIDGE: bridge made of large slabs of stone, some built up to make rough piers and other longer ones laid on top to make the roadway.

CLASSIC: here used to mean the moment of highest achievement of a style.

CLASSICAL: here used as the term for Greek and Roman architecture and any subsequent styles copying it.

CLERESTORY: upper storey of the nave walls of a church, pierced by windows.

COADE STONE: artificial (cast) stone made in the late C18 and the early C19 by Coade and Seely in London.

COB: walling material made of mixed clay and straw.

COFFERING: decorating a ceiling with sunk square or polygonal ornamental panels.

COLLAR-BEAM: see Roof.

COLONNADE: range of columns.

COLONNETTE: small column.

COLUMNA ROSTRATA: column decorated with carved prows of ships to celebrate a naval victory.

COMPOSITE: see Orders.

CONSOLE: bracket (q.v.) with a compound curved outline.

COPING: capping or covering to a wall.

CORBEL: block of stone projecting from a wall, supporting some horizontal feature.

CORBEL TABLE: series of corbels, occurring just below the roof eaves externally or internally, often seen in Norman buildings.

CORINTHIAN: see Orders.

CORNICE: in classical architecture the top section of the entablature (q.v.). Also for a projecting decorative feature along the top of a wall, arch, etc.

COVE, COVING: concave undersurface in the nature of a hollow moulding but on a larger scale.

COVER PATEN: cover to a Communion cup, suitable for use as a paten or plate for the consecrated bread.

CRADLE ROOF: see Wagon-roof.

CRENELLATION: see Battlement.

CREST, CRESTING: ornamental finish along the top of a screen, etc.

CROCKET, CROCKETING: decorative features placed on the sloping sides of spires, pinnacles, gables, etc. in Gothic architecture, carved in various leaf shapes and placed at regular intervals.

CROCKET CAPITAL: see Fig. 5.

Fig. 5

CROSSING: space at the intersection of nave, chancel, and transepts.

CRUCK: big curved beam supporting both walls and roof of a cottage.

CRYPT: underground room usually below the E end of a church.

CUPOLA: small polygonal or circular domed turret crowning a roof.

CURTAIN WALL: connecting wall between the towers of a castle.

CURVILINEAR: see Tracery.

CUSHION CAPITAL: see Block Capital.

CUSP: in tracery (q.v.) the small pointed member between two lobes of a trefoil, quatrefoil, etc.

DADO: decorative covering of the lower part of a wall.

DAGGER: tracery motif of the Dec. style. It is a lancet shape rounded or pointed at the head, pointed at the foot and cusped inside (see Fig. 6).

Fig. 6

DAIS: raised platform at one end of a room.

DEC ('DECORATED'): historical division of English Gothic architecture covering the first half of the C14.

DEMI-COLUMNS: columns half sunk into a wall.

DIAPER WORK: surface decoration composed of square or lozenge shapes.

DOG-TOOTH: typical E.E. ornament consisting of a series of four-cornered stars placed diagonally and raised pyramidally (Fig. 7).

Fig. 7

DOMICAL VAULT: see Vault.

DONJON: see Keep.

DORIC: see Orders.

DORMER (WINDOW): window placed vertically in the sloping plane of a roof.

DRIPSTONE: see Hood-mould.

DRUM: circular or polygonal vertical wall of a dome or cupola.

E.E. ('EARLY ENGLISH'): historical division of English Gothic architecture roughly covering the C13.

EASTER SEPULCHRE: recess with tomb-chest usually in the wall of a chancel, the tomb-chest to receive an effigy of Christ for Easter celebrations.

EAVES: underpart of a sloping roof overhanging a wall.

EAVES CORNICE: cornice below the eaves of a roof.

ECHINUS: quarter round moulding carved with egg and dart pattern, used in classical architecture.

EMBATTLED: see Battlement.

EMBRASURE: small opening in the wall or parapet of a fortified building, usually splayed on the inside. See Loop.

ENCAUSTIC TILES: earthenware glazed and decorated tiles used for paving.

ENGAGED COLUMNS: columns attached to, or partly sunk into, a wall.

ENGLISH BOND: see Brickwork.

ENTABLATURE: in Classical architecture the whole of the horizontal members above a column (that is architrave, frieze, and cornice) (see Fig. 11).

ENTASIS: very slight convex deviation from a straight line; used on Greek columns and sometimes on spires to prevent an optical illusion of concavity.

ENTRESOL: see Mezzanine.

EPITAPH: hanging wall monument.

ESCUTCHEON: shield for armorial bearings.

EXEDRA: the apsidal end of a room. See Apse.

EXTRADOS: outer surface of an arch.

FAIENCE: decorated glazed earthenware.

FAN TRACERY: see Tracery.

FAN VAULT: see Vault.

FERETORY: place behind the High Altar, where the chief shrine of a church is kept.

FESTOON: carved garland of flowers and fruit suspended at both ends.

FILLET: narrow flat band running down a shaft or along a roll moulding.

FINIAL: in Gothic architecture the top of a pinnacle, gable, or

GLOSSARY

bench-end carved into a leaf or leaf-like form.

FLAGON: jug for the wine used in the Communion service.

FLAMBOYANT: properly the latest phase of French Gothic architecture where the window tracery takes on wavy undulating lines.

FLÈCHE: slender wooden spire on the centre of a roof (also called Spirelet).

FLEMISH BOND: see Brickwork.

FLEURON: decorative carved flower or leaf.

FLUSH WORK: Decorative use of flint in conjunction with dressed stone so as to form pattens: tracery, initials, etc.

FLUTING: vertical channelling in the shaft of a column.

FLYING BUTTRESS: see Buttress.

FOIL: lobe formed by the cusping (q.v.) of a circle or an arch. Trefoil, quatrefoil, cinquefoil, multifoil, express the number of leaf shapes to be seen.

FOLIATED: carved with leaf shapes.

FOSSE: ditch.

FOUR-CENTRED ARCH: see Arch.

FRATER: refectory or dining hall of a monastery.

FRESCO: wall painting on wet plaster.

FRIEZE: middle division of a classical entablature (q.v.) (see Fig. 11).

FRONTAL: covering of the front of an altar.

GALILEE: chapel or vestibule at the W end of a church enclosing the porch. Also called Narthex (q.v.).

GALLERY: in church architecture upper storey above an aisle, opened in arches to the nave. Also called Tribune (q.v.) and often erroneously Triforium (q.v.).

GARGOYLE: water spout projecting from the parapet of a wall or tower; carved into a human or animal shape.

GAZEBO: lookout tower or raised summer house in a picturesque garden.

'GEOMETRICAL': see Tracery.

'GIBBS' SURROUND: of a doorway or window. A surround with alternating larger and smaller blocks of stone, quoinwise, or intermittent large blocks, sometimes with a narrow raised band connecting them up the verticals and along the extrados of the arch (Fig. 8).

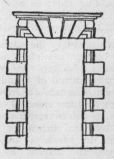

Fig. 8

GROIN: sharp edge at the meeting of two cells of a cross-vault.

GROINED VAULT: see Vault.

GROTESQUE: fanciful ornamental decoration: see also Arabesque.

HAGIOSCOPE: see Squint.

HALF-TIMBERING: see Timber Framing.

HALL CHURCH: church in which nave and aisles are of equal height or approximately so.

HAMMER-BEAM: *see* Roof.

HANAP: large metal cup, generally made for domestic use, standing on an elaborate base and stem; with a very ornate cover frequently crowned with a little steeple.

HEADERS: *see* Brickwork.

HERRINGBONE WORK: brick, stone, or tile construction where the component blocks are laid diagonally instead of flat. Alternate courses lie in opposing directions to make a zigzag pattern up the face of the wall.

HEXASTYLE: having four detached columns.

HIPPED ROOF: *see* Roof.

HOOD-MOULD: projecting moulding above an arch or a lintel to throw off water (also called Dripstone or Label).

ICONOGRAPHY: the science of the contents of works of art.

IMPOST: brackets in walls, usually formed of mouldings, on which the ends of an arch rest.

INDENT: shape chiselled out in a stone slab to receive a brass.

INGLENOOK: bench or seat built in beside a fireplace, sometimes covered by the chimney breast, occasionally lit by small windows on each side of the fire.

INTERCOLUMNATION: the space between columns.

IONIC: *see* Orders (Fig. II).

JAMB: straight side of an archway, doorway, or window.

KEEL MOULDING: moulding whose outline is in section like that of the keel of a ship.

KEEP: massive tower of a Norman castle.

KEYSTONE: middle stone in an arch.

KING-POST: *see* Roof (Fig. 13).

LABEL: *see* Hood-mould.

LABEL STOP: ornamental boss at the end of a hood-mould (q.v.).

LANCET WINDOW: slender pointed-arched window.

LANTERN: in architecture, a small circular or polygonal turret with windows all round crowning a roof (*see* Cupola) or a dome.

LANTERN CROSS: churchyard cross with lantern-shaped top usually with sculptured representations on the sides of the top.

LEAN-TO ROOF: roof with one slope only, built against a higher wall.

LESENE or PILASTER STRIP pilaster without base and capital.

LIERNE: *see* Vault (Fig. 20).

LINENFOLD: Tudor panelling ornamented with a conventional representation of a piece of linen laid in vertical folds. The piece is repeated in each panel.

LINTEL: horizontal beam of stone bridging an opening.

LOGGIA: recessed colonnade (q.v.).

LONG AND SHORT WORK: Saxon quoins (q.v.) consisting of stones placed with the long sides alternately upright and horizontal.

LOUVRE: opening, often with lantern (q.v.) over, in the roof of a room to let the smoke from a central hearth escape.

LOZENGE: diamond shape.

LUNETTE: tympanum (q.v.) or curved opening in a vault.

LYCH GATE: wooden gate structure with a roof and open sides placed at the entrance to a churchyard to provide space for the reception of a coffin. The word lych is Saxon and means a corpse.

MACHICOLATION: projecting gallery on brackets constructed on the outside of castle towers or walls. The gallery has holes in the floor to drop missiles through.

MAJOLICA: ornamented glazed earthenware.

MANSARD: see Roof.

MERLON: see Battlement.

METOPE: in classical architecture of the Doric order (q.v.) the space in the frieze between the triglyphs (Fig. 11).

MEZZANINE: low storey placed between two higher ones.

MISERERE: see Misericord.

MISERICORD: bracket placed on the underside of a hinged choir stall seat which, when turned up, provided the occupant of the seat with a support during long periods of standing (also called Miserere).

MODILLION: small bracket of which large numbers (modillion frieze) are often placed below a cornice (q.v.) in classical architecture.

MOTTE: steep mound forming the main feature of C11 and C12 castles.

MOUCHETTE: tracery motif in

Fig. 9

curvilinear tracery, a curved dagger (q.v.) (Fig. 9).

MULLION: vertical post or upright dividing a window into two or more 'lights'.

NAILHEAD: E.E. ornamental motif, consisting of small pyramids regularly repeated (Fig. 10).

Fig. 10

NARTHEX: enclosed vestibule or covered porch at the main entrance to a church (see Galilee).

NEWEL: central post in a circular or winding staircase; also the principal post when a flight of stairs meets a landing.

OBELISK: lofty pillar of square section tapering at the top and ending pyramidally.

OGEE: see Arch (Fig. 1c).

ORATORY: small private chapel in a house.

ORDER: (1) of a doorway or window: series of concentric steps receding towards the opening; (2) in classical architecture: column with base, shaft, capital, and entablature (q.v.) according to one of the following styles: Greek Doric, Roman Doric, Tuscan Doric, Ionic, Corinthian, Composite. The established details are very elaborate, and some specialist architectural work should be consulted for further guidance (see Fig. 11).

Fig. 11 – Orders of Columns (Greek Doric, Roman Doric, Tuscan, Ionic, Corinthian).
E, Entablature; F, Frieze; A, Architrave; M, Metope; T, Triglyph

ORIEL: see Bay Window.

OVERHANG: projection of the upper storey of a house.

OVERSAILING COURSES: series of stone or brick courses, each one projecting beyond the one below it.

PALIMPSEST: (1) *of a brass:* where a metal plate has been re-used by turning over and engraving on the back; (2) *of a wall painting:* where one overlaps and partly obscures an earlier one.

PALLADIAN: architecture following the ideas and principles of Andrea Palladio, 1518–80.

PANTILE: tile of curved S-shaped section.

PARAPET: low wall placed to protect any spot where there is a sudden drop, for example on a bridge, quay, hillside, house-top, etc.

PARGETTING: plaster work with patterns and ornaments either in relief or engraved on it.

PARVISE: room over a church porch. Often used as a school-house or a store room.

PATEN: plate to hold the bread at Communion or Mass.

PATERA: small flat circular or oval ornament in classical architecture.

PEDIMENT: low-pitched gable (q.v.) used in classical, Renaissance, and neo-classical architecture above a portico and above doors, windows, etc. I may be straight-sided or curved segmentally. *Open Pediment:* one where the centre portion of the base is left open. *Broken Pediment:* one where the centre portion of the sloping sides i 'broken' out.

PENDANT: boss (q.v.) elongated so that it seems to hang down.

PENDENTIF: concave triangular spandrel used to lead from the angle of two walls to the base of a circular dome. It is constructed as part of the hemisphere over a diameter the size of the diagonal of the basic square (Fig. 12).

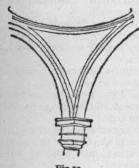

Fig 12.

ERP (PERPENDICULAR): historical division of English Gothic architecture roughly covering the period from 1350 to 1530.

IANO NOBILE: principal storey of a house with the reception rooms; usually the first floor.

IAZZA: square open space surrounded by buildings, in C17 and C18 English sometimes used to mean a long colonnade or loggia.

IER: strong, solid support, frequently square in section or of composite section (compound pier).

IETRA DURA: ornamental or scenic inlay by means of thin slabs of stone.

ILASTER: shallow pier attached to a wall.

PILLAR PISCINA: free-standing piscina on a pillar.

PINNACLE: ornamental form crowning a spire, tower, buttress, etc., usually of steep pyramidal, conical, or some similar shape.

PISCINA: basin for washing the Communion or Mass vessels, provided with a drain. Generally set in or against the wall to the s of an altar.

PLAISANCE: summer-house, pleasure house near a mansion.

PLATE TRACERY: see Tracery.

PLINTH: projecting base of a wall or column, generally chamfered (q.v.) or moulded at the top.

POPPYHEAD: ornament of leaf and flower type used to decorate the tops of bench or stall-ends.

PORTCULLIS: gate constructed to rise and fall in vertical grooves; used in gateways of castles.

PORTE COCHERE: porch large enough to admit wheeled vehicles.

PORTICO: centre-piece of a house or a church with classical detached or attached columns and a pediment. A portico is called *prostyle* or *in antis* according to whether it projects from or recedes into a building. In a portico *in antis* the columns range with the side walls.

POSTERN: small gateway at the back of a building.

PREDELLA: in an altar-piece the horizontal strip below the main representation, often used for a number of subsidiary representations in a row.

PRESBYTERY: the part of the church lying E of the choir. It is the part where altar is placed.

PRINCIPAL: *see* Roof (Fig. 13).

PRIORY: monastic house whose head is a prior or prioress, not an abbot or abbess.

PROSTYLE: with free-standing columns in a row.

PULPITUM: stone rood screen in a major church.

PURLIN: *see* Roof (Figs. 13, 14).

PUTTO: small naked boy.

QUADRANGLE: inner courtyard in a large building complex.

QUARRY: in stained-glass work, a small diamond or square-shaped piece of glass set diagonally.

QUATREFOIL: *see* Foil.

QUEEN-POSTS: *see* Roof (Fig. 14).

QUOINS: dressed stones at the angles of a building. Sometimes all the stones are of the same size; more often they are alternately large or small.

RADIATING CHAPELS: chapels projecting radially from an ambulatory or an apse.

RAFTER: *see* Roof.

RAMPART: stone wall, or wall of earth surrounding a castle, fortress, or fortified city.

RAMPART-WALK: path along the inner face of a rampart.

REBATE: channel or small recess cut into a piece of wood or stone longitudinally to receive the edge of some member that is to be secured in it. The depth of the channel is equal to the thickness of the member to be let into it.

REBUS: pun, a play on words. The literal translation and illustration of a name for artistic and heraldic purposes (Belton=bell, tun).

REEDING: decoration with parallel convex mouldings touching one another.

REFECTORY: Dining hall; *see* Frater.

RENDERING: plastering of an outer wall.

REPOUSSÉ: decoration of metal work by relief designs, formed by beating the metal from the back.

REREDOS: structure behind and above an altar.

RESPOND: half-pier bonded into a wall and carrying one end of an arch.

RETABLE: altar-piece, a picture or piece of carving, standing behind and attached to an altar.

RETICULATION: *see* Tracery (Fig. 19).

REVEAL: that part of a jamb (q.v.) which lies between the glass or door and the outer surface of the wall.

RIB VAULT: *see* Vault.

ROCOCO: latest phase of the Baroque style, current in most Continental countries between c. 1720 and c. 1760.

ROMANESQUE: that style in architecture which was current in the C11 and C12 and preceded the Gothic style (in England often called Norman).

ROOD: cross or crucifix.

ROOD LOFT: singing gallery on the top of the rood screen, often supported by a coving.

ROOD SCREEN: *see* Screen.

ROOD STAIRS: stairs to give access to the rood loft.

ₒOF: *Hipped:* roof with sloped instead of vertical ends. *Mansard:* roof with a double slope, the lower slope being larger and steeper than the upper. *Saddleback:* tower roof shaped like an ordinary gabled timber roof. The following members have special names: *Rafter:* roof-timber sloping up from the wall plate to the ridge. *Principal:* principal rafter, usually corresponding to the main bay divisions of the nave or chancel below. *Wall Plate:* timber laid longitudinally on the top of a wall. *Purlin:* longitudinal member laid parallel with wall plate and ridge beam some way up the slope of the roof. *Tie-beam:* beam connecting the two slopes of a roof across at its foot, usually at the height of the wall plate, to prevent the roof from spreading. *Collar-beam:* tie-beam applied higher up the slope of the roof. *Strut:* upright timber connecting the tie-beam with the rafter above it. *King-post:*

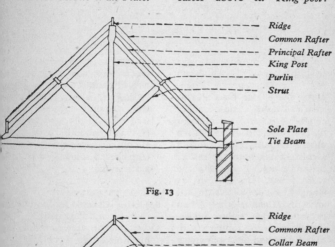

Ridge
Common Rafter
Principal Rafter
King Post
Purlin
Strut

Sole Plate
Tie Beam

Fig. 13

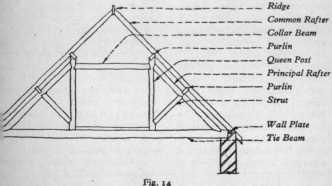

Ridge
Common Rafter
Collar Beam
Purlin
Queen Post
Principal Rafter
Purlin
Strut

Wall Plate
Tie Beam

Fig. 14

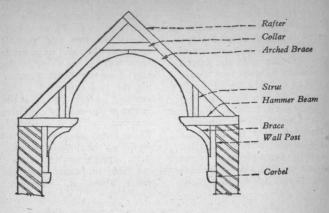

Fig. 15

upright timber connecting a tie-beam and collar-beam with the ridge-beam. *Queen-posts:* two struts placed symmetrically on a tie-beam or collar-beam. *Braces:* inclined timbers inserted to strengthen others. Usually braces connect a collar-beam with the rafters below or a tie-beam with the wall below. Braces can be straight or curved (also called arched). *Hammer-beam:* beam projecting at right angles, usually from the top of a wall, to carry arched braces or struts and arched braces (*see* Figs. 13, 14, 15).

ROSE WINDOW (or WHEEL WINDOW): circular window with patterned tracery arranged to radiate from the centre.

ROTUNDA: building circular in plan.

RUBBLE: building stones, not square or hewn, nor laid in regular courses.

RUSTICATION: Ashlar-work of blocks with the margins only wrought and the faces rough or specially rock-faced: or ashlar-work of smooth-faced blocks with the joints greatly emphasized (smooth rustication). If only the horizontal joints are emphasized it is called banded rustication.

SADDLEBACK: *see* Roof.

SALTIRE CROSS: equal-limbed cross placed diagonally.

SANCTUARY: area around the main altar of a church (*see* Presbytery).

SARCOPHAGUS: elaborately carved coffin.

SCAGLIOLA: material composed of cement and colouring matter to imitate marble.

SCALLOPED CAPITAL: development of the block capital (q.v.) in which the single semicircular surface is elaborated into a series of truncated cones (Fig. 16).

Fig. 16

SCARP: artificial cutting away of the ground to form a steep slope.

SCREEN: *Parclose screen*: screen separating a chapel from the rest of a church. *Rood screen*: screen at the W end of a chancel. Above it on the rood-beam was the rood (q.v.).

SCREENS PASSAGE: passage between the entrances to kitchen, buttery, etc., and the screen behind which lies the hall of a medieval house.

SEDILIA: seats for the priests (usually three) on the S side of the chancel of a church.

SEGMENTAL ARCH: *see* Arch.

SET-OFF: *see* Weathering.

SEXPARTITE: *see* Vaulting.

SGRAFFITO: pattern incised into plaster so as to expose a dark surface underneath.

SHAFT-RING: ring round a circular pier or a shaft attached to a pier.

SILL: lower horizontal part of the frame of a window.

SLATEHANGING: the covering of walls by overlapping rows of slates, on a timber substructure.

SOFFIT: *see* Archivolt.

SOLAR: upper drawing-room of a medieval house.

SOPRAPORTE: painting above the door of a room, usual in the C17 and C18.

SOUNDING BOARD: horizontal board or canopy over a pulpit. Also called Tester.

SPANDREL: triangular surface between one side of an arch, the horizontal drawn from its apex, and the vertical drawn from its springer, also the surface between two arches.

SPIRE: tall pyramidal or conical pointed erection often built on top of a tower, turret, etc. *Broach Spire*: spire which is generally octagonal in plan rising from the top or parapet of a square tower. A small inclined piece of masonry covers the vacant triangular space at each of the four angles of the square and is carried up to a point along the diagonal sides of the octagon. *Needle Spire*: thin spire rising from the centre of a tower roof, well inside the parapet.

SPIRELET: *see* Flèche.

SPLAY: chamfer, usually of the jamb of a window.

SPRINGING: level at which an arch rises from its supports.

SQUINCH: arch or system of concentric arches thrown across the angle between two walls to support a superstructure, for example a dome (Fig. 17).

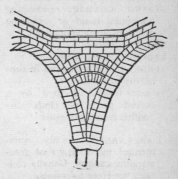

Fig. 17

SQUINT: hole cut in a wall or through a pier to allow a view of the main altar of a church from places whence it could not otherwise be seen (also called Hagioscope).

STALL: carved seat, one in a row, made of wood or stone.

STEEPLE: the tower or spire of a church.

STIFF-LEAF: E.E. type of foliage of many-lobed shapes (Fig. 18).

Fig. 18

STILTED: see Arch.

STOUP: vessel for the reception of holy water, usually placed near a door.

STRAINER ARCH: arch inserted across a room to prevent the walls from leaning.

STRAPWORK: C16 decoration consisting of interlaced bands, and forms similar to fretwork or cut and bent leather.

STRETCHERS: see Brickwork.

STRING COURSE: projecting horizontal band or moulding set in the surface of a wall.

STRUT: see Roof.

STUCCO: plaster work.

STUDS: Upright timbers in timber-framed houses.

SWAG: festoon formed by a carved piece of cloth suspended from both ends.

TABERNACLE: richly ornamented niche (q.v.) or free-standing canopy. Usually contains the Holy Sacrament.

TAZZA: shallow bowl on a foot.

TERMINAL FIGURES (TERMS, TERMINI): upper part of a human figure growing out of a pier, pilaster, etc., which tapers towards the base.

TERRACOTTA: burnt clay, unglazed.

TESSELATED PAVEMENT: decorative floor or wall covering made up of tesserae or small coloured cubes of stone, fitted into a bed of cement.

TESTER: see Sounding Board.

TETRASTYLE: having four detached columns.

THREE-DECKER PULPIT: pulpit with Clerk's Stall and Reading Desk placed below each other.

TIE-BEAM: see Roof (Figs. 13, 14).

TIERCERON: see Vault (Fig. 20).

TILEHANGING: see Slatehanging.

TIMBER-FRAMING: method of construction where walls are built of timber framework with the spaces filled in by plaster or brickwork. Sometimes the timber is covered over with plaster or boarding laid horizontally.

TOMB-CHEST: chest-shaped stone coffin, the most usual medieval form of funeral monument.

TOUCH: soft black marble quarried near Tournai.

TOURELLE: turret corbelled out from the wall.

TRACERY: intersecting ribwork in the upper part of a window, or used decoratively in blank arches, on vaults, etc. *Plate tracery:* early form of tracery where decoratively shaped openings are cut through the solid stone infilling in the head

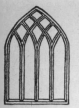  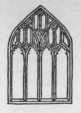 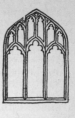

   (a)   (b)   (c)   (d)

Fig. 19

of a window. *Bar tracery:* intersecting ribwork made up of slender shafts, continuing the lines of the mullions of windows up to a decorative mesh in the head of the window. *Geometrical tracery:* tracery consisting chiefly of circles or foiled circles. *Intersected tracery:* tracery in which each mullion of a window branches out into two curved bars in such a way that every one of them runs concentrically with the others against the arch of the whole window. The result is that every light of the window is a lancet and every two, three, four, etc., lights together form a pointed arch (Fig. 19a). *Reticulated tracery:* tracery consisting entirely of circles drawn at top and bottom into ogee shapes so that a net-like appearance results (Fig. 19b). *Panel tracery:* tracery forming upright straight-sided panels above lights of a window (Fig. 19, c & d).

TRANSEPT: transverse portion of a cross-shaped church.

TRANSOME: horizontal bar across the opening of a window.

TRANSVERSE ARCH: *see* Vaulting.

TRIBUNE: *see* Gallery.

TRICIPUT, SIGNUM TRICIPUT: sign of the Trinity expressed by three faces belonging to one head.

TRIFORIUM: arcaded wall passage or blank arcading facing the nave at the height of the aisle roof and below the clerestory (q.v.) windows. (*See* Gallery.)

TRIGLYPHS: blocks with vertical grooves separating the metopes (q.v.) in the Doric frieze (Fig. 11).

TROPHY: sculptured group of arms or armour, used as a memorial of victory.

TRUMEAU: stone mullion (q.v.) supporting the tympanum (q.v.) of a wide doorway.

TURRET: very small tower, round or polygonal in plan.

TUSCAN: *see* Order.

TYMPANUM: space between the lintel of a doorway and the arch above it.

UNDERCROFT: vaulted room, sometimes underground, below a church or chapel.

VAULT: *Barrel vault: see* Tunnel vault. *Cross-vault: see* Groined vault. *Domical vault:* square or polygonal dome rising direct on a square or polygonal bay, the curved surfaces separated by groins (q.v.). *Fan vault:* vault where all ribs springing from one springer are of the same length, the same distance from the next, and the same curvature. *Groined vault* or *Cross-vault:* vault of two tunnel vaults of identical shape intersecting each other at right angles. *Lierne:* tertiary rib, that is, rib which does not spring either from one of the main springers or the central boss. *Quadripartite vault:* one wherein one bay of vaulting is divided into four parts. *Rib vault:* vault with diagonal ribs projecting along the groins.

Ridge-rib: rib along the longitudinal or transverse ridge of a vault. *Sexpartite vault:* one wherein one bay of quadripartite vaulting is divided into two parts transversely so that each bay of vaulting has six parts. *Tierceron:* secondary rib, that is, rib which issues from one of the main springers or the central boss and leads to a place on a ridge-rib. *Transverse arch:* arch separating one bay of a vault from the next. *Tunnel vault* or *Barrel vault:* vault of semicircular or pointed section (Fig. 20).

VAULTING SHAFT: vertical member leading to the springer of a vault.

VENETIAN WINDOW: window with three openings, the central one arched and wider than the outside ones.

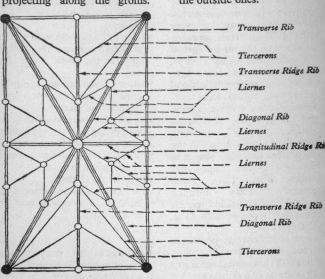

Transverse Rib

Tiercerons

Transverse Ridge Rib

Liernes

Diagonal Rib

Liernes

Longitudinal Ridge Rib

Liernes

Liernes

Transverse Ridge Rib

Diagonal Rib

Tiercerons

Fig. 20

VERANDAH: open gallery or balcony with a roof on light, usually metal, supports.

VESICA: Oval with pointed head and foot.

VESTIBULE: ante-room or entrance hall.

VILLA: according to Gwilt (1842) 'a country house for the residence of opulent persons'.

VITRIFIED: made similar to glass.

VOLUTE: spiral scroll, one of the component parts of an Ionic column (*see* Orders).

VOUSSOIR: wedge-shaped stone used in arch construction.

WAGON-ROOF: roof in which by closely set rafters with arched braces the appearance of the inside of a canvas tilt over a wagon is achieved. Wagon-roofs can be panelled or plastered (ceiled) or left uncovered.

WAINSCOT: timber lining to walls.

WALL PLATE: *see* Roof.

WATERLEAF: leaf shape used in later C12 capitals. The 'waterleaf is a broad, unribbed, tapering leaf curving up towards the angle of the abacus and turned in at the top (Fig. 21).

Fig. 21

WEATHER-BOARDING: overlapping horizontal boards, covering a timber-framed wall.

WEATHERING: sloping horizontal surface on sills, buttresses, etc., to throw off water.

WEEPERS: small figures placed in niches along the sides of some medieval tombs (also called Mourners).

WHEEL WINDOW: *see* Rose Window.

INDEX OF PLATES

INDEX OF ARTISTS

INDEX OF PLACES

The references in brackets indicate the square in which the place will be found on the map preceding the title-page